German Pension Reform

Sozialökonomische Schriften

Herausgegeben von Bert Rürup

Band 34

PETER LANG
Frankfurt am Main · Berlin · Bern · Bruxelles · New York · Oxford · Wien

Christina Benita Wilke

German Pension Reform

On Road Towards a Sustainable Multi-Pillar System

PETER LANG
Internationaler Verlag der Wissenschaften

Bibliographic Information published by the Deutsche Nationalbibliothek
The Deutsche Nationalbibliothek lists this publication in the Deutsche Nationalbibliografie; detailed bibliographic data is available in the internet at <http://www.d-nb.de>.

Zugl.: Mannheim, Univ., Diss., 2008

D 180
ISSN 0172-1747
ISBN 978-3-631-58851-2

Printed in Germany 1 2 3 4 5 7

www.peterlang.de

Acknowledgements

I am grateful to many people for their valuable help and support while I was writing this thesis. First and foremost, I would like to thank my supervisor Axel Börsch-Supan for his always prompt and excellent advice on the many questions that came up during my work. Most of the chapters in this book have benefited from his guidance and example. I am also grateful to David Wise for agreeing to be my second supervisor. Furthermore, I would like to thank my colleague, friend and 'third advisor' Anette Reil-Held for the many valuable comments she gave on my work and all the hours she spent on reading my papers.

I also very much appreciate the feedback of many other academic researchers at conferences, workshops and visits. In particular, I benefited much from the advice of Agar Brugiavini on the more theoretical pension system aspects treated in Chapter 4 which she gave to me during my research stay at Università Ca' Foscari, Venice. I am also particularly thankful for the helpful comments and discussion by Elsa Fornero and Steven Haberman on the conceptual approaches in Chapter 5.

Many other people have backed me during the work on this thesis. In this context I would like to especially thank Johannes Clemens and Stephan Fasshauer for the many fruitful discussions and great insights into the institutional and political aspects of my work. I am also thankful to the Deutsche Rentenversicherung (DRV) for the numerous conferences, graduate colloquiums and workshops that always provided valuable information and an interesting platform for discussion. My special thanks go to all my current and former colleagues and friends at the Mannheim Research Institute for the Economics of Aging (MEA). They all contributed to the uniquely agreeable and familial atmosphere at MEA. They all made this thesis enjoyable and certainly improved its quality. I would also like to take the opportunity to thank Tabea Bucher-Koenen and her husband Johannes Koenen as well as Keren Ladin for their efforts to make this thesis better readable and easier to understand. Special thanks also go to Isabella Nohe and her warm and caring manner. She has helped me deal with the bureaucratic issues of university life innumerable times.

I gratefully acknowledge financial support from the Land Baden-Württemberg, the Gesamtverband der Deutschen Versicherungswirtschaft (GDV) and the EU Research Training Network on the Economics of Aging (RTN). Last but not least, I would like to thank my family, especially my husband Kay who has been an endless source of inspiration. Special thanks also go to my parents and my grandma for their encouragement and support and their unconditional belief in me.

Contents

List of Figures

List of Tables

1. Introduction

The German pension system was the first formal pension system in the world, designed by Bismarck nearly 120 years ago. It has been very successful in providing a high and reliable level of retirement income in the past at reasonable contribution rates, becoming a model for many social security systems worldwide. While the generosity of the German public pension system is considered a great social achievement, negative incentive effects of past reforms in the 1970s and 1980s and population aging are threatening the very core of the pension system. These have led to fundamental pension reforms since 1992. This thesis delivers an assessment of the German pension system and its reforms.

Historical overview. As opposed to other countries such as the United Kingdom and the Netherlands which originally adopted a Beveridgian social security system that provided only a base pension, public pensions in Germany were from the start designed to extend the standard of living achieved during work life throughout retirement. Thus, public pensions are roughly proportional to labor income averaged over the entire lifecourse and feature few redistributive properties. The German pension system is therefore called 'pension insurance' rather than 'social security', as in the United States. Workers used to understand their contributions as 'insurance premia' rather than 'taxes', although this has dramatically changed in recent years with contribution rates rising steadily while pension levels are reduced. The insurance character is strengthened by institutional separation; The German pension insurance system is not part of the government budget but a separate entity. This entity is subsidized by the federal government. Rationale for this subsidy, almost 30% of expenditures, are 'non-insurance benefits' such as benefits paid to German immigrants after opening the iron curtain. Any surplus, however, remains in the system. It is not transferable into a 'unified budget' such as in the United States.

The German retirement insurance started as a fully funded system with a mandatory retirement age of 70 years when male life expectancy at birth was less than 45 years. At the end of the 1990s, life expectancy for men was more than 75 years, but average retirement age had dropped to less than 60[1]. The system was converted to a de facto pay-as-you-go system (PAYG) after most funds had been invested in government bonds between the two World Wars. In 1957, after a long and arduous debate, the German Bundestag decided to convert the system gradually to a pay-as-you-go scheme. The remainder of the capital stock was spent about 10 years later. Since then, the German system has been purely PAYG, with a very small reserve fund lasting from a minimum of 6 to a maximum of 45 days.

A second historical reform took place in 1972. It made the German pension system one of the most generous ones of the world. The 1972 system was generous in two respects. First, the system provided very high pension levels[2], generating net pension benefits of around 70% of average earnings for workers with a 45-year earnings history and average lifetime earnings. Moreover, pension benefits were indexed to the development of gross wages. Second, the 1972 reform abolished the statutory retirement age of 65 years for workers with a service life of at least 35 years. Instead a *window of retirement* between age 63 and 65 was introduced without any actuarial adjustments. In addition to these generous early retirement options, easy ways to claim disability benefits and low statutory retirement ages for women and unemployed further increased the number of beneficiaries and effectively extended the window of retirement to between age 60 and 65.

However, under the increasing pressure of population aging it has become clear that this generosity no longer can be maintained. All industrialized countries are aging. However, Germany, as well as Italy and Japan, will experience a particularly dramatic change in population age structure. The severity of the demographic transition in Germany has two causes: a quicker increase in life expectancy partly due to a relatively low level in the 1970s,

[1]The average retirement age in a given year is the average age of those workers who retired the same year thus receiving public pension benefits for the first time. See Verband Deutscher Rentenversicherungsträger (VDR) (2007).

[2]Note that this pension level is defined as the current pension of a retiree with a 45-year average earnings history divided by the current average earnings of all employed workers. It is different from the replacement rate relative to the most recent earnings of a retiring worker that are usually higher than the life-time average.

and a more incisive baby boom/baby bust transition (e.g., relative to the United States) to a very low fertility rate of 1.4 children per women, only a bit higher than the low fertility rate of 1.2 in Italy and Spain. Consequently, the ratio of elderly to working age persons, the old age dependency ratio, will increase steeply in the next decades. Projections show that the dependency ratio will more than double in the next four decades, from roughly 30% today, to between 60% and 65% in 2050.[3].

This increase in the dependency ratio has immediate consequences for a PAYG based system because fewer workers must finance the benefits of more recipients. The German contribution rate to the public pension system, 19.9% of gross income in 2008, was projected at the end of the 1980s to exceed 40% of gross income at the peak of population aging in 2035, if the accustomed pension levels and the indexation of pensions to gross income were maintained[4]. This led to a major pension reform in 1992. This reform abolished the indexation of pensions to gross wages in favor of net wages. While this is still more generous than indexation to costs of living (as it is the case in the U.S.), it was an important move away from the destabilizing feedback loop in which pensions increased when taxes and contributions increased. In addition, the 1992 reform introduced benefits adjustments to early retirement and abolished the generous window of retirement for women and unemployed. These adjustments, however, are still being phased in and will only be fully implemented in 2017.

It soon became clear that the 1992 reform was too little and too late to put the German system on a stable and sustainable path. Another parametric reform introduced by the conservative government and due to become law in 1999 failed after the change in government in 1998. Three years later in 2001, the secretary of labor, Walter Riester, successfully passed another major reform bill through parliament. This reform abolished the pure pay-as-you-go system and introduced a multi-pillar pension system with small, but growing, supplementary pillars. In addition, it greatly cut future pension levels in favor of a more moderate rise in contribution rates. However, the Riester reform had been based on overly optimistic assumptions. In December 2002, the government therefore established a 'Commission on the financial

[3]See chapter 2.

[4]See Prognos (1987).

Sustainability of the Social Security Systems', commonly referred to as the 'Rürup Commission' after its chairman Bert Rürup. In its reform proposal in August 2003, the commission proposed further cuts in pension levels by introducing a '*sustainability factor*' into the benefit indexation formula, linking the development of benefits to internal system parameters. As a second measure, an increase in the normal statutory retirement age from 65 to 67 was proposed. The first proposition was legislated in 2004, the second with some delay in 2007. At the time of writing of this thesis, further (parametric) reform measures are still being debated.

Assessing pension system reforms. This thesis looks at whether the pension reforms of the past quarter century have been successful enough to bring the system back onto a stable path. Pension reforms can be assessed according to very different dimensions. At its Gothenburg Summit in 2001, the European Commission agreed on three principles of pension reform: (1) adequacy of pensions, (2) financial sustainability of pension systems and (3) modernization of pension systems in response to changing needs of the economy, society and individuals where modernization mainly refers to labor market compatibility, equal treatment of men and women and transparency[5]. The World Bank set up similar goals for pension systems in 2005. According to the bank, pension systems should provide (1) adequate, (2) affordable, (3) sustainable and (3) robust retirement income[6]. Schwarz (2005) extends these goals by two additional dimensions, namely (1) fairness and (2) redistribution. For the purpose of this thesis, I consolidate these different approaches to the following five dimensions that in my view are of particular relevance for the German pension system:

Adequacy The adequacy of pension benefits can be judged according to at least two criteria[7]: (1) The level of benefits compared to the poverty level to determine whether benefits are sufficient to prevent poverty in old age and (2) the level of benefits compared to average wages to determine how benefits compare to the overall wage growth in the economy. In this thesis, I will focus on the second aspect. The key

[5]See Council of the European Union (2001).

[6]See Holzmann and Hinz (2005).

[7]See Council of the European Union (2001) as well as Schwarz (2005).

question is how future pension levels in the German public pension system will develop under the current state of the system, and to what extent this projected development has been driven by the past reforms.

Affordability and Sustainability In view of population aging, financing of adequate pension levels has become increasingly difficult for many pension systems worldwide. Sustainability, in this context, refers to a stable financial situation of the pension system that allows for adjustments in contribution rates and pension levels in a balanced way. This principle has played a crucial role in the German pension reform process. From a macroeconomic perspective, pension systems can only be sustainable if benefits and contributions are linked to the internal rate of return of the system, $n + g$ with n as the population growth rate and g as the per capita economic growth rate. If the system's rate of return is higher, the system is unsustainable in that it transfers a growing burden to younger generations. This concept has been particularly relevant in the discussion on the transition of the PAYG system to a funded system[8]. In this thesis, I will thoroughly investigate the underlying balancing mechanism of the German public pension system that determines the development of pension benefits and contribution rates. In a second step, I will compare the German system to the much appraised Swedish notional defined contribution system (NDC), which also incorporates an automatic balancing mechanism.

Fairness and Redistribution As mentioned above, increases in contribution rates and further cuts in pension levels have led to the problem that the system is no longer perceived to be fair. People tend to regard their contribution payments as taxes rather than contributions. This has negative incentive effects on system participation as a whole, which places the system at further financial distress in the short and medium term. The term fairness here alludes to whether individuals, once they retire, will get fair returns from the contributions they paid into the system. One possibility to measure the fairness of a pension system is

[8] Here, the internal rate of return of the PAYG pension system is compared to the internal rate of return on the capital market which would apply in case of a funded system. See e.g. Börsch-Supan (1998), Breyer (1989), Fenge (1995) and Raffelhüschen (1993) for different points of view in this debate concerning the transition of the German pension system to a fully-funded one.

to look at individual internal rates of return[9]. A key question here is whether rates of return will turn to zero or even negative, such that the system no longer can be perceived as being fair. In this thesis, I will point out two different approaches according to which internal rates of return can be calculated, and show the results for the German public pension system for different demographic groups and across cohorts in order to look at the *inter*generational redistribution. Due to the strict relation of benefits to lifetime earnings, *intra*generational redistribution, by contrast, only plays a minor role in the German pension system.

Robustness Robustness also has become an important issue in times of high fluctuations at the capital markets and political interventions. While public pension systems face high political risks, private pension schemes are confronted to the rate of return risk on the capital markets. In this thesis, I discuss whether the shift from the former monolithic towards a multi-pillar system has turned the German pension system into a more robust one.

Transparency Finally, particularly for Germany, the issue of transparency is crucial. Over the course of the repeated discretionary interventions of the past and its ongoing reform process, the German PAYG system has lost a good deal of its former credibility[10]. Transparency here could help to re-establish some of this credibility and make the reform process more comprehensible.

A simulation model of the German pension system. In order to analyze these questions, I construct a sophisticated simulation model of the German pension system that I will refer to as MEA-PENSIM throughout this thesis[11]. Figure 1.1 gives an overview of the structure of this model.

In the first step, projections for Germany's future demographic and labor market development are computed. This is necessary in order to evaluate

[9]Note that here, the internal rate of return does not refer to the system as a whole but to the individual that pays contributions to and receives benefits from the system.

[10]See Pfeiffer, Braun, Grimm, and Schmidt (2007).

[11]See chapter 3 as well as Wilke (2004) for a thorough description of the model.

Figure 1.1. – Modeling the German Pension System: Structural Overview of MEA-PENSIM

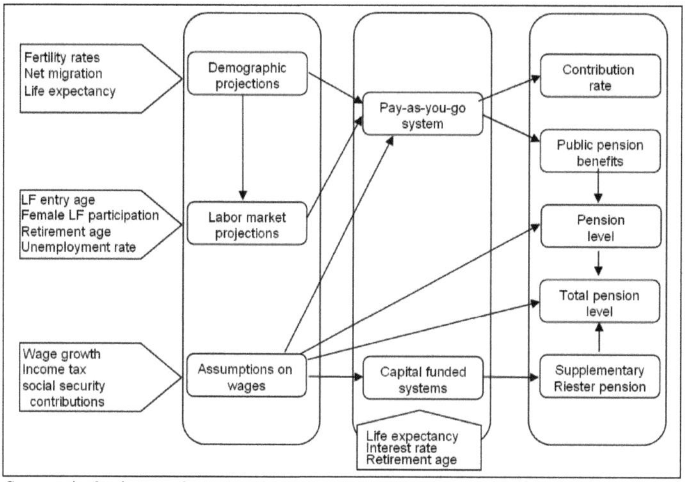

Source: Author's compilation.

the effects of different demographic and labor market assumptions on the future German pension system. As will be shown, different underlying assumptions can have a large impact on the results. The exact modeling of these projections will be described in chapter 2. In addition, assumptions on the future development of wages are necessary. These enter exogenously into the model[12]. In a second step, based on the demographic and labor market forecasts and wage assumptions, the future financial development of the German pension system is computed. This computation is composed of two parts. The first part refers to the financial development of the public PAYG system. The second part refers to the development of the state-subsidized supplementary Riester pensions. This illustrates the observable shift of the German pension system from the former monolithic to a multi-pillar system. The underlying conceptual approaches will be explained in chapter 3. The

[12]This of course is a drawback of the model as feedback effects such as with the labor and capital market cannot be modeled. However, any model has its restrictions and for the purpose of this thesis, it seems more important to build a comprehensive model of the German pension system that allows a thorough evaluation of past and current reform measures.

model's calculation results are summarized in several pertinent system measures, such as the development of contribution rates and pension levels, the pension value and the value of supplementary pensions, as well as the total pension level of both public and private pension income. For the analysis of the NDC approach and the computations of cohort-specific rates of return, this basic setup of the model is extended. Additional underlying assumptions and the computational approach are explained in these chapters.

Structure of this thesis. The remainder of this thesis is structured as follows. Chapter 2 presents demographic and labor market projections for Germany, illustrating the demographic challenges Germany faces and the labor market potentials it can use in order to better cope with these challenges. Chapter 3 describes the basic principles of the German pension system and delivers a first assessment of past reforms, with respect to the adequacy of pension benefits, the long-term financial sustainability and the robustness of the system as a whole. Chapter 4 then looks at whether the NDC approach presents an alternative reform option for a more transparent German PAYG system, and compares the different outcomes of the two systems. In chapter 5, cohort-specific internal rates of return are computed in order to assess the fairness and intergenerational redistribution of the system. Chapter 6 summarizes the main findings and provides some concluding remarks. Overall, it can be said that past reforms have put the German pension system back onto a stable path and moved it towards a multi-pillar system. Some unresolved issues however remain and future reforms seem likely.

2. Demographic Challenges and Labor Market Potentials

2.1. Introduction

Similar to other industrialized countries, Germany too faces enormous demographic challenges in the near future. Its population size is projected to decrease considerably, while the remaining population is projected to age rapidly. This process is driven by three (independent) factors, namely: (1) the great increase in fertility rates between the mid 1950s and mid 1960s (the so-called baby boom) followed by the sharp decline in fertility rates through the mid 1970s (the so-called baby bust), (2) the continuous rise in life expectancy, and (3) the subsequently low fertility rates.

The first effect has led to fundamental changes in the age structure of the population, as aging baby boomers account for a large share of the graying population. This aging process is strengthened even further by the second and third factors as the increasing share of older people will continue to live longer lives with fewer younger people following. The low level fertility rate (approx. 1.4 births/woman) will eventually lead to a decline in the size of the population. At this fertility rate, each generation will only reproduce approximately two thirds of itself. In fact, since 1972, the number of deaths has outweighed the number of births in Germany. Until 2002 this was offset by positive net migration, however since then, net migration (though still positive) was not high enough, leading to a slow decline in the size of the German population.

This change in the size and age structure of the German population will pose enormous challenges for society as a whole. It means that the old age dependency ratio, i.e. the ratio of elderly to working age persons, will increase steeply within the next decades. This will affect the entire economic system and will lead to deep structural changes. The impact on financing social security systems, the topic to be analyzed in the remainder of this thesis, is only one dimension. Other dimensions include the effects on labor, capital and goods markets, on public finances, and foremost on per capita growth. The future development of the labor market is of particular importance. On the one hand, labor supply is directly affected by the described demographic change. On the other hand, it can mitigate the economic consequences of this process if the labor force decreases at a lower rate than the working age population, thereby facilitating for a less pronounced decline in the size of the economically active fraction of the proportion. If Germany succeeds in making use of its labor market potentials this will cushion the demographic burden and positively influence the prospect of all other dimensions.

This chapter provides a detailed overview about how Germany's demographic situation may evolve in the future and which possible labor market developments may accompany it. It is based on an earlier version by Börsch-Supan and Wilke (2007). The chapter is structured as follows: Section 2.2 presents current demographic projections for Germany that show how the population size and structure could develop over the next decades. Based on these scenarios, projections of the possible future development of labor supply are presented in section 2.3. Since labor supply depicts only one side of the labor market, assumptions for the future development of labor demand are added to the labor market projection model in section 2.4 in order to project future employment. Section 2.5 concludes.

2.2. Demographic Projections

This section presents current projections on the future development of the German population. I will refer to the latest German official forecasts and most current frequently applied projections as well as to my own projections, which I will name the MEA[1] projections. Section 2.2.1 describes selected population scenarios and their underlying methodology and assumptions. Projection results are illustrated in section 2.2.2.

[1]MEA stands for the Mannheim Research Institute for the Economics of Aging.

2.2.1. Methodology and Scenarios

The MEA projections are based on the most recent 11th coordinated population projections by the German Federal Statistical Office (GFSO)[2]. The objective was to build a population simulation model that is able to replicate the various variants of these official population projections. I will first briefly outline the basic methodology of these projections, followed by an explanation of the GFSO variants and MEA scenarios. I compare these to the still widely used demographic scenario by the Rürup Commission[3].

Modeling demographic development. The most simple and commonly used projection approach is the cohort-component method[4]. Based on initial age and sex-specific population data for a given country or region, age and sex-specific groups are adjusted according to assumptions on the three main demographic parameters: fertility, mortality, and migration. Each group survives and continues to the next according to assumed age and sex specific mortality rates. In general, five-year age groups are applied[5]. As data is available on an annual basis for Germany, the GFSO defines one-year-age groups. I follow this approach. Migration is accounted for by including age and sex-specific net migration rates that are adjusted according to the set migration assumptions while preserving the initial age pattern. The annual number of births is computed by applying age-specific fertility rates to females in the age groups between 15 and 50 (the reproductive age span). A sex ratio of 0.51 for males is applied to births in order to maintain the population sex ratio.

The German 11th coordinated population projections. The 'medium scenario' of the GFSO population projections includes two variants: variant 1W1, as a lower limit, and variant 1W2, as an upper limit. Note that the

[2]See Statistisches Bundesamt (2006a) for the original German report and Statistisches Bundesamt (2006b) for an English summary.

[3]See Kommission für die Nachhaltigkeit in der Finanzierung der Sozialen Sicherungssysteme (2003a) for the original German report and Kommission für die Nachhaltigkeit in der Finanzierung der Sozialen Sicherungssysteme (2003b) for an English summary.

[4]See O'Neill, Balk, Brickman, and Ezra (2001) for a thorough overview of different population projection methods.

[5]See e.g. the United Nations population projections (United Nations 2006).

first digit refers to the assumptions for life expectancy while the second digit refers to the assumptions for migration[6]. Both variants assume a stagnant birth rate of 1.4 births/woman. With respect to life expectancy, both variants use the base assumption, according to which the life expectancy at birth will rise to 83.5 years for men and 88.0 years for women by the year 2050[7]. With respect to migration, the two scenarios use different assumptions. Variant 1W1 assumes a net migration of 100,000 persons/year and thus follows the declining trend observed over the past few years. Variant 1W2 is based on the observed long-term net migration for Germany of 200,000 persons/year.

The MEA population projections. Based on the desire to create a 'medium' migration scenario and to model life expectancy more realistically, I develop two additional population scenarios. My base scenario 3W1.5[8] assumes a stronger rise in life expectancy than the GFSO projections. In addition, I create a third variant for the 'medium scenario' which I call 1W1.5. Both scenarios use a constant birth rate of 1.4 births/woman and assume a medium net migration of 150.000 persons/year (hence the abbreviation 'W1.5').

Life expectancy assumptions for the base scenario (MEA 3W1.5) presume a continuation of the observable increases of the past decades. By extrapolating the quasi linear trend after the World War II separately for men and women, a life expectancy of 85.7 years for men and 91.7 years for women can be computed for the year 2050. Similar calculations by Schnabel, Kistowski, and Vaupel (2005) that apply more sophisticated extrapolation methods compute 92.6 $\pm$ 3.8 years for men and 94.0 $\pm$ 2.8 years for women (depending on the extrapolation method) for the year 2050. Compared to these calculations, the MEA 3W1.5 scenario is still moderate, but life expectancies are clearly higher than in the case of the GFSO base assumption for the 'medium' scenario and also higher than in the GFSO 'steep rise' scenario. Considering that past GFSO life expectancy projections have repeatedly underestimated actual development, assuming a slightly steeper rise in life expectancy, as is the case in the MEA base scenario, seems appropriate.

[6]The *W* stands for 'Wanderungen', German for 'Migration'.

[7]The GFSO publishes another scenario called 'steep rise' with the variants 2W1 and 2W2 which assumes a life expectancy of 85.4 years for men and 89.8 years for women in 2050.

[8]Note that I adopt the notation used by the German Federal Statistical Office explained above.

Table 2.1. – Overview of Population Scenarios

	Life Expectancy		*Net migration*	*Birth rate*
	Male	*Female*	*[Thousands]*	*[Births/woman]*
Rürup Commission	81.3	86.6	200	1.4
GFSO 1W1	83.5	88.0	100	1.4
MEA 1W1.5	83.5	88.0	150	1.4
GFSO 1W2	83.5	88.0	200	1.4
GFSO 2W1	85.4	89.8	100	1.4
GFSO 2W2	85.4	89.8	200	1.4
MEA 3W1.5	85.7	91.7	150	1.4

Source: Author's compilation based on the 11th coordinated population projections of the German Federal Statistical Office (GFSO) (Statistisches Bundesamt 2006a) and on the demographic scenario of the Rürup Commission (Kommission für die Nachhaltigkeit in der Finanzierung der Sozialen Sicherungssysteme 2003a).

Overview of population scenarios. Table 2.1 gives an overview of the GFSO and MEA scenarios and their underlying assumptions. It also includes the demographic scenario of the Rürup Commission, which was used for its 2003 reform proposal, and is still frequently applied.

2.2.2. Simulation Results

2005 was used as the base year for the projections as it is the last year for which historical population data is available. The projection period ends in 2050.

Development of the total population. Figure 2.1 shows the development of the total population between the years of 2005 and 2050 for the different population scenarios. Since the MEA base scenario 3W1.5 is almost identical to the GFSO variant 1W2, and the MEA 1W1.5 scenario closely reflects the GFSO variant 2W1, the two variants 1W2 and 2W1 were omitted from Figure 2.1 to facilitate clearer illustration.

Compared to a population of 82.4 million in 2005, the MEA 3W1.5 scenario leads to a decline of about 8 million to 74.4 million in 2050. This corresponds to the Rürup Commission projections for the year 2050. However, in contrast to the MEA 3W1.5 scenario, the Rürup Commission assumes additional growth in the size of the total population through 2020. The MEA 1W1.5 scenario shows a much stronger decline of 11.3 million to 71.1 million in 2050. The GFSO variant 1W1 produces a figure 2.3 million below this value (68.8 million). The projected population decline is less pronounced in the GFSO 2W2 variant because of the higher annual net migration.

Changes in the age structure of the population. In addition to the projected decline in total population, the age structure of the German population will change considerably. Figure 2.2 illustrates this change by depicting the development of the old age dependency ratio (OADR) for the different population scenarios. Note that the OADR here is defined as the ratio between persons aged 65+ and persons aged 15 to 64.

The percentaged change in the OADR is significantly larger than the percentaged population decline depicted in Figure 2.1. For the MEA 3W1.5 scenario, the OADR is projected to increase from 0.29 in 2005 to 0.65 in 2050, meaning that there will be only 1.5 persons aged 15-64 compared to one person aged 65+ in 2050. This scenario is realistic and highlights the severity of the German demographic situation. For the MEA 1W1.5 scenario, the rise in the OADR is more moderate and amounts to 0.58 in 2050. Through the year 2030 this increase is nearly identical to the projected increases in the GFSO 1W1 and 2W2 variants. Beyond 2030, the OADR in the GFSO 1W1 and 2W2 rises a bit more rapidly and ends up a bit above the MEA 1W1.5 scenario in 2050. The Rürup Commission scenario shows the most optimistic development where the OADR will climb to 0.53 in 2050. In contrast to the development of the total population, the development of the OADR in the MEA 3W1.5 scenario is now equivalent to the GFSO variant 2W1, while the projected OADR for the 1W1.5 scenario lies in between the GFSO 1W2 and 2W2 variants. Changes in the total population thus do not necessarily translate one to one into corresponding changes in the age structure. Assumptions on future net migration have an especially considerable impact on the projected age structure of the population.

It is important to note that it is this change in the age structure illustrated in Figure 2.2 that represents the core of the aging problem. As shown, the latter is far more severe than the projected population decline [9]

[9]Note that changes in the age structure do not always correspond to simultaneous population declines, as

Figure 2.1. – Development of the Size of the German Population

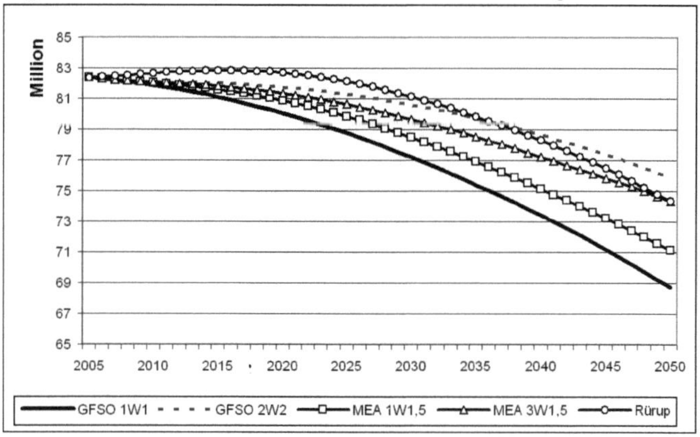

Source: Author's computations based on the 11th coordinated population projections of the German Federal Statistical Office (GFSO) (Statistisches Bundesamt 2006a) and on the demographic scenario of the Rürup Commission (Kommission für die Nachhaltigkeit in der Finanzierung der Sozialen Sicherungssysteme 2003a).

Figure 2.2. – Development of the Old Age Dependency Ratio for Germany

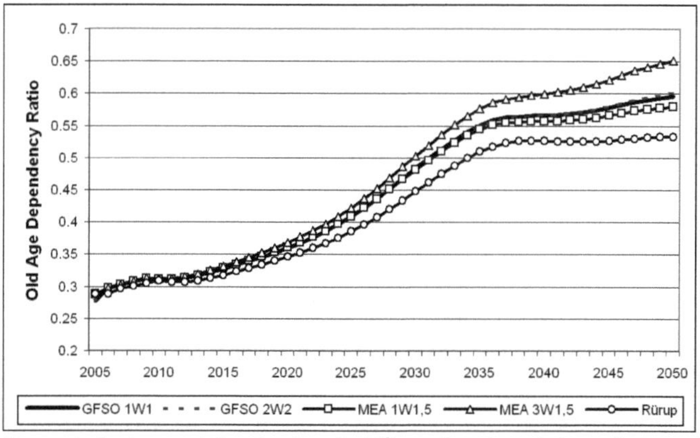

Source: Author's computations based on the 11th coordinated population projections of the German Federal Statistical Office (GFSO) (Statistisches Bundesamt 2006a) and on the demographic scenario of the Rürup Commission (Kommission für die Nachhaltigkeit in der Finanzierung der Sozialen Sicherungssysteme 2003a).

2.3. Projections on Future Labor Supply

The previous section showed that the working age population is projected to decline. How strongly this affects the actual size of the labor force (employees + unemployed) depends on the percentage of working age population seeking employment[10]. This section will provide projections for the future labor supply. The projections are based on the demographic projections described in the previous section. The objective is to develop a realistic scenario for Germany that reflects the currently perceived future labor market prospects.

The projections are based on the methodology applied by Börsch-Supan (2003a) for earlier projections on the German labor market. More recent supply side oriented projections for Germany were published in 2005 by the Institute of Labor Market and Professional Research[11] and by the European Commission[12]. A more demand side oriented projection was constructed by the Rürup Commission in 2003, based on the Commission's demographic projections which were presented in section 2.2.1[13]. I will later compare my projection results with the results of these studies.

In the following, I will first describe the underlying modeling approach of my projections in section 2.3.1. Selected scenarios are then explained in section 2.3.2. Section 2.3.3 shows the projection results. I conclude this section with a sensitivity analysis on the single parameter effects in the labor supply model in section 2.3.4.

is the case in Germany. In the United States, for example, fertility rates have declined much less than in Germany while life expectancy has risen to a similar extent also provoking changes in the population's age structure without declines in the size of the population.

[10]Note that this difference between the size of the working age population and the labor force size is called hidden reserve. Foreigners wanting to join the German labor market are included in the hidden reserve and implicitly incorporated in the migration assumptions of the underlying demographic forecast.

[11]See Fuchs and Dörfler (2005b) and Fuchs and Dörfler (2005a) as well as Fuchs and Söhnlein (2007).

[12]See Carone (2005).

[13]See again Kommission für die Nachhaltigkeit in der Finanzierung der Sozialen Sicherungssysteme (2003a) for the original German report and Kommission für die Nachhaltigkeit in der Finanzierung der Sozialen Sicherungssysteme (2003b) for an English summary.

2.3.1. Modeling Labor Supply

In a first step, future age and sex-specific labor force participation rates[14] are determined by the development of the following three labor supply parameters:

1. **Labor Entry Age.** The mean labor entry age is assumed to decrease in the future. To simulate this effect, the age distribution of labor force participation rates below a certain age limit is shifted to the left. The age limit is the age that marks the current end of the educational period, which in Germany is around 27. After that age, participation rates usually reach the higher levels which are maintained until almost age 50. Participation rates between this initial age limit and the new (lower) age limit are set equal to former participation rates at the initial age limit. Since the youngest recorded working age in the microcensus is age 15, participation rates below this age are assumed to turn zero. The adjustment of participation rates over time from the initial to a specified target distribution is computed linearly.

2. **Female labor force participation.** It is assumed that age specific female participation rates in the future will converge with today's male participation rates. This effect is modeled by reducing the difference between female and male participation rates by a specified factor between zero and one. Again, the adaptation over time for participation rates between the base and target years is done linearly.

3. **Retirement age.** Finally, the mean retirement age is assumed to increase further in the future. To simulate this effect, the age distribution of labor force participation rates above a certain age limit is shifted to the right. The age limit now is the earliest age that marks the beginning of the transition period into retirement, which in Germany is

[14] Participation rates describe the proportion of the labor force to the population. Labor force participation rates are based on the microcensus of the German Federal Statistical Office. The microcensus contains the official representative statistics of the German population and labor market, annually surveying 1% of all households in Germany (continuous household sample survey). However, marginal occupation in the microcensus is underrepresented and total labor force participation is therefore slightly underestimated. I correct for this by calibrating the microcensus-based labor force participation rates with the aggregated labor force participation rate provided by the OECD Labor Statistics multiplied by the size of the aggregate labor force of the base year.

around age 47. After that age, participation rates start to decline as people retire from the workforce. Participation rates between the initial age limit and the new (higher) age limit are again set equal to former participation rates at the initial age limit. Again, the adjustment over time is computed linearly.

In a second step, these rates are multiplied with the age and sex-specific data from the population projections described in section 2.3[15].

2.3.2. Scenarios

Using the parameters introduced in the preceding section, nearly all future development of the labor supply can be modeled, however, it remains to be seen which future development should be considered most realistic. I create four scenarios ('Status Quo', 'Best Case', 'Denmark' and 'Agenda 1005') in order to illustrate the range of possible future outcomes. The scenarios are described below.

The 'Status Quo' scenario. This scenario defines the lower limit of possible future outcomes. It assumes that labor force participation rates will remain constant at current levels. This implies that the mean labor entry age will not decrease, that female participation rates will not converge with those of men, and that the current mean retirement age will not increase further despite the recent pension reforms which are explained in more detail in chapter 3. This scenario seems rather unlikely, but is intended to show the effects of the maximum demographic pressures on the labor supply.

The 'Best Case' scenario. While the 'Status Quo' scenario marks the lower limit of potential future labor supply developments, the 'Best Case' scenario marks the upper limit. In this scenario, participation rates are assumed to increase as much as possible. This assumes that by 2040, the mean labor entry age will decrease by two years, that the gap between female and male participation rates will be closed by 90% while male participation rates will

[15]Note that I do not differentiate between West and East Germany, not least because a projection of the corresponding parameters is very difficult. See e.g. Fuchs and Söhnlein (2007) regarding differences between East and West Germany concerning labor force behavior.

Figure 2.3. – A Comparison of Danish and German Labor Force Participation Rates

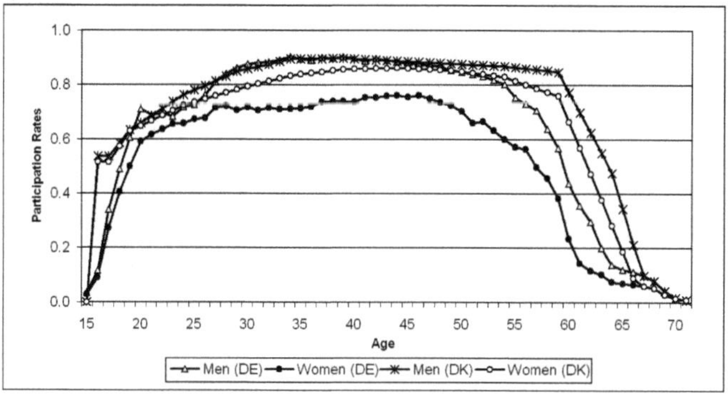

Source: Author's compilation based on the microcensus data of the German Federal Statistical Office and Statistics Denmark (www.statbank.dk).

be lowered to 95% of current levels, and finally that the mean retirement age will increase by three years. This scenario is extremely optimistic. It is intended to illustrate the maximum possible labor supply which is achieved, for example, by US-American participation rates.

The 'Denmark' scenario. In order to find a realistic scenario within these lower and upper limits, I use evidence from Germany's European neighbors. Denmark, together with Switzerland, records the highest participation rates for female and elderly workers in Europe. Figure 2.3 compares German participation rates with the Danish ones. The Danish female participation rates are significantly higher than those of German women for all ages. For men, the participation rates are similar in both countries for younger workers, but diverge later as a significantly higher proportion of Danish men continues working at older ages.

The 'Denmark' scenario assumes that German participation rates will eventually converge with the Danish rates. Convergence by the year 2040 results in: lowering the mean labor entry age by one year, the 90% convergence of female participation rates towards men's rates with a corresponding decrease in male participation rates to 95% of current levels, and an increase in the

Table 2.2. – Overview of Labor Supply Scenarios

	Labor entry age [years]	*Female labor force participation*	*Retirement age [years]*
Status Quo	unchanged	unchanged	unchanged
Agenda 1005	-1	75%	+1
Denmark	-1	90%	+2
Best Case	-2	90%	+3

All projections have 2040 as target year.
Source: Author's compilation.

mean retirement age by two years. The 'Denmark' scenario seems very realistic if current German reform efforts, such as 'Agenda 2010' which was founded by the former Schröder regime, are continued. This assumes that over the next 30 years Germany will be able to execute the necessary labor market reforms implemented in Denmark during the 1990s. A third of the Danish reform speed should thus suffice for this scenario to turn real.

The 'Agenda 1005' scenario. Last, I choose a clearly less optimistic but also realistic scenario that takes into account the recent trend in German politics to undo some of the most recent important labor market reforms. This scenario will be called 'Agenda 1005' scenario, hinting at an only 'half hearted' implementation of the set Agenda 2010. For this scenario, assumptions include a reduction of the mean labor entry age by one year, an increase in female participation rates up to 75% of the different to men's, and an increase in the mean retirement age by one year by 2040.

Thus, the four selected scenarios show the possible range of future developments of the labor supply in Germany. Table 2.2 summarizes the different underlying assumptions for each scenario. Two of the scenarios define the lower and upper bounds, the other two are realistic scenarios, one geared to the current situation in Denmark and the other to current reform trends in Germany.

2.3.3. Simulation Results

The base year for my projections is 2005. I assume constant labor force participation rates through 2008, as the reforms in the 'Agenda 1005', 'Denmark' and 'Best Case' scenarios will require time until fully implemented. Projections are run through the year 2050. However, since adjustments in participation rates are all assumed to take place by 2040, participation rates de facto remain constant after that. Thus, from the year 2040 on, changes in labor supply are only based on the underlying demographic development, for which I choose the MEA 3W1.5 scenario presented in section 2.2.1.

Development of the size of the labor force. While the labor force declines in all four scenarios (Figure 2.4), the extent of this decline varies greatly. While a large decrease of 9.6 million (about 22.7%) to 32.6 million in 2040 is projected in the 'Status Quo' scenario, the labor force only decreases by 2.8 million (about 6.6%) to 39.4 million in the 'Best Case' scenario. The decline in the 'Best Case' scenario thus only amounts to roughly a third of the decline in the 'Status Quo' scenario. In the 'Denmark' scenario the decrease is 3.9 million (about 9.2%) by 2040, one million more than in the 'Best Case' scenario. In the 'Agenda 1005' scenario, the decline in the labor force amounts to 5.8 million (about 13.7%) in 2040, three million more than in the 'Base Case' and two million more than in the 'Denmark' scenario[16].

From the year 2040 on, the decrease in the labor force accelerates in all scenarios and declines at the same rate as in the 'Status Quo' scenario, namely according to the development of the working age population as projected by the underlying demography. The 'Best Case' and 'Denmark' scenarios, where the adjustment of participation rates is so high that it offsets the demographic trends, show a kink in 2040 when participation rates reach their target values while the population continues to decline further. Thus, even if the best possible usage of the labor force potential is assumed will the population decline be reflected in a smaller labor force in the long run.

[16] For my projections I assume a convergence with Danish participation rates by the year 2040. If other transition periods are assumed, the resulting development obviously differs. Appendix A shows the different transitional patterns for different adjustment periods.

Figure 2.4. – Development of the Size of the Labor Force.

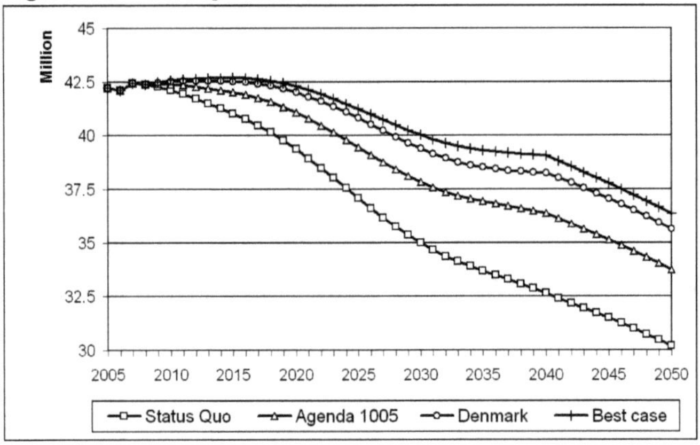

Source: Author's computations.

Figure 2.5. – Labor Force Development under Different Population Scenarios.

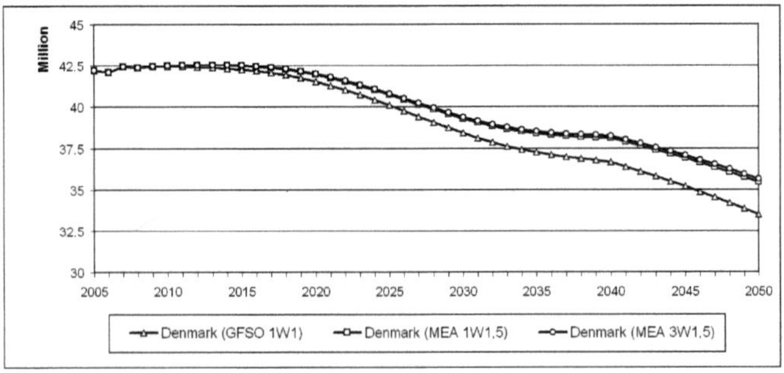

Source: Author's computations.

Consequences of a stronger population decrease. How strongly will these results vary if more pessimistic population projections are used? Figure 2.5 compares the development of the labor force size in the 'Denmark' scenario for both MEA population projections (3W1.5 and 1W1.5) as well as the GFSO variant 1W1.

Differences between the two MEA projections are minimal since these only differ with respect to life expectancy assumptions and hardly play a role with respect to development of the labor force. However, a difference between the MEA 3W1.5 scenario and the GFSO 1W1 variant of around 1.6 million by 2040 results from differing assumptions of net migration (100,000 instead of 150,000 per year) as lower annual net migration considerably reduces the size of the working age population. Analogously, a net migration of 200,000 instead of 150,000 will lead to a labor force increase of 1.6 million. It should be noted that even though a higher net migration generally leads to a larger labor force, it cannot stop the long-term decline of the labor force[17].

Changes in the age structure. In addition to the size, the age structure of the labor force will change considerably during the next decades. Figure 2.6 shows the age structure of the labor force for the 'Denmark' scenario for the years 2010, 2020, 2030, 2040 and 2050. It can be seen that the peak of the distribution first shifts to the right and then disappears between 2020 and 2030, when the baby boomers retire. Subsequently, the age distribution flattens and changes only slightly in the following years.

Figure 2.7 shows the development of the average age of the labor force. In the 'Denmark' scenario, the average age will rise from 39.8 today to 41.7 years in 2025. After that it will slightly decrease for 10 years and then rise again by half a year, finally peaking at 42 years in year 2050. In the 'Best-Case' scenario the development is similar. In the scenarios 'Agenda 1005' and 'Status Quo' the decline of the average age is much stronger after 2025 because a large part of the baby boom generation will have retired at that time already.

The change in the age structure becomes even more evident when looking at the percentage of the labor force aged 55+. Figure 2.8 illustrates the temporary rejuvenation of the labor force when the baby boomers have retired. It becomes evident that the change in the age structure of the labor force is not a temporary phenomenon but a longer lasting development. In the 'Denmark' and 'Best-Case' scenarios, the percentage of the labor force aged

[17]For the role of migration in the discussion about the effects of the demographic changes, see Börsch-Supan (2002b).

Figure 2.6. – Age Structure of the Labor Force

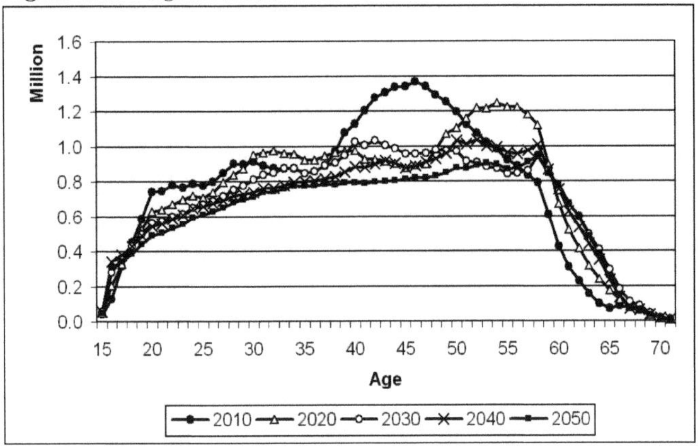

Source: Author's computations.

55+ nearly doubles. In the 'Agenda 1005' scenario increase in the percentage of the labor force aged 55+ is two thirds.

These trends clearly illustrate that future labor supply will increasingly rely on older workers. If we do not succeed in better integrating the elderly population into the labor market and using their potential, we won't be able to offset much of the projected labor force decline under the 'Status Quo' scenario.

2.3.4. Sensitivity Analysis

The labor supply projections presented in the previous section were based on four scenarios which span the possible range of future developments. All scenarios make different assumptions regarding the labor entry age, female participation rates and retirement age, parameters which significantly influence the labor supply. This section looks at how strong the single parameter effects are. Computations refer to the differences to the 'Status Quo' scenario. For this purpose, labor force development in the 'Status Quo' scenario is normalized to one.

Figure 2.7. – Average Age of the Labor Force

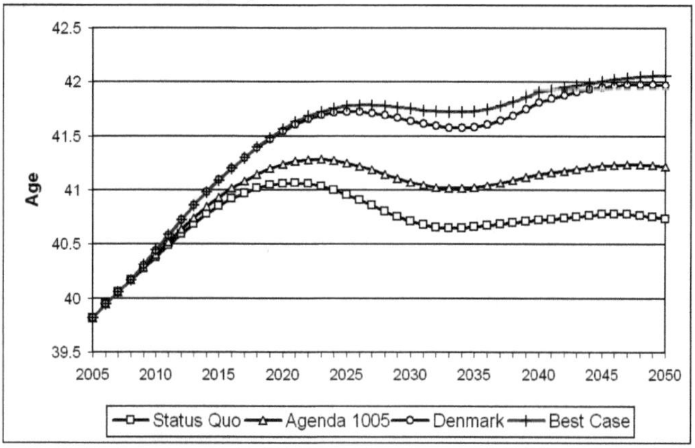

Source: Author's computations.

Figure 2.8. – Fraction of the Labor Force Aged 55+

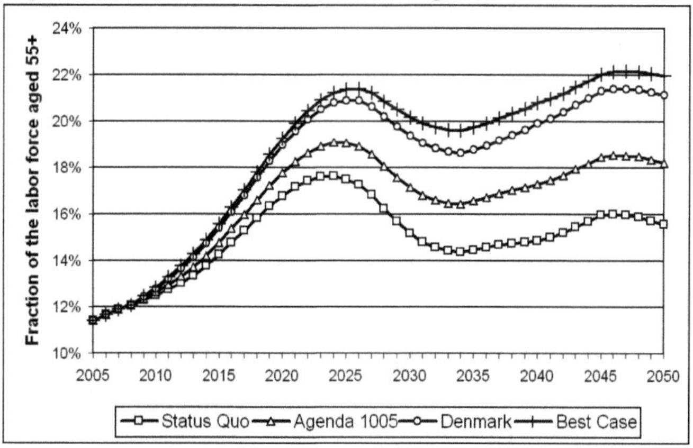

Source: Author's computations.

Increases in the labor entry age. Figure 2.9 shows the effects on the labor force participation rates and thus on the labor force size if the labor entry age (LEA) is reduced by 1 year resp. 2 years by 2040. A reduction by one year leads to an increase of the labor force size by 0.7% by 2020 and 1.5% by 2040 compared to the 'Status Quo' scenario. Reducing the labor entry age by two years will double this effect, reaching 1.4% by 2020 and 3.0% by 2040.

Given the current discussions surrounding the introduction of an 8-year-high-school system (currently it is 9 years) and the introduction of a Bachelor/Master-system instead of the German diploma, a reduction of one year seems realistic. A reduction of two years seems to be a bit far-fetched, as it would place Germany in the group of countries with the shortest education times in the EU. The effects on the labor force size are rather small since cohort sizes are small. Note, however, that a lower labor entry age leads to a slight rejuvenation of the age structure of the labor force.

Increase in female participation rates. A convergence of female participation rates to those of men may have a very large effect on the labor force as Figure 2.10 demonstrates. A convergence of 20% by 2040 will result in a labor force size increase of 1% by 2020 and of 2% by 2040. A higher convergence of 40%, 60% or 80% of the gap in participation rates of men and women will consequently lead to an increase of 2%, 3% and 4% in labor force size by 2020, and of 4%, 6% and 8% by 2040.

The effects here are thus relatively large. Compared to countries like Denmark, Germany still reports relatively low levels of female labor force participation (see Figure 2.3) and as such, there is an ample scope for future adjustment. While in Germany participation rates of women without children are comparatively high, they are comparatively lower when mothers with children are included[18]. A prerequisite for higher female participation rates corresponds to a policy which supports the reconcilability of family and work, diverging from traditional gender roles[19].

[18]See Dressel, Corneließen, and Wolf (2005).

[19]See Wissenschaftlicher Beirat beim Bundesministerium für Wirtschaft und Arbeit (2005).

Increase in the retirement age. An increase in the mean retirement age (RA) also has a relatively large impact on the labor supply as Figure 2.11 shows. An increase in the retirement age by one year by 2040 results in growth of 1.2% in the labor force by 2020, and growth of 2.4% by 2040. An increase in the retirement age by 2 or 3 years leads to nearly proportional results.

As a result of the past German pension reforms (see chapter 3), the average retirement age has increased during the last decade, from 61.2 years in 1995, to 62.7 years in 2003 [20]. If disability pensions are included (from age 50 on), the average retirement age is lower (62.3 years in 2005) but its increase since 1996 is higher[21]. In line with this development a further increase in the mean retirement age by one year is conceivable until the phase-in of the new regulations ends in 2017. With the implementation of the increase in the statutory retirement age from 65 to 67, a further increase of the mean retirement age by 2 or even 3 years also becomes more likely.

Comparison of the effects. Figure 2.12 compares the different single parameter effects[22]. It assumes a decrease in the labor entry age by one year, a convergence of female participation rates to those of men by 90% and an increase in the retirement age by two years. Together, these assumptions correspond approximately to the 'Denmark' scenario but are illustrated as separate effects here.

The decline in the labor entry age by one year increases labor supply by 2040 by 1.6%, higher female participation rates lead to a 8.6% increase and the higher retirement age to a 4.9% increase. Together this corresponds to an increase of 15.1% by 2040. However, this calculation underestimates the joint effects of simultaneous changes in the parameters. A higher retirement age, for example, will eventually also translate into higher female labor force participation if the target male participation rates increase. The single parameter effects thus strengthen each other if more than one parameter is

[20] See Berkel and Börsch-Supan (2004).

[21] See Brussig and Wojtkowski (2006).

[22] In the economic analysis, such comparisons are usually based on elasticities that allow to scale the single effects as percentage changes. However, in this case, the appropriate computational basis is unclear. An increase in the effective retirement age by one year, for example, cannot be related to the whole life span.

Figure 2.9. – Entry Age and Labor Supply

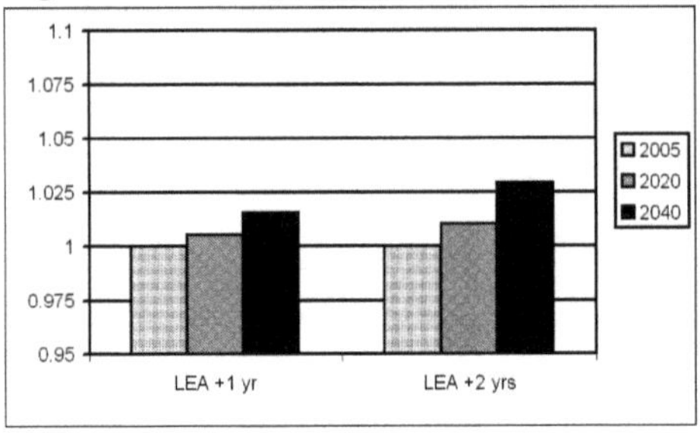

Source: Author's computations.

Figure 2.10. – Female Participation Rate and Labor Supply

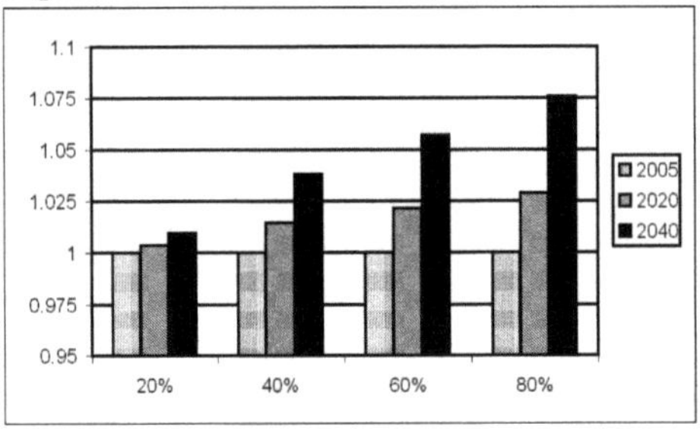

Source: Author's computations.

Figure 2.11. – Retirement Age and Labor Supply

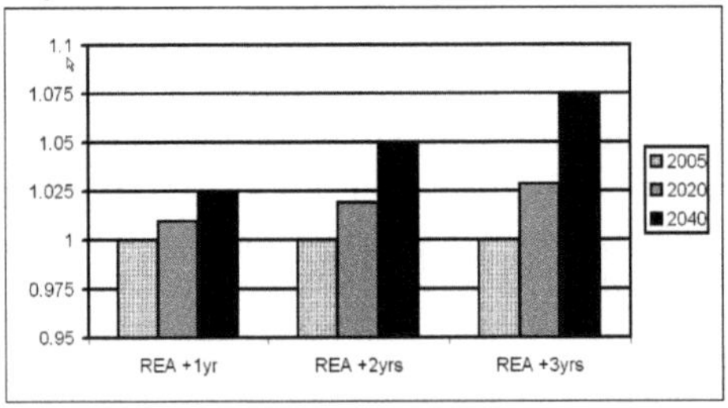

Source: Author's computations.

Figure 2.12. – Comparison of the Single Parameter Effects

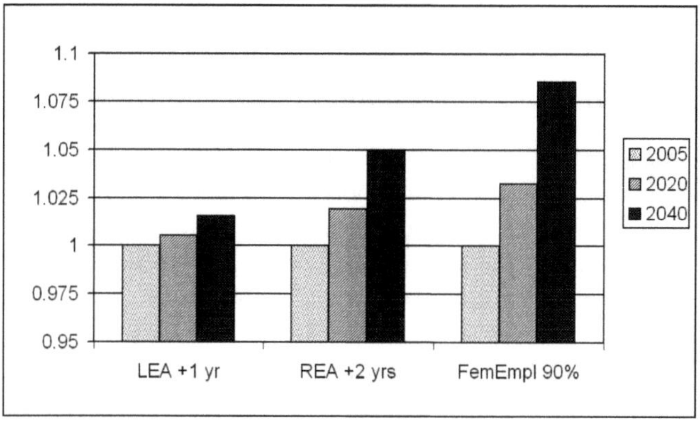

Source: Author's computations.

adapted. This is an interesting aspect that should be taken into account in political incentives aimed to induce the desired parameter changes.

2.4. Projections on Future Employment

The labor force projections of the preceding section have illustrated the magnitude of the demographic pressure and shown to what extent changes in the labor supply may mitigate these demographic effects.

However, labor supply only reflects one side of the labor market. The other side is that of labor demand. If labor demand does not match labor supply (which is usually the case), not all members of the labor force who seek find employment, and thus remain unemployed. The size of employment, however, is the crucial parameter for economic development. It is the employed who contribute to production and economic growth and who pay taxes and social security contributions and also, partially, finance the unemployed.

In this section, I will therefore extend my projection model to also consider the development of labor demand. Section 2.4.1 describes the new modeling approach and the additional assumptions for the four labor market scenarios presented in section 2.2.1. Resulting projections on employment are depicted in section 2.4.2.

2.4.1. Introducing Labor Demand into the Model

While the long-term development of labor demand is mainly influenced by the cost of capital and labor as well as important job market characteristics, such as hiring and layoff costs, the short-term development is greatly influenced by business cycles. For my projections, I will purely focus on the medium- and long-term trends, ignoring short-term fluctuations.

Implicit assumptions. Labor demand is not modeled explicitly in my model[23]. Instead, it is modeled via the development of the long-term business-cycle independent unemployment rate $UR = U/(U + E)$, which is introduced into the model as an exogenous parameter. This requires two implicit assumptions: (1) Changes in the labor supply $(U+E)$ are exclusively modeled by changes in UR and (2) if more people seek employment this does not affect the UR. The second assumption implies that the labor market absorbs all additional capacity with a rate of $1 - UR$.

Unemployment scenarios. This additional assumption regarding the development of the unemployment rate is added to the four selected scenarios presented in section 2.2.1. Base parameter is the aggregated unemployment rate of 9.1% for the year 2005 as defined by the German Federal Employment Office. Table 2.3 gives an overview of the assumptions regarding the future development of the unemployment rate for the different scenarios.

For the 'Status Quo' scenario it is assumed that the unemployment rate remains at current levels and does not decrease despite a shrinking labor force. In the 'Best Case' scenario the unemployment rate is assumed to decline until 2040 reaching the 'natural level' of an economy which the literature estimates at around 4%[24]. For the realistic 'Denmark' scenario, a convergence with the current Danish unemployment rate of 4.8% is assumed. This seems possible

[23]For a current projection of labor demand until 2020 for Germany see Schnur and Zika (2005)

[24]According to the theory of Friedman (1968) the unemployment rate in an economy fluctuates in the long term around this natural, positive rate.

Table 2.3. – Overview of Unemployment Scenarios

Scenario	*2005*	*2040*
Status Quo	9.1%	9.1%
Agenda 1005	9.1%	7.0%
Denmark	9.1%	4.8%
Best Case	9.1%	4.0%

Source: Author's compilation.

as Denmark also reached a similar reduction after its labor market reforms in the last decade. In the case of the 'Agenda 1005' scenario, a long-term decline of the unemployment rate to 7% by 2040 is assumed. As the Agenda 2010 targets the structural causes for persistent high German unemployment rates since the 1980s and is similar to the Danish labor market reform in the 1990s, a partially implemented 'Agenda 1005' is likely to have a considerably lower effect.

As for the participation rates in section 2.3, age and sex-specific unemployment rates are applied. Transitions over time are again computed linearly and the adjustment process begins in 2008 and ends in 2040. Beyond 2040 the unemployment rate is kept constant.

2.4.2. Simulation Results

This section presents the projections of the size of the future employment in Germany. I will first show the projected absolute number of employees and compare it with the projection results from section 2.3.3. Subsequently, relative values, such as the support ratio and the pensioner ratio, will be discussed.

Development of the number of employees. Like the labor force size, the number of employees decreases in all four scenarios (see Figure 2.13). In the 'Denmark' scenario, the number of employees declines by over 2.5 million to 36.2 million by 2040, while the 'Agenda 1005' scenario presents an additional decline of another 2.5 million. The 'Status Quo' scenario doubles the decrease to over 11 million down to 27.4 million employees by 2040, which is equivalent

Figure 2.13. – Development of the Labor Force and the Number of Employees

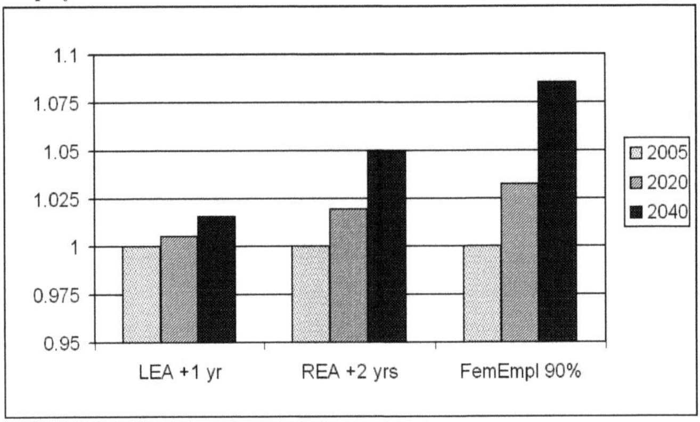

Source: Author's computations.

to a drop of 30% compared to current levels. In contrast, in the 'Best-Case' scenario the number of employees decreases by only one million.

Note also that the difference between the labor force size and the number of employees of today's approximately 3.5 million narrows down to 2.8 million for the 'Status Quo', 2.5 million for the 'Agenda 1005' and about 1.7 million for the 'Denmark' and 'Best Case' scenarios. This is due to two effects. The first effect is that the unemployment rate is based on a diminishing labor force over time. The second effect is the assumed decline in the unemployment rate itself as in the case of the scenarios 'Denmark' and 'Best Case'.

Economic support ratio. We have seen that both the number of employees on the labor market and the total population are projected to decrease in the future. The relative decline in the number of employees, however can be shown to be less than the total decline. This is illustrated in Figure 2.14 which depicts the development of the economic support ratio. The economic support ratio is defined as the ratio of employees to the adult population aged 15+. The latter is assumed to be approximately equal to the number of consumers creating the demand for the goods and services which are produced

Figure 2.14. – Development of the Economic Support Ratio

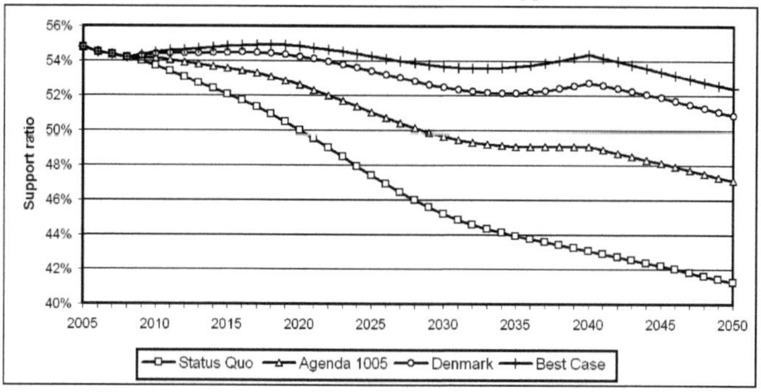

Source: Author's computations.

by the employees.

With the exception of the 'Status Quo' scenario, the relevant decline starts after 2015. For the 'Denmark' scenario, the support ratio falls from current rate of 54.8% to 52.1% by 2035, after which it will increase again until 2040. This is due to the assumed labor market adjustments which affect the number of employees more after 2035 than the increase in life expectancy affects the number of grown-ups. After 2040 the support ratio further decreases under constant labor market participation rates. For the 'Status Quo' scenario where no labor market adjustments are assumed, the support ratio falls steeply and strictly monotonically.

Consequences on growth and productivity. As it has been shown, the labor force size will not only shrink absolutely but also relative to the population size. Relative to the current consumption level of goods and services and the corresponding investments, there will be fewer employees to produce these, and thus a lower standard of living. To consume and invest at current levels, Germany needs a greater increase in productivity than hitherto.

For the 'Denmark' scenario, employees must produce by 2035 nearly 5% more than today to keep the current level of consumer and investment goods per capita as today. This corresponds to a yearly productivity increase of 0.2 percentage points, in addition to the historical normal increase of about

1.4%[25] per year. A yearly productivity gain of 1.6% is not impossible, for some countries it is even normal. It would enable Germany to keep its living standard on one level with its EU-neighbors.

For the 'Status Quo' scenario, the employees would need to produce about 20% more than today by 2035. This would correspond to an additional yearly productivity increase of about 0.63 percentage points. An increase in the current yearly productivity gain to more than 2% per year for the mid-term future does not seem realistic. This scenario implies, given no surprising jump in productivity, that the living standard compared with Germany's EU-neighbors will decrease.

The projections show how important the current and future labor market reforms are to keep our living standard also in future, at least relative with Germany's EU-neighbors.

Pensioner ratio. Even more serious than the decrease of the absolute resp. relative number of employees is the change in ratio of employees to pensioners, the so-called pensioner ratio[26]. Figure 2.15 shows the development of the pensioner ratio for the different labor market scenarios.

In all scenarios the pensioner ratio increases, but the range between the extremes is large. Assuming a very positive labor supply development, as illustrated in the 'Best Case' scenario, the pensioner ratio reaches about 73.1% by 2040. In the 'Status Quo' scenario, it nearly reaches 105% by 2040 which means that one employee needs to finance more than one pensioner. In the 'Denmark' scenario, the pensioner ratio is about 4 percentage points higher than in the 'Best Case' scenario. This shows again that a good usage of the labor supply potential may not prevent the long-term trend completely but the inevitable increase of the pensioner ratio may be softened considerably.

Consequences of a stronger population decrease. In order to see how the depicted increases in the pensioner ratio depend on the underlying population

[25]See Buchheim (1994). The IAB (Institut für Arbeitsmarkt- und Berufsforschung) calculates only with 1.3% for their long-term projection of labor demand until 2020, see Schnur and Zika (2005).

[26]Note that pensioners here are defined as all persons who retire from the labor market. Since self-employed persons as well as civil-servants are included in the employees, this definition leads to a lower pensioner ratio than the classical definition of the German pension insurance which takes only account of those retirees that can claim a public pension.

Figure 2.15. – Development of the Pensioner Ratio

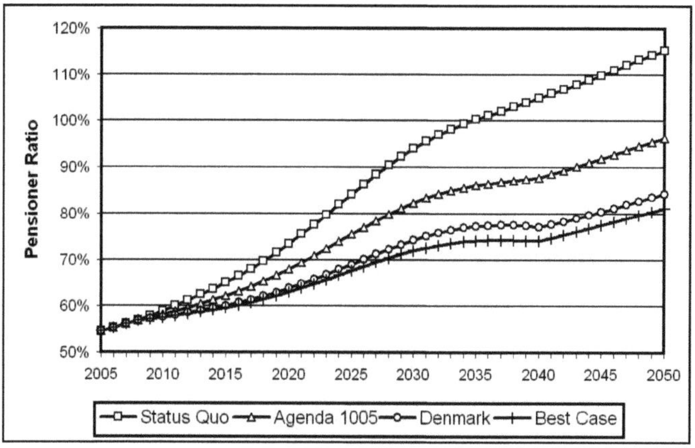

Source: Author's computations.

projection, Figure 2.16 compares the development of the pensioner ratio in the 'Denmark' scenario for both MEA population projections (3W1.5 and 1W1.5) as well as the GFSO 1W1 variant.

Assuming that life expectancy rises less rapidly (MEA 1W1.5), the pensioner ratio remains lower given the same amount of employees (see Figure 2.5) now faces fewer pensioners. If, in addition, lower annual net migration is assumed (1W1), the moderate assumptions with respect to life expectancy which generally flatten the increase of the pensioner ratio are offset partly by the lack of younger migrants.

The pressure on the social security systems may, consequently, be cushioned only partly by the labor market. Higher life expectancy may only be compensated to a certain degree by higher labor participation of seniors. Even under more pessimistic life expectancy assumptions, the pressure remains high. Even in the 'Best Case' scenario, the pensioner ratio will rise by at least 15 percentage points until 2040. This means an additional burden of more than a fourth by 2040 alone for employees.

Figure 2.16. – Development of the Pensioner Ratio Under Different Population Scenarios

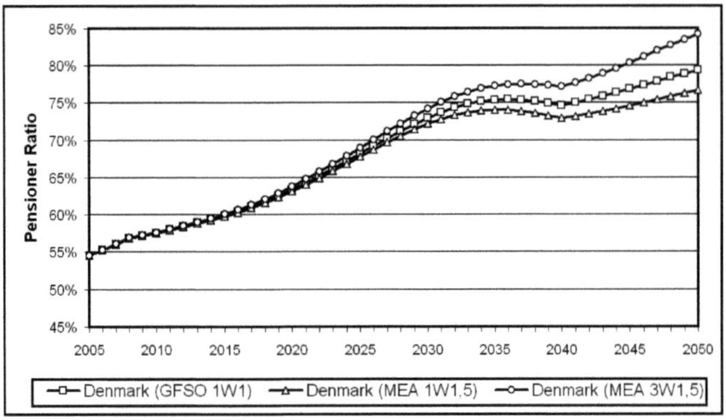

Source: Author's computations.

2.5. Conclusion

This chapter showed projected future developments of the German population as well as the German labor market through 2050. It was shown that the extent to which the demographic pressures translates to the labor market depends significantly on the success of the current labor market reforms in triggering the necessary changes with respect to labor supply and labor demand.

After 2020, at the latest, both the labor force size and the number of employees will decline due to the population decline. Neither the best usage of the labor supply potential nor an increased net migration may stop this trend completely. In the 'Denmark' scenario, the labor force size will already slowly start to decline from 2015 onwards. Similar trends for Germany have been projected by the IAB (Institut für Arbeitsmarkt- und Berufsforschung) in their labor market projections and long-term calculations of the labor force potential[27] and the European Commission[28], although the projections differ in detail because of different population and labor market assumptions.

[27] See Fuchs and Dörfler (2005b) and Fuchs and Dörfler (2005a) and Fuchs and Söhnlein (2007).
[28] See Carone (2005).

It is an important insight, however, that targeted reforms that create the necessary incentives for an increase in labor force size may significantly reduce the projected labor force decline and cushion the demographic effects.

In any case, the age structure of workers will change enormously. The average age of the labor force will increase over the next decades. Especially, the fraction of employees aged 55+ will increase considerably. This change of the age structure is inevitable and requires corresponding adjustments from both employers and employees. Nevertheless, large increases in the pensioner ratio seem inevitable.

It was also shown that besides shorter education times and the resulting lower average labor entry age, higher female participation rates and an increase in the retirement age have large impacts on the labor supply. In addition, increasing the retirement age does not only positively affect labor supply, but also reduces the number of pensioners, thereby reducing the rise in the pensioner ratio. This also has significant positive effects on the financial situation of the social security systems. It is important for Germany's current labor market policy to set the right incentives in this context.

Note however, that participation rates and the share of employed and unemployed persons do not reflect the labor market situation completely. One important aspect which was left out of the labor market projections presented in this chapter is labor volume, that is the total number of hours worked by the labor force. This is extremely difficult to model. For example, the increases in female participation rates during the 1990s in Germany were based nearly completely on part-time jobs[29]. In general, the work volume in Germany has decreased during the last decades because of fewer working hours per week, a higher vacation entitlement, a lower participation rate of seniors and last but not least because of a high unemployment rate[30]. But there is some evidence, that the work volume will increase when work patterns of women converge with those of men as expected[31]. Across EU-countries a clear correlation between child care and the working hour difference of women and men can be found. The better the child care offer, the less the working hour difference[32]. Thus, working volume needs to be kept in mind when

[29]See Bothfeld, Klammer, and Klenner (2005) and Dressel (2005).

[30]See Börsch-Supan (2000b).

[31]See Allmendiger and Ebner (2005).

[32]See European Commission (2000).

political incentives are targeted at increasing the labor supply.

Apart from this quantitative development, the future qualitative development of the labor market plays an important role. This means foremost education. If education is not promoted enough, there will be a shortage of qualified persons in the future as the total labor force declines and the demand for highly educated workers cannot be filled[33]. At the same time the problem of employing less educated persons will persist. A corresponding political focus on education and lifelong learning thus seems crucial in order to increase the share of the better educated in the labor force and prevent such mismatches. In any case, the accumulation of human capital will become increasingly important over the next decades.

An active labor market policy, both quantitatively and qualitatively, will become essential for Germany to tap its full labor market potentials. If such a policy takes place it could mitigate the demographic effects on the labor market and the pressure on the remainder of the economy, including the social security systems. Halting current reforms or regressing, in contrast, will have clearly restrictive consequences for the future living standard as well as for the financing of social security systems.

The demographic and labor market projections in this chapter will form the basis for the computations in the following chapters. However, I do not choose the MEA projection scenarios and corresponding labor market scenarios as the base scenario for subsequent calculations, but the population and labor market scenarios by the Rürup Commission. The reason is that these correspond most to the projections that are currently applied for official pension system computations. In fact, a comparison of the calculated number of employees and ratios for the 'Denmark' scenario shows a strong correspondence to the results of the labor force projections of the Rürup Commission. This is surprising since the Rürup Commission's projections are based on much more optimistic population projections and also model explicitly the future development of labor demand, which has not been done in this chapter. However, it makes it easier for me to use their projections and interpret resulting effects correctly.

[33]See Reinberg and Hummel (2003).

3. A Quarter Century of Reforms: An Evaluation of the German Pension Reform Process

3.1. Introduction

Until recently, the German public pension system has been one of the most generous in the world. Today, the system is in great financial distress. On the one hand, expenditures have risen as pensions have to be financed for a longer time due to continuous increases in life expectancy and an early retirement age induced by generous early retirement options. On the other hand, revenues have not kept up as younger working cohorts have become smaller, thus accounting for fewer contributors. This situation is projected to deteriorate even further when the baby boom generation will enter retirement around 2015.

A series of parametric reforms in the 1990s attempted to curtail the generosity of the system by imposing stricter retirement options narrowing down the retirement window. More fundamental reform measures were instituted in 2001, 2004 and 2007. Since then, the system has been subject to major changes, converting the once exemplary and monolithic Bismarckian pension insurance system into a complex, sustainable multi-pillar system. This chapter will give an overview of the German pension system and its ongoing reform process. Moreover, it will assess whether these reforms will solve the pressing problems of a prototypical pay-as-you-go system of old age provision, hopefully illustrating lessons for other countries to learn[1].

This chapter is structured as follows. Section 3.2 explains the basic principles of the German pension system before past and current reforms from

[1]This chapter is an update and extension of Börsch-Supan and Wilke (2003), Börsch-Supan, Reil-Held, and Wilke (2004) and Wilke (2004).

the 1990s until today are described in section 3.3. In order to evaluate the long-term effects of these reforms, I develop a detailed simulation model of the German pension system which I introduce in section 3.4. Based on this model, section 3.5 presents projections on the future financial development of the public pension system. Further projections are presented in section 3.6 which looks at the future role of supplementary pension income in Germany. Section 3.7 concludes.

3.2. Basic Principles of the German Pension System

Pension systems can be best described in pillars. According to the definition of the World Bank five pillars can be distinguished[2]:

0. Pillar The objective of the zero pillar is to prevent poverty in old age. In Germany, before 2002, retirees with no or low pension claims were covered by the same social assistance as a needy German of any age. Financial resources of the family had to be used first before state subsidies were paid. As a consequence, older people who did not want to burden their children did not apply for social assistance. Until 2002, this had applied only to a small fraction of retirees, but in the face of the planned future cuts in public pension levels in the context of the 2001 Riester reform, it was clear that this needed to be changed. The 2001 Riester reform introduced a minimum social security guarantee (*'Grundsicherung'*) for old age as well as those, whose earning capacity is reduced. Effectively, this is a means-tested minimum pension at a level of around 15% higher than the German social assistance[3]. However, it is financed by taxes and contributions. Its purpose is to shield workers in the lowest income deciles from future benefit cuts in public pensions.

1. Pillar The first pillar refers to public pension systems, financed on a pay-as-you-go (PAYG) basis. Public pension systems are usually mandatory

[2] See Holzmann and Hinz (2005).

[3] See Deutsche Rentenversicherung Bund (DRV) (2007b) for a description of the new regulations.

and provide old age pensions in addition to disability and survivor pensions. The German pension insurance (*'Gesetzliche Rentenversicherung (GRV)'*) has provided extremely generous old age as well as disability and survivor pensions until recently, accounting for about 85% of retirement income of current pensioners[4]. This is changing slowly as the demographic transition and misled incentive effects of past reforms have set the German PAYG system under financial pressure.

2. Pillar According to the World Bank, the second pillar comprises mandatory, private capital-funded pension schemes. For Germany, such a mandatory private coverage does not exist. Instead, voluntary company pension schemes embody the second pillar. They are offered by the employer and are capital-funded. Traditionally, company pension schemes have played a minor role in Germany (roughly 10% of old age income[5]), particularly when compared to other countries, such as the Netherlands. This will change as a result of the reforms described below.

3. Pillar The third pillar comprises voluntary, private individual pension arrangements in the form of regular payments from some annuitized capital stock. In Germany, these were traditionally life insurance policies that comprised around 5% of old age income[6]. As the second pillar, the third pillar will play an increasing role for future retirees.

4. Pillar Finally, real-estate assets, cheap access to health services etc. are comprised under the fourth pillar. In Germany, property plays a large role for pensioners. Access to health services is provided via the public (as well as additional private) health insurance system that in the past, similarly to the pension system, provided generous services but currently faces similar pressures to the public pension system.

[4] See Börsch-Supan, Miegel, Brombacher Steiner, Bovenberg, Mijdam, Disney, Wise, and Schmidt-Hebbel (1999).

[5] See Börsch-Supan, Miegel, Brombacher Steiner, Bovenberg, Mijdam, Disney, Wise, and Schmidt-Hebbel (1999).

[6] See again Börsch-Supan, Miegel, Brombacher Steiner, Bovenberg, Mijdam, Disney, Wise, and Schmidt-Hebbel (1999).

In the remainder of my thesis, I will focus on the first, second and third pillars. The basic features of the first pillar will be described in this section. Supplementary pensions (second and third pillar) will be discussed in the context of the German pension reform process discussed in section 3.3 and taken up again in section 3.6.

3.2.1. Coverage and Contributions

The German public pension system features very broad mandatory coverage of workers. Only civil-servants and the self-employed are not subject to mandatory coverage[7]. Contributions are administered like a payroll tax, levied equally on employees and employers. Total contributions are 19.9% of the first 4.550 Euro (end of 2007) of monthly gross income (upper earnings threshold, about twice the average monthly gross wage). The contribution rate has been steadily rising since the late 1960s, and the upper earnings threshold has been used as an additional financing instrument, increasing considerably faster than wage growth.

These contributions finance roughly 70% of the budget of the German pension insurance. The remaining 30% are financed by subsidies from the federal government. These subsidies are also used to fine-tune the PAYG budget constraint because the system has a reserve of only 0.2 to 1.5 months worth of benefit expenditures. As opposed to a unified budget such as in the U.S., transfers can be made from the government to the public pension insurance, but not in reverse.

3.2.2. Pension Benefits and Pension Levels

The German public pension system provides old age pensions for workers aged 60 and older, disability benefits for workers below age 60 which are converted to old age pensions latest at the statutory retirement age (currently age 65) and survivor benefits for spouses and children. In addition, pre-retirement (i.e. retirement before age 60) has been possible through several channels (mainly unemployment) in the past and, until recently, women and

[7]Until 1998, workers with earnings below the official minimum earnings threshold (15% of average monthly gross wage) also were exempted from the public pension system contributions.

workers with a long service history were allowed to retire earlier than the statutory retirement age with full benefits.

Benefit computation. Benefits are strictly work-related and are computed over the lifetime. They can be interpreted as the product of three elements: (1) the 'earnings points' (EP) which reflect the employee's relative earnings position in each year, (2) an adjustment factor (AF) according to the pension type and (since the 1992 reform) the retirement age, and (3) a reference pension value - the 'current pension value' (PV). The annual value of a pension $P_{t,i}$ in year t for pensioner i can be computed as follows:

$$P_{i,t} = EP_{i,RA} \times AF_{i,RA} \times PV_t \tag{3.1}$$

Earnings points (EP) The German point system dates back until 1957, when the PAYG system was introduced. Earnings points are expressed as a multiple of the average annual contribution (roughly speaking, the relative earnings position) in each working year: one EP corresponds to average earnings in that year, 0.5 EPs to 50% of average earnings, and 2 EPs to earnings twice as large as average earnings in that year. These earnings points are granted for each year of service life and are accumulated at retirement. Years of service life comprise not only years of active contributions but also years of contributions on behalf of the employee (e.g. during periods of unemployment) and years that are counted as service years even when no contributions were made at all. These include years of military service, some allowance for advanced education (only for older cohorts), three years for each child's upbringing for one of the parents etc. Unlike in many other countries there is neither an upper bound of service years entering the benefit calculation, nor can workers choose certain years in their earnings history and drop others. However, a minimum number of service years (at least 5) has to be reached in order to become eligible for the different benefit types.

Adjustment factor (AF) Before 1992, the adjustment factor took on values between 0.25 and 1 depending on the applicable benefit type (old age, disability or survivor pension). It is one for a normal old age pension.

Since the 1992 reform, the adjustment factor has an additional second element: it adjusts pension entitlements to the retirement age (RA), reducing the pension base in the case of early retirement and increasing the pension base in the case of retirement after the statutory retirement age.

Current pension value (PV) This is the crucial link between worker's earnings and pensioners' benefits. The current pension value is indexed to the annual changes in the level of wages and salaries net of pension contributions and thus enables pensioners to share in the rising prosperity generated by the economy. This link between changes in workers' earnings and pensioners' benefits is specified as a mathematical 'benefit indexation formula' in the law.

The first two factors make up the 'personal pension base', while the third factor determines the income distribution between current workers and the stock of pensioners. The combination of the first three factors is unique to the German pension system and provides a strong link between lifetime income and pension benefits. Hence, differently from the U.S., redistribution plays only a minor role in the German pension system[8].

The current reform process will not change this. Rather, since 1992, the cost cutting reforms have largely concentrated on the fourth factor and redefined how changes in the average earnings of workers affect the size of pensions. Note the formula is applied to the entire stock of pensioners, not only to new entrants. Hence, the German system is time, not cohort, oriented. This crucial difference makes reform easier, than in other pension systems (e.g. Italy and Sweden), if burden sharing is an agreed principle among voters. I will come back to this in chapter 4.

[8]See e.g. Casmir (1989) for a comparison across countries. Note also that there have been elements of redistribution in the individual benefit indexation formula in the past. One such element was introduced in 1972 when earnings points could not fall below 0.75 for years of contributions before 1972 provided a worker had a service life of at least 35 years. A similar rule was introduced in the 1992 reform: for contributions between 1973 and 1992, annual earnings points below 0.75 are multiplied by 1.5 up to the maximum of 75, effectively reducing the redistribution for workers with relative wage positions below 50%. In 2001, this system has been abolished in favor of the guaranteed minimum pension (*'Grundsicherung'*) (see above).

Disability pensions. There are three ways to claim disability benefits (*'Erwerbsminderungsrente' (EM)*). One has to (1) be physically disabled to at least 50%, or (2) pass a strict earnings test, or (3) pass a weaker earnings test. The strict earnings test is passed if the worker is unable to work at least 3 hours a day. In this case the full old age benefits are paid. The weaker earnings test is passed if the worker can only work less than six hours a day. In this case, disability pensions are only half of the applicable old age pension unless the worker remains unemployed, then full benefits are also paid[9].

This definition of disability and the associated earnings tests are relatively new and were implemented as a part of the Riester Reform in 2001. Previously, the term disability applied not only to health but also to labor market reasons, meaning that a person could receive disability pensions when he was no longer capable to work at his job. Under these old regulations, the strict earnings test was passed if the earnings capacity was reduced below the minimum earnings threshold for any reasonable occupation (*'Erwerbsunfähigkeit' (EU)*). The weaker earnings test was passed when no vacancies for the worker's specific job description were available and the worker had to face an earnings loss of at least 50% when changing to a different job (*'Berufsunfähigkeit' (BU)*). In the 1970s and 1980s, the rules were frequently used as a device to keep unemployment rates down and German jurisdiction interpreted both rules very broadly, especially the applicability of the first rule. Jurisdiction also overruled the earnings test during disability retirement. This lead to a share of *EU*-type disability pensions for more than 90% of all disability pensions[10].

After average retirement ages had dropped considerably for more than two decades setting the system under financial stress, this generous interpretation was amended in the form of the 2001 Riester Reform. For cohorts born before February 1961, protection of confidence regulations still allow acquiring *BU*-type disability pensions in form of the lower new *EM*-type pension if the person can only work less than six hours in his job but is capable of working at least six hours in another job. Under the new plan, persons who received a disability pension in December 2000 maintain their entitlements as long as the original reasons persist, regardless of whether these entitlements were

[9]For a thorough description of these rules, see Deutsche Rentenversicherung Bund (DRV) (2007a).

[10]See e.g. Riphahn (1995) for an analysis of German disability rules.

temporary or for an unlimited period.

Survivor pensions. Survivor pensions are 55% (*'large widow pension'*) of the deceased spouse's applicable pension, and given to surviving spouses aged 45 and up, or if there children are in the household, otherwise 25% (*'small widow pension'*). These regulations have also only recently been adjusted following the 2001 Riester reform, as before, there was a large widow pension of 60%. Instead, there is now a bonus for raising a child under the age of three. Since 2002, the smaller widow pension has been restricted to a period of two years. Certain earnings tests apply if the surviving spouse has his own income or pension. However, this is only relevant for a very small (below 10%) share of widows among today's pensioners. Since 2002, upon retirement,couples can decide to split their total earnings points in half and each receive a pension which is continually paid if one spouse dies (*'Rentensplitting'*)[11].

Pre-retirement. In addition to benefits from the public pension system, transfer payments (mainly unemployment compensation) have, until recently, enabled what is referred to as *'pre-retirement'*. At the end of the 1990s, labor force exit before age 60 was frequent. About 45% of all men retired by the age of 59. Approximately half retired due to disability, whereas the other half made use of one of the many official and unofficial pre-retirement schemes.

Unemployment compensation has been used as pre-retirement income in an unofficial scheme inducing very early retirement. Workers entered such a scheme much earlier than age 60 and were paid a negotiable combination of unemployment compensation and a supplement or severance pay, as pension for the unemployed could then start at age 60. As the rules of unemployment pensions and the duration of unemployment benefits changed, so did the unofficial retirement ages. Age 56 was particularly frequent in West Germany because unemployment compensation is paid for up to three years for elderly workers. It is followed by the lower unemployment aid. Earlier retirement ages could be induced by paying the worker the difference between the last salary and unemployment compensation for three years; and for further years

[11] An overview of these rules can be found in Deutsche Rentenversicherung Bund (DRV) (2007d).

the difference between the last salary and unemployment aid. This was dependant on the *social plan* which a firm would negotiate with the workers before restructuring the work force. In addition, early retirement at age 58 was made possible by an official pre-retirement scheme in which the employer received a subsidy from the unemployment insurance if a younger employee was hired. While the first (and unofficial) pre-retirement scheme was very popular and presented a convenient way to overcome the strict German labor laws, the (official) second scheme was less commonly used[12].

Exceptional rules for women and long-time insured. Last, special regulations apply for women as well as workers with a contribution history of at least 35 years. Both groups could retire earlier than the statutory retirement age (age 60 for women and age 63 for the long-time insured) with full benefits as a result of the 1972 reform[13]. However, this has been changed over the course of the 1992 reforms.

Standard pension level. In Germany, the size of pension benefits is typically measured in relation to average wages. These pension levels in the official statistics are displayed for the so-called standard pensioner. The standard pensioner is a fictitious person who worked for 45 years, earned the average wage in each year and retired at the statutory retirement age of 65. He is thus credited 45 earnings points EP_{Strd}, which multiplied by the current pension value PV_t in a specific year t gives his annual pension income[14]. The pension level PL_t is defined as this standard pensioner's pension divided by average wages of the labor force of the same year.:

$$PL_t = \frac{(EP_{Strd} \times PV_t)}{AGW_t} \tag{3.2}$$

The pension level is to be distinguished from the replacement rate or level that describes the individual pension income relative to the last or average

[12]See Bundesministerium für Arbeit und Sozialordnung (BMA) (2002) for a description of the institutional rules as well as Bäcker (1999) for an assessment of the set incentive effects.

[13]For a description of possible pathways to retirement for women, see Deutsche Rentenversicherung Bund (DRV) (2007c).

[14]Note that $AF = 1$ for the standard pensioner.

individual wage income during the working life[15]. Pension levels generally can be expressed in gross or net terms. However, their precise definition has been changed repeatedly over the past decade[16]. Currently, gross pension and (modified) net pension levels before tax are the two prevailing measures. The latter became important following the 2005 Old Age Income Act, which introduced deferred taxation for old age income. As this new regulation is phased in slowly with different applicable tax rates for different cohorts, net pension levels can no longer be displayed for the whole pensioner stock. As a result, net pension levels are now displayed before tax.

Until recently, the German public pension system recorded comparably high pension levels (70% of net wages and approximately 48% of gross wages). These were maintained until the end of the 1990s, causing substantial increases in the contribution rate. A main element of the latest pension reforms was to reduce pension levels and further limit increases in the contribution rate, as we will see in the next section.

3.3. The German Pension Reform Process

Since the 1972 reform, five dates have marked the pension reform process in Germany: the 1992/1999 pension reforms which introduced the first cost cutting measures after the overly generous 1972 reform, the Riester Reform in 2001 which pushed the system away from the former monolithic towards a multi-pillar one, the 2004 reform which further strengthened this paradigm shift, and finally, the 2007 reform which increased the statutory retirement age from currently 65 to 67. In this section, I will concentrate on these major reforms. An overview of German pension reforms since Bismarck until today is provided in Appendix B.

[15]There is a vast literature on replacement rates. For the theoretical concept of replacement rates and alternative measures, see Hurd and Rohwedder (2006). See e.g. Hauser (1998) for a comparison of replacement rates on a household level for 14 OECD countries, including Germany. For replacement rates based on an individual level concept, see e.g. Burniaux, Dang, Fore, Förster, Mira d'Ercole, and Oxley (1998).

[16]See appendix C for an overview of the different pension level concepts.

3.3.1. The 1992 and 1999 Reforms: Containing Early Retirement

One of the main changes of the 1992 reform was to anchor benefits to net, rather than to gross, wages. This has implicitly reduced benefits since taxes and social security contributions have increased, reducing net relative to gross wages. This mechanism will become particularly important when population aging increases, as it implies an implicit mechanism of burden sharing between generations.

The second important element of the 1992 reform was the introduction of 'actuarial' adjustments of benefits to retirement age. Before 1992, adjustment of benefits to retirement age was only implicit via the number of service years accomplished. Since the 1992 reform, age 65 has been deemed to be the 'pivotal age' for benefit computations. For each year of earlier retirement benefits are reduced by 3.6% (in addition to the effect of fewer service years). The 1992 reform also introduced rewards for later retirement in a systematic way. For each year of retirement postponed past the statutory retirement age, the pension is increased by 5% in addition to the 'natural' increase via the number of service years. There has been a discussion in the German pension literature on whether these 'actuarial' adjustments are truly actuarially fair in a mathematical sense. I will come back to this in chapter 4.

The 1999 pension reform was supposed to lower pension levels according to a pre-specified 'demographic factor', which was a function of life expectancy and several correction factors. However, it was revoked after the change of government in 1998. A side effect of this reform, which was not revoked, was a gradual change of eligibility ages for pensions for women and unemployed from age 60 to age 65 and disability pensions from age 60 to 63[17]. These changes are expected to be fully implemented by 2017, and effectively leave a 'window of retirement' for healthy workers only if they have at least 35 years of service. This practically abolished early retirement options for women and the unemployed.

These changes, together with the introduced actuarial adjustments, have effectively reduced incentives to retire early. As a result, average retirement

[17]This increase in eligibility ages for all pension types actually had already been determined under the 1992 reform. However, the 1999 reform greatly accelerated implementation of these changes.

ages for men have risen by 1.2 years, for women by 0.8 years between 1995 and 2004[18]. Note that in the context of the 2007 reform, age limits have been modified once more and increased further. An overview of the cohort-specific eligibility regulations and adjustment paths for the various pension types is thus given later in Figure 3.1 on page 58, under the 2007 reform.

3.3.2. The 2001 Reform: Shifting Towards a Multi-Pillar System

On May 11, 2001, a new pension reform act was ratified in Germany, popularly referred to as the 'Riester reform' after the then labor minister, Walter Riester. The key objective of the Riester reform was to stabilize contribution rates. The law actually states that contribution rates to the public pension system must stay below 20% until 2020 and 22% until 2030 ('Riester limits'). In order to reach these objectives, pensions were to be gradually reduced by a rather complex new benefit indexation formula from the level of 70% of average net earnings in 2000 to around 67% by the year 2030. The decline in public pensions was to be offset by supplementary (occupational and private) pensions. In order to achieve this aim, supplementary pensions were subsidized, either by tax deferral and tax deduction, or by direct subsidies to individual and occupational pension plans. These supplementary pensions are, however, not mandated. Since many restrictions apply, it remains to be seen, how many workers actually start building up private pensions[19].

Changes in the benefit indexation formula. Before the 2001 reform, the objective of safeguarding standards of living in old age was considered to be met if pensions were worth 70% of average net wages. The system was es-

[18] Own calculations based on the results by Berkel and Börsch-Supan (2004). For a further discussion about the effects of early retirement options on the retirement age also see Schmidt (1995), Riphahn and Schmidt (1997) and Siddiqui (1997).

[19] The main restriction is on payment plans. Since additional private pension schemes are intended to supplement or replace benefits from the public pension scheme, the government decided that incentives will only be available for investment vehicles which guarantee payment of a life annuity, payable from the date of retirement. Investment vehicles which provide lump-sum disbursements are not subject to state subsidies. This restriction was met with considerable criticism in the public debate, as it excludes other forms of provision for old age (such as investments in old age or nursing homes). For a detailed overview of the restrictions, see appendix D.

sentially run by adapting the contribution rate to 70%, the standard pension level. Thus, pension benefits more than maintained their purchasing power over the entire retirement period. In 2001, the Riester Reform introduced a rather complex new adjustment formula, which relates changes in the current pension value (PV_t) to lagged changes in gross income (AGW_t), modified by the actual contribution rate to public pensions (τ_t) and a fictitious contribution rate to the new private pension accounts (AVA_t)[20], gradually increasing from 0.5% in 2003 to 4% in 2009. In addition, a somewhat awkward 'sensitivity factor' d_t was introduced. It was set to 100 until 2010 and was supposed to decrease to 90 in 2011 which effectively would have increased the sensitivity of PV to increases in τ after 2010.

$$PV_t = PV_{t-1}\frac{AGW_{t-1}}{AGW_{t-2}} \times \frac{\frac{d_t}{100} - AVA_{t-1} - \tau_{t-1}}{\frac{d_t}{100} - AVA_{t-2} - \tau_{t-2}} \qquad (3.3)$$

The complex design of the formula reflects the balance between the two opposing aims of the reform: (1) to keep the contribution rate below a fixed level (20% until 2020, 22% until 2030), and (2) to keep the redefined standard pension level above 67% until 2030[21]. Both conflicting aims are now part of the German pension law. If either of these aims are violated, the law requires government action. Note that the awkward jump in the sensitivity factor d_t reflects these aims since the system dependency ratio remains still flat until 2010 and then quickly rises.

Direct savings subsidy and tax deductible special expenses for individual Riester pensions. All employed and certain self-employed workers who pay personal contributions to a certified retirement pension policy are entitled to receive a direct retirement savings subsidy. The subsidy is paid directly into the beneficiary's saving account. A basic subsidy and a child subsidy for each child for which child benefits were received during the previous year is paid. Child subsidies are payable to the mother. In the case of married couples, both partners receive a basic subsidy if they have each taken out their own supplementary private pension policy. In addition, non-entitled partners

[20] AVA = *'Altersvorsorgeanteil'*.

[21] See again appendix C for an overview of the various pension level definitions in Germany.

Table 3.1. – Direct Savings Subsidies

From [year] on	*Savings rate*	*Basic subsidy [€/year]*	*Child subsidy [€/year]*
2002	1%	38	46
2004	2%	76	92
2006	3%	114	138
2008	4%	154	185

Source: Author's compilation based on current legislation.

Table 3.2. – Minimum Savings

Year	*Number of children*		
	None	*One*	*Two or more*
2002 – 2004	45	38	30
As of 2005	90	75	60

Source: Author's compilation based on current legislation.

(such as mothers not in paid employment) are also entitled to receive the full subsidy for their own retirement pension policy provided that the respective married partner who is subject to compulsory insurance contributions has paid his minimum personal contribution to their supplementary retirement pension policy (see below).

Table 3.1 shows the maximum incentive subsidies available as of 2002. In order to qualify for the maximum subsidy, the beneficiary must invest a specified percentage of his gross earnings (denoted as 'savings rate'). This percentage increases until 2008 in four steps ('Riester staircase'). The percentage is applied to the actual earnings level, capped at the same level as the PAYG contributions are (about twice average earnings). If less money is invested, the state subsidy is reduced accordingly. The scheme is complicated by the fact that the subsidy is included in the savings amount. Hence, the actual savings rate necessary for the maximum subsidy is lower than the percentages indicated in the second column of Table 3.1. In turn, certain minimum amounts are necessary, see Table 3.2.

Table 3.3. – Maximum Savings

From on	*[year]*	*Tax deductible special expenses [€/year]*
2002		525
2004		1,050
2006		1,575
2008		2,100

Source: Author's compilation based on current legislation.

Alternatively, qualifying retirement savings can be deducted as 'special allowances' from income taxes. This is usually more advantageous for workers with higher than average earnings. Savings rates, caps etc. are the same as in the subsidy case. Table 3.3 shows the maximum tax-deductible contributions to private retirement savings accounts.

As shown in Tables 3.1– 3.3, the subsidies for private old age provision are being phased in rather slowly. Together with the restriction in investment plans, this has led to a rather slow uptake of Riester pensions. The Riester reform did not produce the 'big bang' which a fundamental reform might need in order to change habits of old age provision.

Note that while old age pension contributions will be tax exempt during the saving phase, pension payments during the benefit phase will be taxed in full as normal income. This applies to all benefits regardless of whether these accrue from contributions, subsidies or capital gains. One may regard this as another form of subsidy (an implicit tax credit), since taxes occur later in life and usually at a lower rate due to progressivity[22].

Direct salary deduction for occupational pension schemes. The Riester reform remained largely undecided regarding the role of occupational pensions versus individual accounts. Traditionally, occupational pensions have played a minor role in Germany, particularly compared to other countries. On the other hand, occupational pensions should not provide a psychological substitute for private pensions. In the end additional subsidies were intro-

[22]For a further discussion of taxation principles for pensions, see Börsch-Supan and Lührmann (2000).

duced with the Riester-Reform in order to strengthen occupational pensions. Arrangements may be based both on gross or net pay. If they are based on net pay, there is a large implicit subsidy since the converted salary may not only be subject to deferred taxation, but can also be exempt from social security contributions. If they are based on gross pay, contributions may enjoy the same direct subsidies or tax relief as contributions to individual accounts, as long as the occupational pensions meet certain criteria which are less restrictive than the criteria for individual pension plans. Which contribution rules apply depends on the chosen investment vehicle and the incentives they attract[23]. Collective bargaining agreements, however, have precedence over the right to convert salary.

3.3.3. The 2004 Reform: Introducing the Sustainability Factor

When it became obvious that the Riester reform measures would not suffice to meet the contribution rate and pension level targets, a new reform commission, the 'Commission for Sustainability in Financing the German Social Insurance Systems', popularly referred to as the Rürup Commission after its chairman, Bert Rürup, was established in November 2002[24]. Its twin objectives were those of the Riester reform: to stabilize contribution rates while ensuring appropriate future pension levels.

The Rürup Commission met in 2003, and faced a very different situation than Riester had in 2001. Unexpectedly high unemployment rates, the poor performance of the German economy, and extremely low growth rates precipitated a short-run financial crisis of the pension system and created a sense of urgency for reform. Moreover, the electorate became increasingly aware that stabilizing social security contributions in total labor compensation would be essential to enhance future growth. This paradigm shift away from thinking about pension claims towards thinking about financing possibilities had a noticeable impact on the commission's work.

[23]See appendix E for an overview of the various investment vehicles and how they are subsidized.

[24]The commission was in charge of making reform proposals for the pension system, the health care and the long-term care insurance. In the following I will only refer to the pension proposals.

In 2003, the Rürup Commission published a reform proposal that comprised two major elements: a gradual increase of the normal retirement age from 65 to 67 years, and a further modification of the pension benefit indexation formula linking benefits to the system dependency ratio[25]. Introduction of the 'sustainability factor' came into effect with the pension reform in spring 2004, while the shift in the retirement age was legislated three years later under the 2007 reform.

The sustainability factor. The commission proposed to extend the Riester benefit indexation formula by a 'sustainability factor'. This factor reflects the development of the relative number of contributors to pensioners, the system dependency ratio (SDR), which is the most important long-term determinant of pension financing[26]. The new benefit indexation formula looks as follows:

$$(3.4)\quad PV_t = PV_{t-1}\frac{AGW_{t-2}}{AGW_{t-3}} \times \frac{1 - AVA_{t-2} - \tau_{t-2}}{1 - AVA_{t-3} - \tau_{t-3}}\left(\left(1 - \frac{SDR_{t-2}}{SDR_{t-3}}\right)\alpha + 1\right)$$

It includes the sustainability factor in the inner brackets, weighted by α, and replaces the one-time shift in the somewhat awkward 'sensitivity parameter' d_t, see section 3.3.2. If α equals zero, the former Riester pension adjustment formula would remain unchanged. If α equals one, the new indexation formula would imply a purely income-oriented pension benefit adjustment policy. A weighting factor α of 0.5 would spread the additional financial burden resulting from the demographic challenges somewhat equally between contributors and beneficiaries. The commission set the value of α at 0.25 by arguing that this would fulfill the Riester objectives to keep the contribution rate under 20% until 2020 and under 22% until 2030[27]. I later show in section 3.5 that this is the case, however only under the underlying demographic, labor market and economic assumptions, and after both proposed

[25]See Kommission für die Nachhaltigkeit in der Finanzierung der Sozialen Sicherungssysteme (2003a) for the original German report and Kommission für die Nachhaltigkeit in der Finanzierung der Sozialen Sicherungssysteme (2003b) for an English summary.

[26]Strictly speaking, the sustainability factor will link benefits to the 'equivalized system dependency ratio' in order to avoid distortions created by extremely low contributions and/or pension benefits. This ratio standardizes the number of pensioners by converting standard pensions into the number of 'equivalence pensioners'. The number of 'equivalence contributors' is likewise calculated by standardizing the average earner.

[27]For a simulation analysis on the effects of alternative α see Börsch-Supan, Reil-Held, and Wilke (2003).

reform measures (the sustainability factor and the increase in the statutory retirement age) have been implemented.

The new pension formula led to further decreases in pension benefit levels vis-à-vis the path planned by the Riester reform. In contrast to the earlier proposed but never enforced 'demographic factor' in 1999, the sustainability factor considers not only the development of life expectancy but the entire demographic development (including changes in migration and notably in birth rates), as well as the development of the labor market. This is important as the inevitable reduction of the working-age population can be compensated by a higher labor force participation of women and elderly workers, as was shown in chapter 2. The introduction of the sustainability factor directly links pension adjustments to the crucial factors determining pension financing, namely the number of contributors and benefit recipients. This gives the new pension benefit indexation formula a self-stabilizing effect.

Further strengthening of second and third-pillar pensions. In order to compensate for the larger decrease in pension levels, further strengthening of the second and third-pillars pensions was necessary. Since the uptake of the funded supplementary Riester pension had been modest in the first years after the introduction, the commission proposed a host of administrative changes to occupational and private pensions in order to make the system easier to handle, and thus more popular. Among these were the expansion of the group of entitled persons to all tax payers, dynamic pension benefits and increased transparency in the private pension provision. These administrative changes accompanied the proposed introduction of an EET-type ex post taxation of private pensions[28].

3.3.4. The 2007 Reform: Raising the Statutory Retirement Age to 67

The Rürup Commission had proposed a step-wise increase of the normal retirement age from 65 to 67 by 2035. This increase would corresponded to roughly two-thirds of projected changes in life expectancy. The idea was to

[28] A parallel commission, also headed by Bert Rürup, proposed to keep pension contributions and capital gains tax exempt (symbolized by 'EE'), and to tax benefits (symbolized by 'T').

offset future increases in the total value of accumulated benefits generated by a prolonged life span through later retirement. In order to prevent substitution into early retirement and disability pensions as a result of the increase in the retirement age, the commission also proposed an increase of eligibility ages for early retirement (at the same extent and schedule as the normal retirement age). These propositions were finally implemented in spring 2007.

Increases in the statutory retirement age are phased in slowly, starting in 2012 and ending in 2030[29]. Between 2012 and 2029, the statutory retirement age is adjusted first each year by one month from age 65 to 66, and then each year by two months from age 66 to 67. The phase-in is cohort-oriented, it will affect cohorts younger than 1947. For the 1964 and younger cohorts a statutory retirement age of 67 finally applies.

In addition, eligibility ages for disability pensions are raised from age 63 to 65 from 2017 to 2029 for handicapped persons. Early retirement with deductions is raised from age 60 to 62. Maximum deductions for early retirement are thus 10.8%. For long-time insured workers, disability pensions can still be received at age 63 without deductions if workers have at least 35 service years (until 2023) or 40 years (from 2024 on).

Since there were additional worries about the coverage for workers subject to extreme physical wear and tear due to long years of hard work, a new pension type was introduced making it possible for workers with a service life of at least 45 years to retire two years earlier without any actuarial adjustments. Figure 3.1 summarizes the eligibility regulations for all pension types[30].

3.4. A Simulation Model of the German Pension System

In order to evaluate how the reforms described in the previous section will affect the long-term financial sustainability of the public pension system and which role supplementary pensions will play in the future, I develop a detailed simulation model of the German pension system. The model comprises two

[29] See Fuchs (2007).

[30] For a thorough historical overview of the changes in eligibility regulations, see Kaldybajewa and Kruse (2006).

Figure 3.1. – Changes in Eligibility Ages Due to the 1992, 1999 and 2007 Reforms

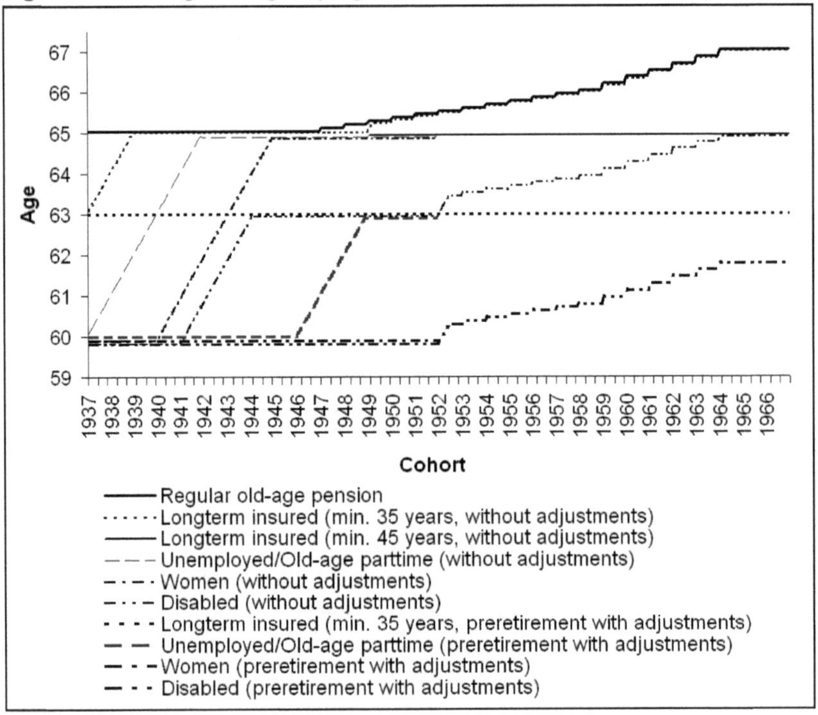

Source: Author's compilations based on data by the German Pension Insurance (DRV, www.deutscherentenversicherung.de) and the Ministry of Labor and Social Welfare (BMAS, www.bmas.de).

parts. The first part models the financial development of the public PAYG system. The second part models the development of the state-subsidized supplementary Riester pensions under the assumption that workers will save the recommended (and subsidized) savings amount of 4% of wages (recall Figure 3.1). Both parts of the model are described below.

3.4.1. Modeling the German PAYG System

This part of the model is based on an aggregate, macro level approach. Each year, the number of contributors and pensioners in the system is derived from the underlying population and labor market projections presented in chapter 2. The system's revenues and expenditures are then computed according to the development of wages, social security contribution rates and existing pension claims. Pension claims are derived from accumulated cohort-specific earnings points that account for different labor force participation across cohorts. The current pension value that determines pension levels and the value of pension claims is annually recalculated according to a specified benefit indexation formula. Each year, revenues and expenditures have to match. If this is not the case, the contribution rate is adjusted up or down. This is done in an iterative process until the budget constraint is met. Note that changes in the contribution rate are reflected also in the development of the current pension value in subsequent years.

Revenues

There are three main sources of revenues for the German pension insurance:

1. contributions by employees and employers
2. contributions by the German Federal Employment Office for the currently unemployed and
3. government subsidies.

Contributions by employees and employers. The size of the mandatory contributions by employees and employers C_t^{LAB} in a given year t can be derived from Equation 3.5:

$$C_t^{LAB} = \tau_t \times AGW_t \times \beta \times LAB_t \tag{3.5}$$

Here, τ_t is the contribution rate for the pension system and AGW_t is the average gross wage of the insured labor force in year t. $\beta \times LAB_t$ designates the size of the insured labor force, with LAB_t representing the number of employed persons in year t and β representing the share of those with mandatory insurance. This share is approximately 80[31]. In terms of the model, β can be chosen without restrictions, but must remain constant in the course of the simulation.

Contributions by the German Federal Employment Office for the Unemployed. Since 1995, the German Federal Employment Office has been paying contributions to the pension system for those unemployed receiving benefits. As a basis for the calculations, the office uses 80% of the wage compensation payments[32]. In general, these will amount to 60%[33] of the last overall net wage that the unemployed has earned. Therefore, the German Federal Employment Office pays about 48% of the contributions that the individual would have paid if he were employed. I make the simplifying assumption that unemployment lasts for one year, as this ensures that there exists an average net wage from the previous year that can be used as the basis for computations. This leads to the following Equation 3.6 for the payments by the German Federal Employment Office C_t^U into the pension system:

$$C_t^U = \tau_t \times 0.48 \times ANW_{t-1} \times U_t \tag{3.6}$$

ANW_{t-1} denotes the average net wage of the insured labor force in the previous year, and U_t is the number of unemployed in year t.

Government Subsidies. In addition to the contributions by employees, employers and the employment office, the pension system receives a number of government subsidies. Since 1998 one has to distinguish between the regular and the additional federal subsidy.

- The *'Regular Federal Subsidy'* (RFS) is computed on a yearly basis, extrapolating according to the development of average gross wages and

[31] See Verband Deutscher Rentenversicherungsträger (VDR) (2002), pp. 248–249.

[32] Cf. §166(1) SGB VI.

[33] Cf. §129 SGB III states certain conditions according to which receivers of unemployment benefits can claim an increased rate of 67%. Only the rate of 60% is applied for calculations in the model.

salaries as well as the contribution rate to the pension system, as described by Equation 3.7[34].

$$RFS_t = RFS_{t-1} \times \frac{AGW_{t-1}}{AGW_{t-2}} \times \frac{\tau_t}{\tau_{t-1}} \tag{3.7}$$

- The *'Additional Federal Subsidy'* (AFS) is an additional flat-rate payment to cover benefits that are not funded by contributions[35]. It is adjusted to changes in the value added tax[36] T^{VA} on a yearly basis. In addition, it is raised by an additional supplement Sup, which is funded from additional revenues from the petroleum and electricity taxes and extrapolated according to the development of wages (Equation 3.8).

$$AFS_t = AFS_{t-1} \times \frac{T_t^{VA}}{T_{t-1}^{VA}} + Sup_t \times \frac{AGW_{t-1}}{AGW_{t-2}} \tag{3.8}$$

Besides the federal subsidies discussed above, the federal government provides additional contributions, in order to finance child support supplements to pensions. These contributions are not included in the model. Consistently, the numerous rules and regulations concerning credits for child support will also not be portrayed on the expenditure side of the model.

Other Sources of Revenues. In addition to these three main sources, there are further revenue items, e.g. the long-term care insurance contributions[37], contributions from sick-pay[38], contributions from voluntarily insured persons and reimbursements from public funds. These items account for a very minor share of the total budget and are therefore not included in the model.

[34] Cf. §213(2) SGB VI.

[35] Cf. §213 SGB VI.

[36] Note, that the value added tax is assumed to remain constant for the computations presented in this thesis.

[37] Cf. §44 SGB XI as well as §166(2) SGB VI.

[38] Cf. §166(1) SGB VI.

Expenditures

The main expenditures of the system are the following:

1. pension payments to pensioners,
2. contributions of the pension insurance to the health insurance for pensioners,
3. expenditures for rehabilitation measures and
4. administration costs.

Pension Payments. The pension payments P_t to pensioners in year t are computed according to Equation 3.9:

$$P_t = PV_t \times \sum_{c=t-RA}^{c=t-a_{max}} (RET_{c,t} \times EP_c) \qquad (3.9)$$

PV_t designates the current pension value, i.e. the value of one earnings point in year t, $RET_{c,t}$ is the number of pensioners of a cohort c in this year and EP_c is the sum of earnings points for a cohort c.

The current pension value PV_t is updated yearly using the applicable benefit indexation formula. The model allows to choose from various historical, current and potential alternative benefit indexation formulas.

The group of pensioners receiving benefits through the pension system $RET_{c,t}$ is composed of members of different cohorts c that have retired. The earliest time of retirement is RA (RA = retirement age) – therefore the youngest cohort whose members are among the current pensioners is the cohort $c = t - RA$. a_{max} designates the highest age that a pensioner can attain – therefore the oldest cohort whose members are among the current pensioners is the cohort $c = t - a_{max}$.

To determine the pension claims of the current pensioners, i.e. the sum of earnings points over all cohorts, cohort specific earnings points EP_c are computed. Each pensioner is assigned the cohort-specific earnings points of his cohort. The pension claims of each cohort are calculated on the basis of the cohort's specific employment history $H_{c,a}$. This history is derived

Figure 3.2. – Sex-specific Wage Profiles for Germany

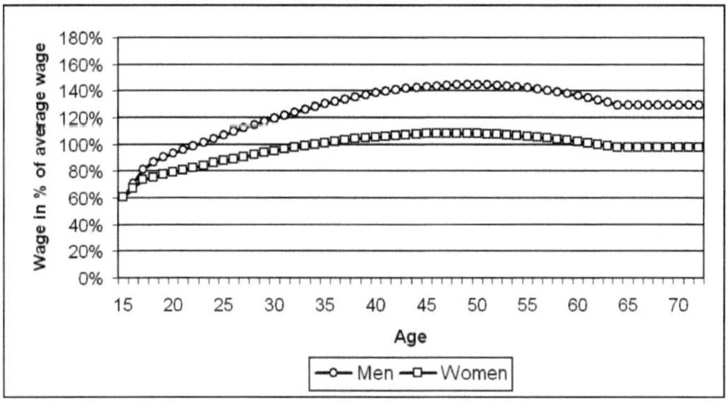

Source: Author's compilation based on Fitzenberger, Hujer, McCurdy, and Schnabel (2001).

by calculating the share of employed men in the labor force (and women respectively) for each age a of a cohort c and multiplying it with the age and sex-specific wage profile $WP_{a,s}$ which applies to all cohorts equally, see Equation 3.10. These sex-specific wage profiles are derived from estimated wage profiles for Germany by Fitzenberger, Hujer, McCurdy, and Schnabel (2001) and are depicted in Figure 3.2.

(3.10)

$$H_{c,a} = \sum_s \frac{LAB_{c,a,s}}{\max\limits_{a_0->RA-1}(LAB_{c,a,s})} \times WP_{a,s}\texttt{, with}\quad WP_{a,s} = \frac{AGW_{a,s}}{\sum\limits_a \sum\limits_s AGW_{a,s}}$$

Thus, if a cohort used its full labor force potential, the cohort's earnings would correspond exactly to the age and sex-specific wage profile. Taking the sum of the employment histories over all years in which members of the cohort were potentially employed – starting from the earliest possible entry into the labor market at age a_0 and ending with the latest possible exit from the labor market at age $RA - 1$ – yields the cohort specific earnings points EP_c, see Equation 3.11[39]:

[39]Note that in addition, the accumulated sum of earnings points for members of the cohort that retire prior to their statutory retirement age is reduced by the applicable adjustment factor.

(3.11)
$$EP_c = \sum_{a=a_0}^{RA-1} H_{c,a}$$

Contributions to the Health Insurance of Pensioners. In addition to the pension payments, the public pension insurance also pays half of pensioners' health insurance contributions. The contribution rate to the health system τ_t^H enters exogenously into the model. Therefore the payments to the health insurance E_t^H in year t can be computed according to Equation 3.12:

(3.12)
$$E_t^H = 0.5 \times \tau_t^H \times P_t$$

Here, P_t designates the pension benefit payments (see Equation 3.9).

Pensioners are also obligated to make a 1.7% contribution to the long-term care insurance, which exists since 1995. Prior to April 2004, the public pension insurance covered half of these contributions, since then the pensioners are solely responsible for these payments. Therefore the contributions to the long-term care insurance are no longer among the expenditures of the public pension insurance.

Rehabilitation Measures. Rehabilitation measures include actions to maintain, improve and recover (reduced) earnings capacity. Their aim is to reduce the number of disability pensions. The amount of rehabilitation payments E_t^{Reha} is updated according to the development of average wages on a yearly basis as shown in Equation 3.13:

(3.13)
$$E_t^{Reha} = E_{t-1}^{Reha} \frac{AGW_{t-1}}{AGW_{t-2}}$$

Administration Costs. The yearly adjustment of the expected administration costs E_t^{Admin} takes both changes of the current wage level and of the amount of current pensioners into account. The costs are described by Equation 3.14:

(3.14)

$$E_t^{Admin} = E_{t-1}^{Admin} \times \frac{AGW_{t-1}}{AGW_{t-2}} \times \left(1 + \theta \times \left(\frac{RET_{t-1}}{RET_{t-2}} - 1\right)\right) \quad \texttt{with } 0 \leq \theta \leq 1$$

Clearly, there is no one-to-one relationship between changes in the number of current pensioners and the administration costs in reality. For this reason, the factor θ is introduced to the model, which measures the relationship between changes in the number of pensioners and changes in the administration costs. For the calculations in the model, a value of 0.1 is used, which is the actually observed average value over the past decade[40].

Other Expenditures. There are two additional expenditure categories which only play a minor role and are therefore not included in the model. These are reimbursements of contributions and payments between different sub-insurances within the public pension insurance.

Budget Restriction

From the revenue and expenditure items discussed above the following budget restriction can be derived:

$$C_t^{LAB} + C_t^U + RFS_t + AFS_t = P_t + E_t^H + E_t^{Reha} + E_t^{Admin} \tag{3.15}$$

This budget restriction entails that the expenditures of the public pension insurance in every year t must be financed from the revenues of the same year[41]. In principle, there are three possible approaches to this:

Defined benefit system In the *defined benefit* approach, pension levels are annually adjusted according to a fixed benefit indexation formula. In order to ensure an annually balanced budget, the contribution rate is

[40]See Verband Deutscher Rentenversicherungsträger (VDR) (2007). Note that in 2006, administration costs amounted to 3.7 Mio. euros, i.e. around 1.6% of the total budget.

[41]As the condition that revenues exactly correspond to expenditures in every year will generally not be satisfied in reality, the law (§158 SGB VI) provides that the contribution rate for the following year has to be set in such a way that the so-called sustainability reserve is worth no less than 20% and no more than 150% of the total monthly expenditures of the pension insurance (§216ff. SGB VI). This sustainability reserve is not included in the model since it has little impact on the long-term financial development of the pension insurance.

adjusted such that the new pension level can be financed given the budget restriction. An example of this approach is the German gross wage adjustment from 1957 to 1992.

Defined contribution system In contrast to the defined benefit approach, the *defined contribution* approach assumes a fixed contribution rate and adjusts pension levels such that the budget restriction is met. An example of this approach are the so-called freezing scenario[42] where the contribution rates is set constant. A similar approach also applies to notional defined contribution (NDC) systems that will be treated in more detail in chapter 4.

Hybrid systems In addition to these pure system forms, one can think of *hybrid forms* that are a mixture of the defined benefit and defined contribution approaches since they incorporate elements of both approaches.

The current German system can be described as such a hybrid system[43]. Even though pension levels are annually adjusted according to a pre-specified formula and contribution rates adjust in order to finance this adjustment ('*defined benefit*'), the link in the benefit indexation formula to the development of contribution rates and the sustainability factor introduce elements of '*defined contribution*' that limit increases in the contribution rate at the expense of pension levels. For the projections in the remainder of this chapter, I therefore use this third approach that represents the current situation of the German PAYG pension system.

3.4.2. Modeling the State Subsidized Private Riester Pension

In order to model the state subsidized private Riester pension a representative '*Standard Riester Pensioner*' is introduced, who is defined by the following characteristics:

[42]See e.g. Börsch-Supan (2002a) for a simulation analysis on a freezing ´scenario for Germany.

[43]See Börsch-Supan (2004b) for a discussion on the German pension system as a hybrid in between defined benefit and defined contribution systems.

1. The person is a standard pensioner who worked for 45 years, always earned the average wage and retired at the statutory retirement age of 65.

2. The person signs a 'Riester contract' either immediately upon entering the workforce (at the age of 20[44]) or in 2002 when the 'Riester pension' was introduced, if the person was older than 20 years at this point of time.

3. The person pays the maximum contribution that receives subsidies by the state every year without interruption[45].

Based on this 'Standard Riester Pensioner' the resulting savings in the course of the contribution phase and the resulting pensions are computed. Note that the underlying 'Standard Riester Pensioner' is different for every cohort, since each cohort enters the Riester savings scheme at a different point in time.

Contribution phase

The respective 'Riester savings' $S_{c,t}$ of cohort c in year t are computed according to Equation 3.16:

$$S_{c,t} = sr_t \times AGW_{t-1} \tag{3.16}$$

s_t designates the savings rate in year t and AGW_{t-1} is the average gross wage of the previous year. This yearly savings amount of c is accumulated throughout all years of employment of this cohort until the end of the working period to total savings S_c, with the already accumulated capital each year earning the interest rate r, which has to be chosen in the model. Therefore the following relationship results:

$$S_c = \sum_{t=c+20}^{t=c+64} \left(S_{c,t} \prod_{v=c+20}^{v=c+64} (1 + r_v) \right) \tag{3.17}$$

[44] A standard pensioner, who retires at the legal pension age of 65, must have started working at the age of 20 in order to have worked for 45 years.

[45] In the course of the model, I assume that until 2008 savings are accrued according to the 'Riester staircase' and starting from 2009 4% of wages are saved annually.

S_c represents the accumulated value of the savings of the 'Standard Riester Pensioner' of cohort c over the entire working life.

Pension phase

The payments from the Riester savings scheme are calculated based on the accumulated savings S_c at the time of retirement. Cohort-specific 'Riester pensions' are either computed as constant or rising life-long annuities. The two approaches are described below[46]. For the computations in this thesis, rising annuities are assumed.

Constant life-long annuity. The constant life-long annuity R can be derived from Equations 3.18 and 3.19:

$$S_c = A \times (1+i)^{1-n_c} \times \frac{(1+i)^{n_c} - 1}{i} \tag{3.18}$$

$$A = \lambda \times S_c \times (1+i)^{n-1} \times \frac{(1+i) - 1}{(1+i)^n - 1} \tag{3.19}$$

with n_c ... conditional survival probability at age 65 of cohort c,
i ... discount rate.

To take the fact into account that the 'Riester products' provide (costly) annuities, the calculation is amended by the factor λ, which represents risk- and profit components, which are generally included in these products. For $\lambda = 1$ the calculated pension is actuarially fair. Factoring in risk- and profit components as well as administrative costs, the value decreases to $\lambda < 1$. Von Gaudecker and Weber (2004) find in an empirical study that the resulting net present value of pension payments after controlling for these additional components in Germany is around 90% of the actual present value.[47] In the model therefore λ is set to 0.9.

[46] Note that advanced payments are assumed. For an overview of different calculation approaches regarding life-long annuities, see Gerber (1997), pp. 35ff.

[47] See Von Gaudecker and Weber (2004), Table 10.

Progressive life-long annuity. In the case of progressive life-long annuities, the model assumes that pensions increase by a constant factor γ each year. Therefore pensions grow geometrically, and the following relationship holds for the net present value S_c:

$$S_c = A_{RA} \times (1+i) \times \frac{\left(\frac{\delta}{1+i}\right)^{n_c} - 1}{\delta - (1+i)} \tag{3.20}$$

Rearranging Equation 3.20 yields the baseline pension in the first payment year A_{RA} for cohort c – again taking heed of the factor λ:

$$A_{RA} = \lambda \times S_c \times \frac{1}{(1+i)} \times \frac{\delta - (1+i)}{\left(\frac{\delta}{(1+i)}\right)^{n_c} - 1} \tag{3.21}$$

All later payments A_t result from increasing the previous year's pension by the factor δ:

$$A_{t=c+64+z} = A_{RA}\delta^{z-1} \quad \texttt{for } z = 1, \ldots, n_c \tag{3.22}$$

3.5. Projections on the development of the German PAYG System

We can now analyze to what extent the past reforms have stabilized the public pension system. The Riester reform was quite bold in writing into the law that the net standard pension level must not fall below 67% while the contribution rate at the same time must not exceed 20% until 2020 and 22% until 2030. This section looks at whether these promises can be kept. Are the past reforms sufficient in order to counteract the foreseen consequences of demographic change and stabilize the system?

Based on the simulation model described in section 3.4 and the demographic and labor market forecasts used by the Rürup Commission depicted in chapter 2, this section presents projections of the future development of contribution rates and pension levels in the German public PAYG pension system. Computations are based on the additional assumptions of a long-term real wage growth rate of 1.5%, an inflation rate of also 1.5% and almost stable contribution rates to the unemployment, health and long-term care insurances[48]. Section 3.5.1 shows the projection results based on the current status quo after all the reforms of the past decades and looks at whether the Riester targets can be met. Section 3.5.2 then illustrates how the future development of contribution rates and pension levels has been affected by each of the described reforms. Finally, section 3.5.3 displays projections under different demographic, labor market and economic growth assumptions in order to show to what extent projection results are affected by the set underlying assumptions.

3.5.1. Future Contribution Rates and Pension Levels

Figure 3.3 shows how contribution rates and pension levels are projected to develop after the latest pension reform in 2007. It can be seen that the contribution rate is slightly above 20% in 2020 but holds the set target of 22% in 2030. Net standard pension levels decrease to 62% in 2030 and thus drop way below their 67%-threshold.

However, as it was mentioned in section 3.2.2, net pension levels are no longer an appropriate measure since the introduction of deferred taxation for retirement income under the 2005 Old Age Income Act that will be phased-in until 2040. Instead, a modified net pension level before tax was defined and Riester pension level targets were redefined accordingly to 46% in 2020 and 43% in 2030. Another possible measurement is gross pension levels for which no target values were manifested by law but can be translated to 38% (2020) and 35% (2030) accordingly. As gross pension levels require the least additional assumptions and mirror best the core mechanisms of the German public PAYG pension system, I will refer to their development in the following as well as in most remaining parts of this thesis. Figure 3.4 displays projected pension levels according to these different definitions. Note that the original net pension level definition according to which pension levels under the old

[48]Contribution rates to the unemployment insurance are assumed to remain constant at a level of 6.5% and contribution rates to the health system are assumed to remain constant at a level of 13.9%. Contribution rates to the long-term care system are assumed to rise from 1.7% to 1.95% from July 2008 on as it was decided by law.

Figure 3.3. – Development of Contribution Rates and Pension Levels

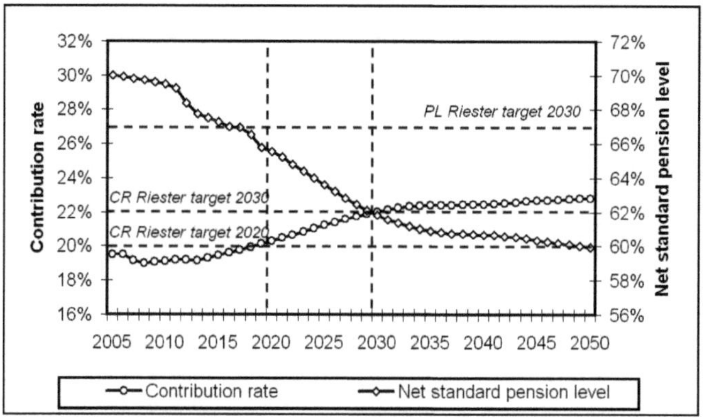

CR = contribution rate, PL = pension level *Source: Author's computations.*

net wage adjustment remained stable at roughly 70% until the late 1990s and which was redefined in the context of the 2001 Riester Reform is also included in the graph.

First, it can be seen that pension levels generally, independent of their specific definition, follow the same decreasing trend and run surprisingly parallel. Only between the old and new definition of net pension levels can the effect of the Riester staircase be observed. This postpones the decrease of newly defined net pension levels (section 3.2.2 and appendix C). Given the projections' underlying assumptions where total social security contributions other than to the public pension system quasi remain stable this pattern is to be expected. Worth noting, however, is that the modified standard pension level before tax remains above the set limits for both 2020 and 2030 while the set limits defined for net pension levels are violated (recall 3.3). The redefinition of the Riester targets from 67% of net pension levels to 46% (2020) and 43% (2030) of net pension levels before tax thus implicitly but considerably softened the Riester targets on pension levels.

Under the assumed population, labor market, economic and (other) social security branches development and the status quo of the German PAYG pension system, the contribution and pension level targets codified in the

Figure 3.4. – Development of Pension Levels According to Different Pension Level Definitions

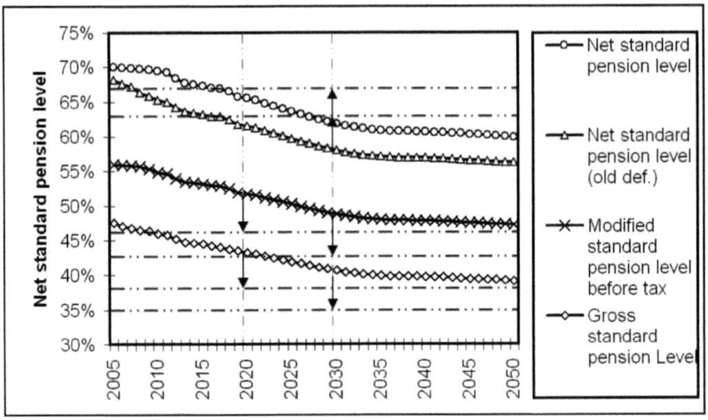

Source: Author's computations.

context of the 2001 Riester Reform and redefined with the introduction of the Old Age Income Act in 2005 can therefore be met.

The scale of the reductions in pension levels also clearly demonstrates that public pension benefits will no longer be sufficient without supplementary pension provision, in safeguarding pensioners' standards of living in old age. We will come back to that in the next section (3.6).

3.5.2. Stepwise Reform Effects

If the Riester reform targets can now be met, to what extent did the different past reforms contribute to the development of contribution rates and pension levels? In the following, we will look at the stepwise reform effects. Figure 3.5 illustrates the projected development of contribution rates and pension levels after each of the reforms.

It shows that under the net indexation adjustment after the 1992 reform, contribution rates would have developed to roughly 30% by 2050, while gross standard pension levels would have not even dropped by 5% to a level of

Figure 3.5. – Stepwise Reform Effects

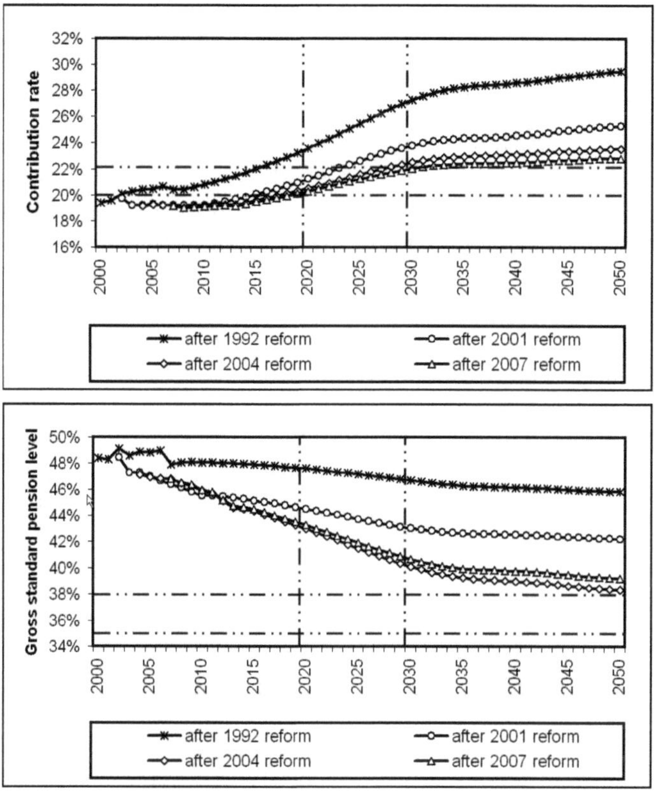

Source: Author's computations.

around 46% over the same time period[49]. This clearly would not have been a sustainable system. The 2001 Riester Reform took a large step towards stabilization in that it reduced the projected increase in contribution rates

[49]Recall that net pension levels (according to their original definition) would have remained roughly stable at a level of 70%. The reason that gross pension levels drop is that the wage gap between net and gross wages widens due to the increase in the contribution rate to the pension system. As for pensioners, the difference between gross and net pensions is much lower than the gap between gross and net wages, gross pensions decrease relative to average gross wages.

by roughly half. This came at the expense of pension levels that in return dropped by almost 9% by 2050. However, as Figure 3.5 shows, the Riester Reform itself would have not been sufficient to meet its own targets. Contribution rates still rise to 21% by 2020 and 24% by 2030, while the gross pension level of 42% corresponds to a net pension level of 63% to 64% and thus would have remained above the set lower threshold[50].

The apparent failure of the Riester reform to reach its main objectives was not accidental. As mentioned earlier, overoptimistic demographic and economic assumptions as a projection basis had been chosen in a fragile political compromise between reformists and unions that enabled the Riester reform package to pass the parliamentary hurdles. When the Rürup Commission took up its work in winter 2002, it was clear that more realistic population and labor market forecasts were needed. Recall that these are the ones most projections in this thesis are based on. But as only half of the commission's proposed reform package was put into law under the 2004 reform, namely the introduction of the sustainability factor, it can be seen from Figure 3.5 that this still proved not to be sufficient in order to reach the set targets. Only when the second part of the reform package, the proposed increase in the statutory retirement age from 65 to 67, became law in 2007 did projected contribution rates and pension levels finally meet the targets[51].

3.5.3. Demographic, Labor Market and Economic Growth Effects

To what extent are these results driven by the underlying assumptions? Figure 3.6 depicts the projected development of contribution rates and gross standard pension levels under different population assumptions[52].

[50] See also Bonin (2001) and Prognos (2001) for similar projection results at that time.

[51] Note that the computations in this subsection are all based on the same demographic and labor market projections. Whether a rather optimistic labor market forecast, for example, with presumed increases in the mean retirement age by two years until 2040 would have been realistic before the 2007 reform is questionable, though. The presented projections here neglect these potential behavioral effects. For future projections on the development of the German PAYG pension system that explicitly take such behavioral effects into account, see Bucher-Koenen and Wilke (2008).

[52] Note that a different population forecast also implies different labor market outcomes as the labor market projections are based on the demographic input. In order to be able to show how different population assumptions affect the simulation results, I therefore replicate the Rürup Commission's labor market forecast with the labor market simulation model illustrated in chapter 2 and underlying Rürup Commis-

Figure 3.6. – Development of Contribution Rates and Pension Levels Under Different Population Scenarios

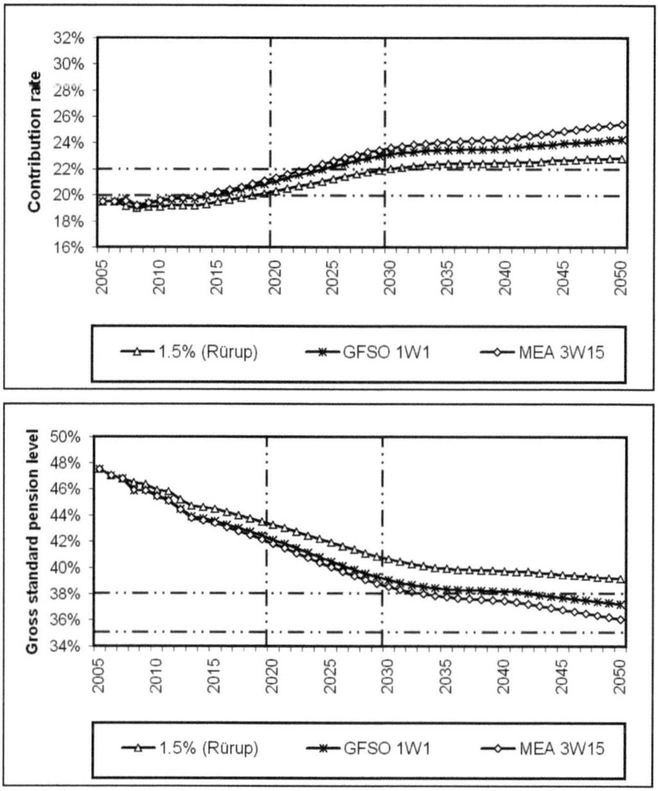

Source: Author's computations.

Compared to the Rürup Commission's projections, the GFSO 1W1 and MEA 3W1.5 population scenarios both lead to a higher level of contribution rates. For the GFSO 1W1 scenario, a difference of 1.5 contribution points results by 2050, while in the case of the MEA 3W1.5 scenario the difference

sion's population projections. It shows that the Rürup labor market forecast is equivalent to a scenario where until the year 2040, the female labor force participation rises to 0.7, the mean retirement age increases by 2 years, the labor entry age is reduced by 1 year and unemployment rates fall to 4.8%.

turns out even larger with approximately 2.5 contribution points. Pension levels in turn drop by 2 percentage points more under the GFSO 1W1 scenario, and 3 percentage points more under the MEA 3W1.5 scenario. This development is a result of the higher old age dependency ratios (OADR) in both the GFSO 1W1 (around 60% in 2050 in contrast to around 54% under the Rürup Commission's projections) and the MEA 3W1.5 scenario (OADR of 65% in 2050).

What are the effects if the labor force responds differently? Figure 3.7 shows how contribution rates and pension levels develop under the 'Status Quo' and 'Agenda 1005' scenario that were presented in chapter 2. Note that the Rürup scenario can be considered to be less optimistic than the Denmark scenario but more optimistic than the Agenda 1005 and status quo scenario that were presented in chapter 2. It can be seen that a more optimistic labor forecast, given the same underlying population assumptions, leads to lower contribution rates and higher pension levels. Under the 'Agenda 1005' scenario, contribution rates would turn out 0.6 contribution points higher, under the 'Status Quo' scenario even 2.5 contribution points higher. Pension levels in return drop by 0.7 percentage points more under the 'Agenda 1005' and 2.8 percentage points more under the 'Status Quo' scenario.

Last, we examine the effects of different wage growth. Figure 3.8 illustrates the projected development of contribution rates and pension levels for real wage growth rates of $g = 0\%$ and $g = 3\%$. Higher wage growth rates thereby lead to lower contribution rates and also to lower pension levels. A 1.5 percentage points higher wage growth rate decreases the rise in the contribution rate by 0.5 and increases the drop in pension levels by 0.3 percentage points. Note that the effects of a lower wage growth rate are symmetric. The explanation for this level effect is as follows: A higher wage growth rate leads to higher contribution revenues that allow the contribution rate to decrease in the following year. Pension levels are then adjusted to this higher rise in wages and lower contribution rate, however, only partly. Since the pure adjustment to wages now would be higher (pension levels would decrease less), the sustainability factor is applied to a larger basis and exerts a larger effect on pension levels. The net effect is negative as can be seen from Figure 3.8. Thus, even if higher wage growth more easily allows to stabilize the contribution rate, the effect on pension levels is the opposite.

Figure 3.7. – Development of Contribution Rates and Pension Levels Under Different Labor Market Scenarios

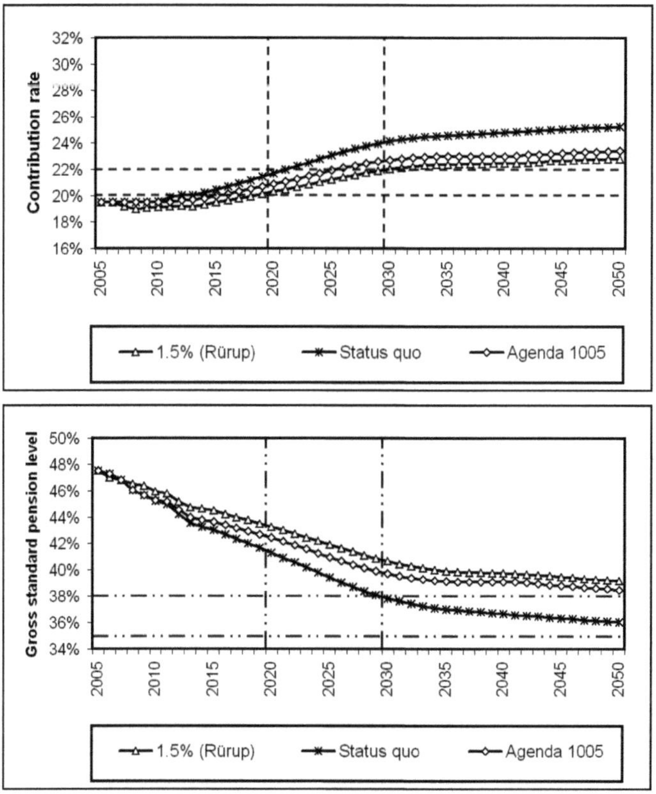

Source: Author's computations.

Overall, the sensitivity analysis of this section shows that the Riester targets will be met only under very few restrictive population, labor market and economic growth assumptions. Higher increases in life expectancy, only moderately increasing labor force participation rates or lower wage growth can shift the Riester off target. If this happens, further reforms are likely[53].

[53]Note however, that potential behavioral effects as well as economic feedback effects such as between labor market participation and wage growth have been neglected here in order to show the simple demographic,

Figure 3.8. – Development of Contribution Rates and Pension Levels Under Different Growth Scenarios

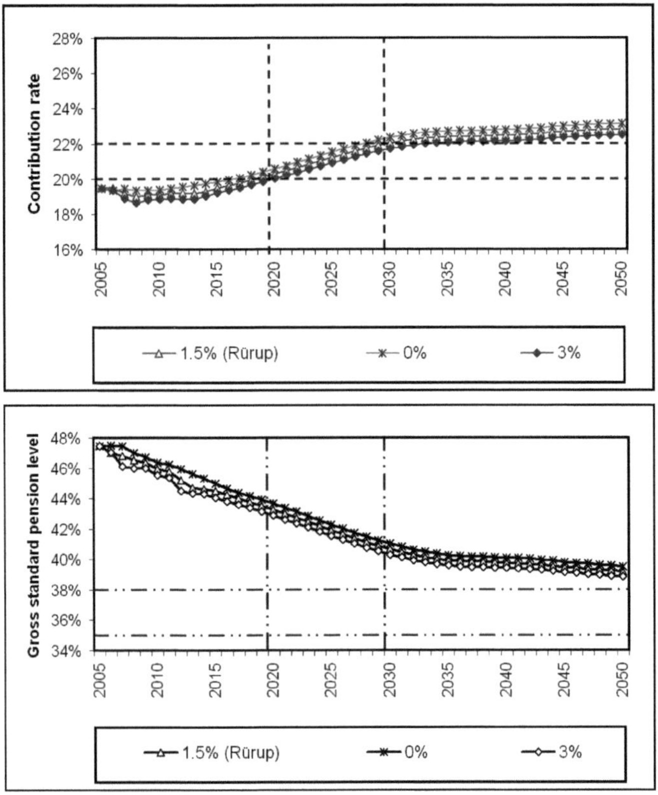

Source: Author's computations.

3.6. Projections on the Future Role of Supplementary Pensions

The previous sections made clear that deductions in future pension levels are inescapable. Thus, if people want to maintain their standard of living

labor market and growth effect.

in retirement they have to make supplementary private savings. With the state-subsidized Riester pension the government has tried to set an incentive for people to build up these necessary additional private old age provision. But is a savings rate of 4% sufficient to fill the upcoming pension gap? And how large will the share of supplementary pension income compared to public pension income then be? These questions will be addressed in this section.

3.6.1. Can the Riester Pensions Fill the Public Pension Gap?

The main point of introducing the Riester pensions was to compensate for the reductions in the public pension system. Figure 3.9 illustrates the growing pension gap (defined as the difference between today's and forecasted future gross pension levels) and the level of additional benefits provided by the Riester pension based on different assumptions regarding rates of return. The model calculations show that an envisaged savings rate of 4% of gross wages is sufficient to close the gap which will open up in old age provision as a result of the cuts in state pensions[54].

While the Riester pensions can fill the pension gap in the long run, they are not sufficient for older cohorts. These cohorts will need to save more than the envisaged maximum savings rates in Table 3.1 in order to close this gap entirely during their lifetime. Younger cohorts born after 1970, in contrast, will be in a position to build up even higher pension entitlements than current pensioners if supplementary pension savings are taken into account. Obviously, rather than a slow increase to a fixed 4% savings rate such as the Riester staircase, initial savings rates have to be high and tailored to each cohort if pension gaps are to be closed.

3.6.2. Future Share of Public and Private Pension Income

Given the projections illustrated in Figure 3.3 on page 71, the future composition of retirement income will be quite different from the current monolithic

[54]Note that it is assumed that individuals have started to save these additional 4% directly in 2002 (first year of Riester pensions) or their first year of work respectively if they were not yet a part of the labor force in 2002. Moreover, as for the standard public pension level, a retirement age of 65 is assumed so that remaining life expectancy at this age is used for the annuity transformation.

Figure 3.9. – Development of the Total Pension Level

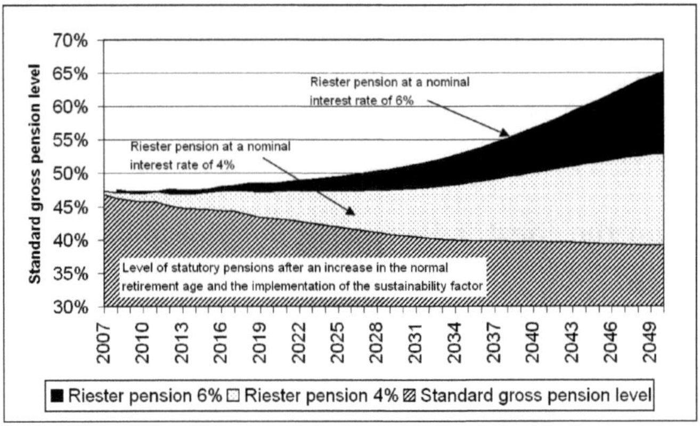

Source: Author's computations.

one. Figure 3.10 outlines this development by birth cohort in the year of their retirement. As for the standard pensioner, retirement is again assumed to be at age 65. Note that the increase in the statutory retirement age to 67 is not taken into account here[55]. Moreover, it is assumed that cohorts have adhered to the recommended Riester savings rates of Table 3.1 on page 52 from the beginning of 2002 or their working life, respectively.

Figure 3.10 shows that the German public pension system will remain the dominant pillar for old age provision also in the future. Riester pensions will make up about 35% or 40% of state organized retirement income by 2050. Should other income sources (currently about 15% of total retirement income)[56] stay as they are, this would yield a share of PAYG pensions in total retirement income at about 55 to 60%. Some crowding out of existing occupational pensions and other private pensions by the new Riester pensions seems likely, however. First evidence on this is found by Corneo, Keese, and

[55]If this increase was considered, the composition would shift even more towards the supplementary private pensions since the saving period would be prolonged by two years and remaining life expectancy at age 67 would form the basis for the annuity computations. Public pensions would also rise, however not to the same extent as returns on the capital market are higher.

[56]See Börsch-Supan, Miegel, Brombacher Steiner, Bovenberg, Mijdam, Disney, Wise, and Schmidt-Hebbel (1999) as well as Börsch-Supan and Schnabel (1999).

Figure 3.10. – Composition of Public and Private Pension Income by Cohort

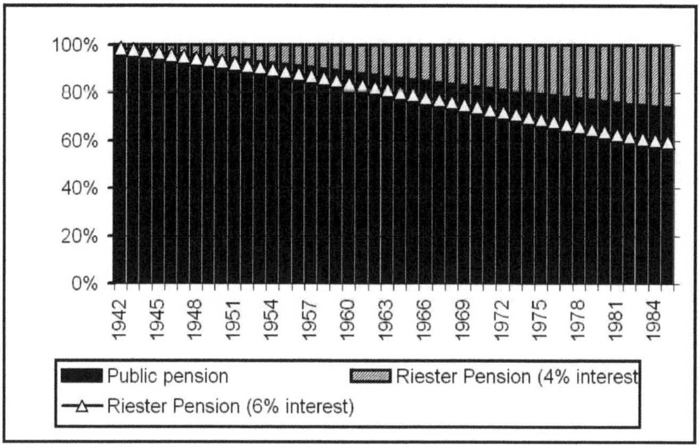

Source: Author's computations.

Schröder (2007). However, the study is based on very rough savings data that in addition tends to underestimate contractual savings. A study by Coppola (2008) on much more detailed savings data in contrast shows the opposite results, namely a crowding in of savings.

3.6.3. Rate of Return Risk

It could be argued that the capital rates of returns of 4% and 6% nominal (corresponding to a real rate of return of 2.5% and 4.5%) illustrated in Figures 3.9 and 3.10 are too optimistic. One cause of concern among critics is the *asset meltdown hypothesis* according to which demographic developments will result in an oversupply of financial assets thus leading to decreasing capital returns on such assets. However, model calculations have shown that the demographically-induced fall in rates of return will not be as dramatic as often predicted in the popular press[57]. Nonetheless, the situation on capital

[57]See e.g. (Börsch-Supan, Ludwig, and Winter (2006) and Ludwig and Krüger (2007) who find that the capital market rate of return, owing to demographic factors, will fall by merely one percentage point if diversification within the EU region is assumed. For the asset meltdown hypothesis, see also Poterba

markets since 2001 provides an unmistakable warning that lengthy periods of below average, or even negative capital returns are certainly a risk that needs to be considered. Calculations by Essig and Reil-Held (2003) have shown however, that this rate of return risk is less important if capital returns do not fluctuate more than during the past 40 years.

3.6.4. On the Voluntary Nature of Riester Pensions

As said before, the projection results presented in this chapter are based on the assumption that individuals save the subsidized 4% of their wage. However, it is by no means certain that households, particularly low-income households, are willing and/or able to set aside additional savings for old age on a consistent basis. Empirical findings confirm that lower income groups are less willing and able to make additional savings for their old age pensions, and that this is exacerbated by these groups being less well informed about financial matters[58]. The especially high Riester incentives for the lowest income group are meant to overcome the first problem, that low-income earners are not able to save. Non-willingness is more difficult to overcome.

Thus, an important question is whether the new voluntary Riester pensions will be accepted by the German workers who have been used to the generous German public pension system. How many will build up supplementary pensions? At this point, seven years since their introduction, a first assessment can be done.

The depth of Riester incentives. Two aspects need to be taken into account when assessing the benefits offered by the Riester incentives. First, the subsidies/tax exemptions during the contribution phase and second, any tax-related advantages or disadvantages which arise during the disbursement phase. The direct subsidies during the contribution phase are very deep for those who have relatively low income and those who have children. The reverse is the case for the tax-deductible special allowances, due to the progressive tax system. Here, households with higher incomes benefit more.

(2001) as well as Abel (2001) who investigates the role of bequests in this context.

[58]See e.g.Bulmahn (2003) on this topic.

Figure 3.11. – Depth of Riester Pension Subsidies

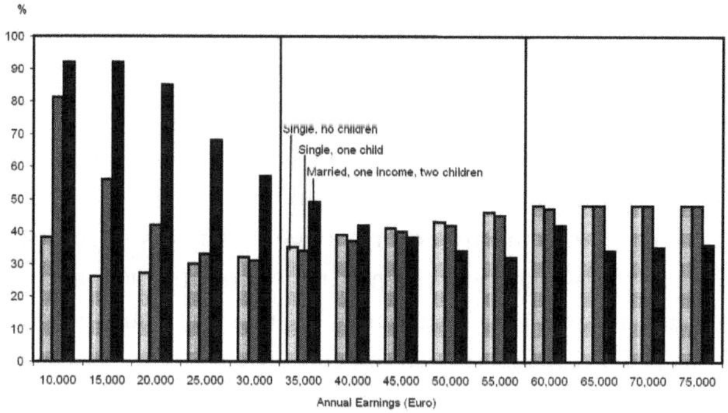

Note: Direct subsidy/tax advantage as percentage of savings in form of the new supplementary pensions. *Source: Own illustration based on Deutsche Bundesbank (2002).*

This results in a U-shaped relationship between subsidies and income, visible in Figure 3.11 which shows the subsidy as a percentage of savings in form of the new supplementary pensions[59].

For lowest income households, the subsidy is almost as large as the contribution itself. Even for the well-to-do, subsidy rates are high around 40–50%. Given these deep subsidies, uptake is likely to be high. The picture of Figure 3.11, however, is misleading insofar as this U-shaped curve is flattened out during the disbursement phase when pension benefits will be taxed. This flattening effect is due to the impact of progressive taxation. Taxation will not affect pensioners in the lower half of the income distribution because their pension income is below a generous exemption for retired households. It will, however, considerably reduce the effective lifetime subsidy to households with incomes above average.

The form of the Riester incentives. While the depth of the Riester incentives makes the Riester pensions rather attractive, the Riester pension is less flexible than other retirement investment products. One of the main

[59]Note that the word 'subsidy' here refers to both the direct subsidy and the tax-deductible special allowance.

complaints is that most of the capital has to be annuitized and can therefore not be used as collateral or bequeathed. The argument lacks a certain logic, as the very objective of the Riester pensions is to provide annuity income in order to fill the pension gap emerging from the reduced PAYG pillar. This widely voiced argument thus rather is a clear indication that most workers have not yet realized that they will depend on supplementary Riester pensions for a reasonable retirement income.

The extensive certification requirements which severely restrict private providers' scope to develop new private insurance products and which lead to higher costs are also disadvantageous. Certain cost items can result in total costs of up to 20%, compared with around 10% for a normal capital sum life insurance policy[60]. However, this has been improved when the certification requirements were redefined under the 2004 reform. Still, the certification rules merely serve to create a formal product standard without creating the transparency needed in order to compare different investment vehicles and the relative rates of return they offer. As a result, customers are often not in a position to make truly informed private investment decisions.

Last, the guarantee of the nominal value of contributions does ensure that, upon retirement, at the very least the nominal capital saved is available as pension capital. However, there are no rules which prescribe the sort of pension dynamisation which is needed in order to ensure that the value of pension benefits paid out from the saved capital can be maintained over the long term. Non-dynamised Riester benefits will very quickly lose their value, even at very modest rates of inflation.

Evidence on take-up rates. First survey results shortly after the introduction showed that demand for Riester products was sluggish: only around 9% had actually taken out a policy by mid 2002; a further 16% planned to conclude a policy by the end of 2002 (Schnabel (2003)). This came during a growing trend for workers to enroll in supplementary pension plans. Only around half of those planning to enroll in such plans are considering doing so in the framework of a Riester policy. The other half prefer other savings and insurance products, and/or occupational pensions[61]. By the end of 2006,

[60] See Stiftung Warentest (2002).
[61] See Leinert (2002).

however, a total of more than 8 million pension plans eligible for subsidy support had been concluded corresponding to a coverage of about 23% of all eligible workers[62].

Still, so far the direct and tax subsidies of Riester pensions are still far from providing universal coverage. Moreover, many households, especially in the higher income brackets, merely may restructure their existing pension plans in order to reap Riester subsidies. At this point, we do not have much hard evidence on such substitution. Should these households have a fixed pension target, financing state subsidies via general taxation can actually have perverse effects which lead to a lower savings rate[63].

Do we need mandatory private pensions after all? Surveys have shown that a large section of the population would actually welcome the introduction of mandatory supplementary private pensions[64]. This preference may be explained by savers' lack of confidence in their ability to exercise the discipline needed to build up additional old age provision by themselves and the fiscal externality imposed by those who speculate on general social assistance or now the minimum pension rather than save.

The arguments generally cited in favor of mandatory supplementary old age provision are poverty in old age and adverse selection on the insurance market[65]. Poverty in old age, however, is currently not an important problem in Germany. This may change in the future because of the benefit cuts in public pensions, but has been addressed by the 2001 Riester reform through the introduction of the new minimum pension. As far as adverse selection is concerned, compulsory provision could lead to a monopoly position being established by a single provider if this product and the offers it generates proves to be unattractive for smaller competitors in which case coercion would bring about even less rather than more product variety.

[62]See Bundesministerium für Gesundheit und Soziale Sicherung (BMGS) (2005) and Sommer (2004) for a detailed overview of take-up rates so far.

[63]See Börsch-Supan and Lührmann (2000).

[64]See Boeri, Börsch-Supan, and Tabellini (2001), Boeri, Börsch-Supan, and Tabellini (2002b) and Boeri, Börsch-Supan, and Tabellini (2002a).

[65]See e.g. Börsch-Supan (2000a).

Another strong argument against mandatory old age provision is the tax-like character it gives to savings and the resulting negative incentive effects[66]. The very idea of reducing the tax and payroll-tax-like contribution burden in order to stimulate economic growth would be jeopardized.

As an alternative to mandatory old age provision, *opting-out* contracts, in the context of company pension plans have been discussed extensively in Germany in the past few years. These are old age provision savings contracts that automatically start with employment in the firm if the worker does not explicitly refuses. In the U.S., such provision plans have increased coverage to over 85% while *opting-in* contracts where individuals have to actively to decide to participate only lead to coverage rates of a third. However, the detailed design of such opting-out contracts is more difficult than at first sight thought. Providing an opting-out option implies the existence of a standard product, and thus drags again the argument of a monopoly position behind it that was already pointed out above[67].

3.7. Conclusion

This chapter described the basic principles of the German pension system and its current reform process. Moreover, it presented projections on the long-term financial development of the public PAYG pillar as well as on the future role of supplementary private pensions. The main findings are that the past reforms have turned the system from a monolithic into a more sustainable and more robust multi-pillar system that still seems to allow for adequate pension benefits – at least if the anticipated demographic and labor market developments come true.

In terms of *adequacy* of pension benefits, the projections showed that the Riester targets of 46% in 2020 and 43% in 2030 for (modified) net pension levels before tax can be just met if the demographic and labor market projections by the Rürup Commission are assumed. However, it was also shown that higher increases in life expectancy, only moderately increasing labor force participation rates or lower wage growth already can quickly shift the

[66]Summers (1989).

[67]See Leinert (2003), Ruprecht (2004), Ippolito (2001) and Gunderson and Luchak (2001) for a discussion of the opting-out concept.

Riester targets out of sight. The scale of the reductions in pension levels also clearly demonstrates that public pension benefits will no longer be sufficient alone – that is without supplementary pension provision – to safeguard pensioners' standards of living in old age. The introduction of the minimum pension guarantee under the 2001 Riester reform is to be seen in this context.

The introduction of the *sustainability* factor into the German benefit indexation formula in 2004 linked the development of benefits to the development of the pensioner ratio, the most crucial internal system parameter. Depending on the size of α, the system now technically can either follow a defined benefit approach ($\alpha = 0$) or a defined-contribution approach ($\alpha = 1$). With the setting of $\alpha = 0.25$ the German public pension system thus was effectively shifted from the formerly defined-benefit to a defined-contribution oriented system. In the next chapter we will see that it now provides a similar self-stabilizing mechanism as the so much promoted NDC schemes.

Finally, thanks to the shift from the former monolithic to a multi-pillar system, the *robustness* of the German pension system has increased as risks are better diversified. Public pension benefits of course are still subject to political risk even though the introduction of a somewhat automatic balancing mechanism with the sustainability factor has reduced this risk considerably. However, several ad hoc rulings with regard to benefit adjustments since 2004 as well as the current debate on an intermission of the Riester staircase for 2008 and 2009 in favor of a higher pension adjustment in these years show that even such an automatic balancing mechanism provides no guarantee against further discretionary interventions. Supplementary private old age income in contrast is subject to the rate of return risk on the capital market. However, as it was discussed, pertinent model calculations show that the demographically-induced fall in rates of return will not be as dramatic as often predicted in the popular press.

4. An NDC System for Germany – A Reform Alternative?

4.1. Introduction

Notional defined contribution (NDC) systems have been debated at length in the worldwide pension literature in the past years. They can be regarded as a new wave of pension reform following the wave of pre-funded systems that were promoted by the World Bank in the mid-eighties[1]. In contrast to these pre-funded systems, the NDC approach does not require a transition to a fully funded system, but can be regarded as a complementary strategy that aims at restructuring the first, PAYG financed pillar. It thus preserves existing PAYG systems, offering a reform alternative to those countries that wish to keep a substantial public PAYG pillar, as it is the case in Germany. Still, the conversion of an existing PAYG pillar to an NDC system does not exclude a partial transition to pre-funding. Indeed, both reform options may complement each other in a multi-pillar approach.

The NDC approach is based on two main ideas. (1) Intragenerational redistribution within the PAYG pillar is to be minimized by establishing a set of individual accounts where contribution payments are recorded and from which individual pension benefits can be directly derived at the time of retirement, accounting for individual life expectancy. (2) In order to ensure the long-run sustainability of the PAYG system, demographic and labor market changes are directly reflected in the interest accrued on the accumulated contribution payments on the individual account.

This chapter looks at whether such a NDC system would be a reform alternative for the German public pension system. In fact, the German public pension system already bears some resemblance to an NDC system[2]. Thanks

[1]See World Bank (1994).

[2]See Börsch-Supan (2004b).

to its point system, which goes back to the introduction of the PAYG system in 1957, the German public pension system is based on a similar concept of individual accounts. Furthermore, the actuarial adjustments depending on the time of retirement entry, that have been phased in following the 1992 and 1999 reforms, mimic the automatic adjustment to changes in life expectancy in an NDC system. Finally, the sustainability factor proposed by the Rürup Commission and implemented with the 2004 pension reform, introduces a self-stabilizing feedback mechanism that responds to changes in demography and labor market development, similar to the one in an NDC system. However, there remain crucial differences between the two systems.

An NDC system, in principle, could have some valuable advantages over the present German PAYG pension system[3]. First, the NDC system provides great flexibility regarding the choice of the retirement age, which could set an end to the ongoing eligibility discussion in the German PAYG system. A second advantage would be the enhanced transparency of an NDC system. This could be extremely helpful for Germany, where the public pension system is composed of a very complicated set of numerous regulations, which obscure the actual size of pension benefits that can be expected from the system as well as the need for private old age pension. Moreover, increased transparency might help to re-establish some of the credibility that the German PAYG system has lost over the course of the repeated discretionary interventions of the past. Another advantage would be that such discretionary interventions would no longer be easy in an NDC system.[4]

Thus, a conversion of the German PAYG system to an NDC system in principle could bring about some crucial benefits. Moreover, such a conversion should be relatively easy due to the existing analogies between the two systems. This chapter analyzes the effects a hypothetical introduction of an NDC system would have on the financial situation of the German PAYG system. The chapter is structured as follows: Section 4.2 gives an introduction into the NDC concept before section 4.3 describes the parallels between the two systems. Section 4.4 presents a thorough simulation and sensitivity

[3]These advantages are partly due to the individualization achieved by the underlying concept of individual accounts. For a general discussion of this concept, see Holzmann and Palacios (2001).

[4]These are only some selected aspects of NDC systems. A thorough discussion of advantages and disadvantages of NDC systems can be found in Barr (2003).

analysis of the effects such an introduction would have on pension levels and the budget of the German pension insurance. Section 4.5 concludes.

4.2. Notional Defined Contribution Systems

The NDC concept was first designed in Sweden, where the system passed legislation in 1994, and was introduced in 2001 with a 16 years transition period[5]. However, it can be argued that the basic underlying principles of the NDC system were already present in earlier concepts like the one presented by Buchanan in 1968[6] or the German and French point systems respectively[7]. Soon after the system had been legislated in Sweden, Latvia and Poland took up the concept and integrated it into their ongoing pension reform processes[8]. They thus became the first countries to introduce an NDC system for the first pillar in 1995[9]. At the same time, Italy also legislated an NDC approach for its first pillar in the context of the Dini reform. However, the system will not become effective before 2040, due to an extremely long transition period[10]. Apart from these European countries, NDC systems have also been introduced in Brazil and the Kyrgyz republic[11].

In the literature, NDC systems remain disputed. While they are perceived quite positively by those who have experienced and accompanied their introduction (e.g. Palmer (2000); Chlon, Góra, and Rutkowski (1999)), they receive some serious criticism from other economists observing the process from the outside (e.g. Disney (1999); Valdés-Prieto (2000)).

This section gives a brief introduction to the NDC system approach. The basic concept is explained in section 4.2.1. Section 4.2.2 provides a mathematical description. Last, section 4.2.3 and section 4.2.4 discuss some selected aspects of system design and system behavior.

[5]See Sundén (2000) for a brief overview of the Swedish NDC system. A thorough description of the system can be found in Palmer (2000).

[6]See Valdés-Prieto (2000).

[7]See Disney (1999) and Valdés-Prieto (2000).

[8]See Disney (1999) and Valdés-Prieto (2000).

[9]A first assessment on the Polish pension reform can be found in Chlon (2003).

[10]See Franco and Sartor (2003) and Brugiavini and Galasso (2004) for an evaluation of the Italian pension reform process.

[11]See Brooks and Weaver (2003) for a description of the NDC system in Brazil and Palmer (2003) for a brief description of the NDC system in the Kyrgyz republic.

4.2.1. Basic Concepts

The NDC system is a PAYG system that in principle is based on a *defined contribution* (DC) instead of the conventional *defined benefit* (DB) approach that has been the basis for PAYG systems in most countries until recently.

Defined benefit (DB). In the conventional DB based PAYG system the size of pension benefits is determined annually via a specified benefit indexation formula, such that a predefined desirable (often stable) pension level for a reference pensioner[12] can be maintained. Pension benefits thus are not directly linked to the amount of previously paid contributions but depend to a large extent on the shape of the benefit indexation formula. In order to ensure an annually balanced budget, the system's contribution rate is raised accordingly if estimated revenues under the present rate are not sufficient to cover arising pension claims. Given the increasing demographic and economic pressures, this has led to continually rising contribution rates in many countries in the past decade.

Defined contribution (DC). The DC approach, commonly used in the capital market for private pension arrangements, derives pension benefits directly from the amount of previously paid contributions by converting the accrued pension wealth into a lifelong pension annuity. This happens only once at the time of retirement. The contribution rate is hereby set exogenously[13].

An NDC system combines this DC approach with the basics of a PAYG system. Contributions to the pension system are recorded on individual accounts so that subsequent pension benefits can be calculated as a lifelong annuity on the basis of the accumulated capital stock at the end of the

[12]Recall that for Germany, the reference pensioner is the so-called standard pensioner who worked for 45 years, always earned the average wage and retired at the statutory retirement age of 65. In the German point system he is thus credited 45 earnings points.

[13]Note that the distinction between defined benefit and defined contribution systems can be made from different perspectives. In the range of PAYG systems, a defined contribution approach can also refer to a PAYG system, where the contribution rate is exogenous while benefits are determined endogenously under the annual budget constraint, see e.g. Lindbeck and Persson (2003). However, in this chapter, the notion 'defined contribution' refers solely to the annuity mechanism used on capital markets that establishes a tight link between contribution payments and pension benefits.

working period. However, since contributions in a PAYG system are needed to finance current pension expenditures, they can only notionally be recorded on the accounts, without any real money transfer, which is why the system is referred to as a *notional* defined contribution (NDC) system. There is no annual budget constraint in this system as is conventional for PAYG systems. The contribution rate enters exogenously, and thus can be held constant or follow a predetermined, desired path.

4.2.2. Mathematical Description

As it was explained above, in an NDC based PAYG system annual contributions are accumulated on notional individual accounts (contribution phase) such that, at the time of retirement, a lifelong pension annuity can be calculated from the accrued notional capital (pension phase).

Contribution phase. Given the annual gross wage income $AGW_{i,t}$ of an individual i, contributions to the pension system $C_{i,t}$ in year t by the individual i can be determined as follows:

$$C_{i,t} = \tau_t \times AGW_{i,t} \tag{4.1}$$

The contribution rate to the pension system τ_t can either be fixed ($\tau_t = \tau$) or follow a predetermined (desirable or acceptable) path, since the system is no longer subject to an annual budget constraint as under the conventional PAYG system approach.

The individual's working life covers the period from a_0 to $RA-1$, where the first working year is $t = 1 = a_0$ and the last working year is $t = RA - 1$ (e.g. 40 years). At the time the individual retires (at time RA), its accumulated notional pension wealth PW_i amounts to:

$$PW_i = \sum_{t=a_0}^{RA-1} \left(C_{i,t} \prod_{v=t}^{RA-1} (1 + r_v) \right) \tag{4.2}$$

The chosen interest rates r_t are crucial for the calculation. This issue will be discussed in more detail below.

Pension phase. Pension benefits $P_{i,t}$ for an individual i in year t can be calculated from the accrued notional pension wealth at retirement PW_i as an annuity:

$$P_{i,t} = \frac{PW_i}{G} \tag{4.3}$$

Most simply, the annuitization divisor G[14] can be set equal to remaining life expectancy at retirement n_{RA}:

$$G = n_{RA} \tag{4.4}$$

Subsequent changes in life expectancy after the time of retirement do not have effects on the size of pension benefits. However, Equation 4.4 only holds if no interest is granted on the remaining capital on the notional account at any time $t > RA$ and if pension benefits are assumed to be equal for all years t. Loosening the first restriction and assuming that some form of (constant) interest r^* is accrued on the remaining notional capital, the annuity divisor G changes as follows:[15]

$$G = (1 + r^*)^{1-n_{RA}} \frac{(1 + r^*)^{n_{RA}} - 1}{(1 + r^*) - 1} \tag{4.5}$$

In order to calculate this annuity, the notional interest rate r has to be defined a priori, and therefore can only depend on estimated future values of r^*.[16] Again, the interest rate chosen is crucial.

If the second restriction is also lifted, pension benefits may rise over the course of the retirement period, i.e. they can be indexed to a certain reference rate. This can be captured by introducing an indexing factor δ into the formula of the annuity divisor G:

$$G = (1 + r^*) \frac{\left(\frac{1+\delta}{1+r^*}\right)^{n_{RA}} - 1}{\delta - r^*} \tag{4.6}$$

[14] In the literature this annuity factor is also referred to as G-value. See e.g. Chlon (2003).

[15] It is assumed that pension benefits are paid in advance, at the beginning of the year or month respectively.

[16] It therefore is sufficient to assume a constant interest rate r since even if changes in r are expected in the future, it is reasonable to take an average value of r for the calculation of the pension annuity.

For simplicity, δ is assumed to be a constant percentage ($0 < \delta < 1$). Possible indexing factors will be discussed in the following section.

4.2.3. System Design

If the contribution rate to the pension system is fixed and pension benefits are determined from accrued pension wealth according to the annuity mechanism, how can the system be stabilized? The answer to this question refers to the chosen system design. There are numerous design features for an NDC system[17]. As it was already pointed out in the previous section, the interest rate r_t that is accrued on the accumulated contributions and the parameters n_{RA}, r^* and δ that are applicable for the calculation of the life-long pension annuity are crucial to the essence of the system. The same applies for the choice of the contribution rate. However, this is an issue that is highly country specific and will therefore be dealt with in the context of the simulation analysis in section 4.4. The other aspects will be discussed below.

Interest rate on contributions. Börsch-Supan (2004b) points out that from a macro-economic perspective, the NDC system can only be sustainable if the chosen interest rate r_t is the internal rate of return of the PAYG system, i.e. the growth rate of the contribution bill. This internal rate of return can be measured as the change in the number of contributors and their labor productivity growth[18]. In this case, changes in demography, employment, and productivity are accurately reflected in the rate of return. So far, this approach has not been implemented in any of the countries that introduced an NDC system. In Latvia and Poland, contributions are granted interest according to the ex-post growth rate of the covered wage bill, thereby only accounting for changes in productivity and neglecting changes in the number of contributors. Italy follows a similar approach by using a moving average of nominal GDP growth[19] as an index. As long as it is assumed that

[17]See Palmer (2003) for a comprehensive list and discussion of possible design features.

[18]This corresponds to the Samuelson-Aaron condition, where the internal rate of return of the system is given by n + g with n = population and g = productivity growth (Samuelson (1958) and Aaron (1966)). A description of possible calculation methods of the rate of return of PAYG systems can be found in Settergren (2003). For an evaluation of the internal rate of the German PAYG system, see Schnabel (1998).

[19]The moving average is computed over 5 years of GDP in order to smooth business cycle effects.

the productivity growth of the economy is closely mirrored by the development of earnings, these approaches are basically identical. Sweden indexes contributions to a moving average of ex-post per capita wage growth[20], but established an automatic adjustment mechanism in case the financial stability of the system is threatened[21]. Brazil in turn does not grant any interest on contributions[22].

Pension annuity. The life-long pension $P_{i,t}$ is derived on the basis of the accumulated pension wealth PW_i considering three parameters:

Remaining life expectancy (n_{RA}) The remaining life expectancy at the time of retirement differs for men and women, but in general unisex survival rates are applied, so that the annuity is equal for men and women[23]. In order to obtain the appropriate life expectancy data, cohort specific life tables must be available. So far, cohort life tables are still not freely disposable in many countries, which creates potential sources of political manipulation.

Interest rate (r^*) The choice of the interest rate that is accrued on the notional pension capital follows the same rule as the interest rate on contributions. However, in order to calculate the annuity, the applicable interest rate r^* has to be defined a priori, and therefore can only depend on estimated future values and not on actual ex-post values, as in the case of the interest rate r_t on contributions. In Sweden, a real rate of return of 1.6% is used, which is in accordance with both the projected long-run rate of return as well as the economy's expected real growth rate.

Indexing factor (δ) The indexing factor allows for increases in pension benefits over the retirement period. The decision whether benefits shall be indexed to a reference rate over the course of the retirement period or not has to be made at the time of retirement ($t = RA$) when the

[20]The moving average is computed over 3 years of wage growth.

[21]For a thorough description of the automatic balancing mechanism, see Settergren (2001a).

[22]For a description of the so-called 'accumulation factor' applied in Brazil, see Brooks and Weaver (2003).

[23]This e.g. is the case in Sweden. In contrast, private pension funds on the capital market usually apply sex specific survival rates.

lifelong pension $P_{i,t}$ is calculated. There are three options as to how to set the indexing factor δ:

- $\delta = 0$ means that pension benefits during the retirement period remain constant, but only in nominal terms[24].
- $\delta = \pi$ indexes pension benefits to the (projected or actual) inflation rate π, so that benefits remain constant in real terms. This approach is used in Sweden.
- $\delta = g$ indexes pension benefits to the (projected or actual) annual rise in nominal wages or productivity respectively, so that pension benefits remain a constant fraction of wages.

The fact that the computation of the pension annuity heavily depends on estimated values introduces a certain level of uncertainty for political discretion. If benefits are indexed to actual rates and projected rates are higher, pension benefits become cheaper than initially calculated. Whereas, if pensioners live longer than estimated, pension expenditures become more expensive than initially calculated and if the ex-post increase of the interest rate r^* is lower (higher) than the estimated increase, pension benefits are harder (easier) to finance with the available contribution revenues. However, these are uncertainties that every private insurance business has to cope with.

4.2.4. System Behavior

Although the NDC system maintains the PAYG system approach, it behaves quite differently compared to conventional PAYG systems regarding both the development of pension levels and the pension insurance's budget.

Cohort-specific and total cohort pension levels. In contrast to conventional PAYG pension systems, where pension levels are annually readjusted by the benefit indexation formula[25] and where this readjustment equally affects the size of benefits of all pensioners, pension levels in the NDC system are cohort-specific. Thus, the future development of cohort-specific pension

[24] In this case, Equation 4.5 instead of Equation 4.6 is then applied for the calculation of the annuity.
[25] See chapter 3 for an explanation of the current German benefit indexation formula.

levels in an NDC system therefore highly depends on the past and forecasted demographic and labor market development as well as the country's historic and future economic performance. In order to reflect the development of pension levels across as well as for specific cohorts, an annual universal pension level can thus no longer be applied. Instead, two separate measures have to be considered. Pension levels for specific cohorts can be illustrated by displaying for each year t only the pension level of the cohort whose respective reference pensioner retires in that year[26]. This will be referred to as the *cohort-specific pension level at retirement* in the remainder of this chapter. An annual pension level reflecting the situation across reference pensioners of all cohorts can then be calculated as the average of reference pensions over all cohorts weighted with the respective cohort sizes. In the following, this will be referred to as the *total cohort pension level.*

Short-term and long-term budget effects. In each year t the public pension system receives revenues R_t in form of contributions by the labor force and pays expenditures E_t in form of pension benefit payments to the pensioners:

$$R_t = \sum_{i=1}^{LAB_t} \tau_t \times AGW_{i,t} \quad \text{and} \quad E_t = \sum_{i=1}^{RET_t} P_{i,t} \tag{4.7}$$

with LAB_t... size of labor force in year t and
RET_t... size of stock of pensioners in year t.

For the short term, the crucial question is whether revenues R_t match expenditures E_t, i.e. whether the annual pension budget is balanced. In conventional PAYG systems, the contribution rate to the pension system τ_t is recalculated each year such that estimated revenues R_t^* equal estimated expenditures E_t^*. Alternatively, the contribution rate τ_t can be fixed ($\tau_t = \tau$) so that pension levels have to be adjusted in order to balance the budget. In each case, the annual budget balance can be achieved by the appropriate adjustments. In an NDC system this annual (short-term) budget balance is

[26]For the standard pensioner in Germany that retires at age 65 the cohort-specific pension level for e.g. the year 2005 would thus correspond to the pension level of the 1940 cohort.

no longer assured. The reason is that the contribution rate is given, while at the same time, pension benefits cannot be adjusted freely since their value is no longer recalculated annually is determined only once at the time of retirement as a lifelong pension. In the short-run, there are no possibilities to balance the system unless ex-post adjustments are made to the applicable interest rate r^* or the indexing factor δ.

As a result, the existence of an appropriate reserve fund is crucial for the introduction of an NDC system. Sweden for example disposes of a large reserve fund that amounts to about 4 years of expenditures[27]. In contrast, the German system's reserve fund only amounts to several days[28].

Although NDC systems cannot ensure the short-term balance of the pension budget, one of their main characteristics is said to be balancing the budget long-term. In other words, NDC systems are supposed to make the pension system financially sustainable[29]. This is disputed in the pension literature, though[30]. In principle, this only holds if the system operates with its internal rate of return. In this case, demographic and labor market changes are directly reflected in pension benefits, allowing the systems restoration from demographic or economic shocks and thereby ensuring a balanced system in the long run[31].

In general, short and long term balance cannot coexist in an NDC system. If e.g. the annual budget constraint was to be maintained within an NDC framework, this would mean that the contribution rate could no longer be predetermined but would instead result as a residual from the annual budget calculation as it is the case in conventional PAYG systems. This, however, would affect subsequent pension levels. Thus, depending on the country-specific case, pension expenditures as well as contribution rates of such a system might just explode.

[27]See Settergren (2001b), p.4.

[28]In 2000, the buffer fund of the German pension system amounted to 14 billion Euros in relation to total annual system expenditures of 214 billion Euros (Verband Deutscher Rentenversicherungsträger (VDR) (2002)). Under the 2004 reform, this reserve was turned into a so-called sustainability reserve that amounts to 0.2 to 1.5 of monthly pension expenditures and is supposed to be built up in 'good' years and is melted down as soon as the upper 1.5 limit is reached.

[29]Financial stability in this context can be defined as 'the ability of a pension plan to adjust to financial shocks without legislative intervention' (Valdés-Prieto (2000)).

[30]See e.g. Valdés-Prieto (2000) for a mathematical analysis of the system's long-run effects.

[31]On the issue of financial sustainability see also Gronchi and Aprile (1998).

4.3. Parallels to the German Public Pension System

It was already mentioned several times that the German pension system in fact is quite similar to such an NDC system described above. These parallels are discussed in the following.

4.3.1. The German Point System

In Germany, the point system dates back until 1957, when the PAYG system was introduced. Point-based systems, as they are also present in France, can be regarded as an indirect source of the NDC approach[32]. There is an analogy of accumulated earnings points in the German and currency-based contributions in an NDC system:

- Both relate to the entire working life (in contrast to PAYG systems, where only some selected years of the earnings history are considered).
- Redistributive features (e.g. special acknowledgement for child bearing) can be easily embodied in both systems by a transfer of additional earnings points/ notional contributions by the pension insurance.

The German earnings point system however differs in the following aspects:

- At a fixed contribution rate, all earnings points of an individual count equally while in the NDC system equal contributions in percent of salary are valued higher in earlier periods of the working life due to compound interest.
- At a rising contribution rate, earnings points count equally but in fact are cheaper for earlier contributions. In the NDC system, later earnings may overweigh earlier contributions despite of compound interest.

We will see later that these differences play a crucial role regarding the development of cohort-specific pension levels and distributional as well as budgetary effects.

[32]See Disney (1999) and Valdés-Prieto (2000).

4.3.2. Actuarial Adjustments to Retirement Age

Adjustments of benefits to retirement age for early and late retirement entry respectively were introduced in Germany with the 1992 pension reform and have been phased in since 1997[33]. 0.3% are deducted from pension benefits for every month an individual retires before and 0.5% are granted for every month an individual retires after the statutory retirement age. These adjustments shall prevent that people actually gain from early retirement and receive the same pension as later retirees but for a longer pension period. Whether these adjustments are also neutral in terms of labor supply (dis)incentives, however, is highly disputed in the literature[34].

In an NDC system, such adjustments are implicit. Since the individual pension is calculated as an annuity taking into account the remaining life expectancy at the time of retirement, the system is automatically actuarially neutral. Thus, in contrast to the German system, no discretionary adjustments are necessary, which avoids potential sources of manipulation. Moreover, while the current German system needs to set a statutory retirement age, the retirement age in an NDC system can be flexible[35]. In addition, changes in life expectancy have a direct impact on pension benefits in an NDC system[36] while in the German system they can only be accounted for via unpopular moves in the statutory retirement age.

4.3.3. The Sustainability Factor

Finally, the sustainability factor introduces a mechanism similar to the long-run sustainability of an NDC system that uses the internal rate of return. As in such an NDC system, pension benefits are adjusted downwards once the system dependency ratio worsens. However, in contrast to the NDC system, these adjustments affect all pensioner cohorts alike. In this regard, the German PAYG pension system is time not cohort-oriented. Another difference

[33] Refer to Berkel and Börsch-Supan (2004) for details of the transition process.

[34] See Ohsmann, Stolz, and Thiede (2003) who justify the current rates, versus Börsch-Supan (2000b) who argues they should be higher. The German Reform Commission on the Sustainability of the Social Security Systems (2003) takes a neutral view.

[35] In practice, a minimum retirement age is recommended as soon as some form of guaranteed pension is provided that may create labor supply disincentives. In Sweden, the minimum retirement age is 61.

[36] At least to the extent they can be projected at the time of retirement when the pension is calculated.

is that changes in the benefit indexation formula are politically more easily possible than changes to the size of pension benefits in the NDC system, where pensions are directly attributable to the individual pensioner. Such discretionary interventions of course are not desirable but provide a tempting policy option to short-term oriented politicians. In fact, since the introduction of the sustainability factor in 2004, several discretionary interventions have already been made.

4.4. Simulating a Hypothetical Introduction of an NDC System for Germany

In the previous section it could be seen that the German public pension system already incorporates some of the basic characteristics of an NDC system. However, if it was replaced completely by the genuine NDC mechanisms such as described in section 4.2, what would be the effects on pension levels and the pension insurance's budget? Would it have been an alternative to the 2004 and 2007 reforms that maybe would have achieved an even better and more robust financial sustainability than the past reforms have? This question is addressed in this section. The subsequent simulation analysis covers the period from 2005 to 2050, assuming that an NDC system replaces the current German public pension system in 2005.

In the following, I first briefly describe how I model the transition of the German public pension system towards an NDC system in section 4.4.1. Section 4.4.2 presents the underlying assumptions for my projections. Projection results are illustrated in section 4.4.3. Last, sections 4.4.4 looks at what happens if the underlying assumptions are altered and points out some exclusive aspects.

4.4.1. Modeling an NDC system

In order to model the transition towards an NDC system, I modify the underlying benefit indexation formula and budget restriction of my model on the German pension system that I described in chapter 3. Now, the contribution rate enters exogenously into the system and the annual budget constraint does not hold any longer. The computation of revenues and expenditures is done as explained in section 3.4 but simplified as follows.

Revenues. In each year t all cohorts c that are part of the labor force pay a certain amount of contributions $C_{c,t}$ depending on the contribution rate τ_t, the level of average wages AGW_t and their respective age-specific wage profile WP_a:

$$C_{c,t} = \tau_t \times AGW_t \times WP_a \tag{4.8}$$

The age-specific income profile WP_a is expressed as a ratio of average wages AGW_t[37] and is the same for all cohorts but varies across age so that in each year t a different income profile $WP_{a=t-c}$ is ascribed to each cohort c. Total revenues R_t in one year t are thus:

$$R_t = \sum_{c=1}^{LAB_t} C_{c,t} \times LAB_{c,t} \tag{4.9}$$

with $LAB_{c,t}$ ... number of members of cohort c in year t and LAB_t ... here: number of cohorts in year t where members are still in the labor force.

Expenditures. Similarly, total system expenditures E_t result from the existing pension claims $P_{c,t}$ of all cohorts c that are part of the pensioner stock:

$$E_t = \sum_{c=1}^{RET_t} P_{c,t} \times RET_{c,t} \tag{4.10}$$

with $RET_{c,t}$ ... number of members of cohort c in year t and RET_t ... here: number of cohorts in year t where members are retired.

[37] It is assumed that cohorts have reached the average wage income at age 35 and that subsequent wage income will be higher than the average wage. Thus for a=35 the income profile is set equal to one, while it is set to values larger than one for $a > 35$. This income profile is derived from an empirical study for Western Germany by Fitzenberger, Hujer, McCurdy, and Schnabel (2001).

4.4.2. Scenarios and Underlying Assumptions

For the subsequent simulation analysis, I consider two scenarios:

- The reference scenario corresponds to the post-reform 2004 scenario that was presented in section 3.5.2 and that accounts for the introduction of the sustainability factor but not yet for the rise in the statutory retirement ages to 67.

- The NDC scenario assumes a transition of the German public pension system under its status quo after the 2004 reform to a genuine NDC system.

Both scenarios are based on the demographic and labor market projections by the Rürup Commission presented in chapter 2 that also served as the basis for the projections on the long-term development of the German pension system in chapter 3. Since the labor market forecast here already assumes a further shift in the mean retirement age for the future, I refrain from explicitly modeling the retirement entry behavioral effects that result from the automatic adjustment of pension benefits to life expectancy in the NDC model. This is also the reason why I chose to use the 2004 post-reform instead of the 2007 post-reform scenario as the reference scenario. I thereby also implicitly abandon the potential retirement entry behavioral effects in response to the increase in the statutory retirement age under the 2007 reform[38].

For the NDC scenario, a number of additional assumptions are necessary in order to specify the system's design which will be explained below.

Contribution rate τ_t. As it was explained in section 4.2, the contribution rate enters exogenously into the system. For the simulation analysis it is assumed to develop as under the reference scenario. This way, resulting

[38]So far, no data is available that quantifies how this new regulation will influence retirement behavior nor is the outcome straightforward and clear. For the following simulation analysis I therefore do not consider the effects of the 2007 pension reform. For an assessment of the reform's effects on the future development of contribution rates and pension levels where behavioral effects are explicitly taken into account, see Bucher-Koenen and Wilke (2008)

pension levels for the NDC scenario can be more easily compared to those projected for the reference scenario[39].

Interest rate r_t on contributions. Contribution payments accumulated on the notional accounts are assumed to receive annual interest equal to the internal rate of return[40] of the German PAYG system, i.e. the annual growth rate of the contribution bill, in order to allow for a balanced system in the long-run. Since this rate has been widely fluctuating over the past decades, annual actual nominal values are smoothened by taking a 5 years moving average[41]. In addition, rates are capped at an absolute nominal level of 6%, so that extremely high rates — as they occurred in Germany in the 1960s and 1970s — are given less weight. The difference between adjusted and actual (nominal and real) values is illustrated in Figure 4.1.

Remaining life expectancy n_{RA}. Life expectancy at the time of retirement is assumed to develop in accordance with the demographic projections by the Rürup Commission presented in chapter 2. This means an increase from 15.8 in 2000 to 19.3 years in 2050 for men and from 19.5 to 23.6 years for women.

Interest rate r^* on notional pension capital. In analogy to the interest accrued on contributions, the internal rate of return is chosen as the applicable interest rate for the annuity calculation. Since the future long-run rate is unknown at the time of the annuity calculation, the rates average value over the last ten years previous to the respective retirement date is used as an approximation of the projected long-run rate, that is to be used if the system shall achieve long-run sustainability. Ten years are necessary if business cycle effects shall be smoothened out. If the rate was averaged over five years only, people would have an incentive to retire earlier in periods of economic slow

[39]Note that a stable contribution rate as it is implemented in many NDC systems provides no serious reform option for the German public pension system. Such a *freezing scenario* would lead to a too large drop in pension levels. See e.g. Börsch-Supan (2002a) for a discussion of this issue and corresponding projections for Germany.

[40]Note that the concept of the internal rate of return is a long-term concept. However, for the purpose of the analysis in this chapter, the internal rate of return will be calculated on an annual basis and in nominal terms.

[41]This follows the Italian approach, where the applicable interest rate is also smoothened over 5 years.

Figure 4.1. – Past and Future Development of the Internal Rate of Return of the German PAYG System

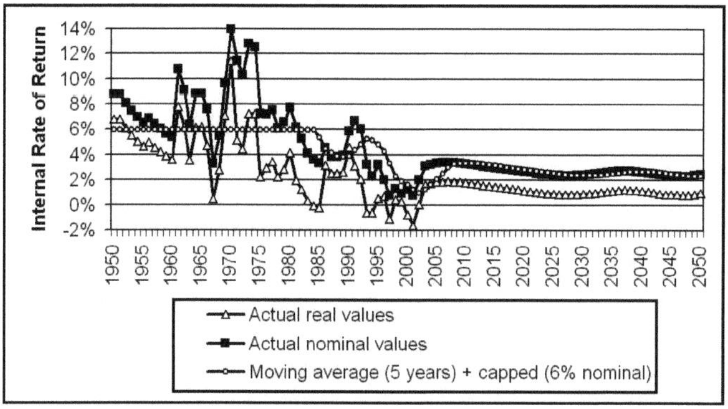

Source: Author's computations. Historical values are based on data by the German Federal Statistical Office (www.destatis.de).

down and later in periods of economic boom. This might be a valuable policy tool, but shall not be further evaluated at this point.

Indexation factor δ**.** It is assumed that pensions are indexed to annual nominal wage growth, so that pension benefits remain a constant fraction of wages during the whole retirement period. In accordance with the labor market projections presented in chapter 2 this means an indexing factor δ equal to 3% nominal.

Transition. A transition period of 10 years is assumed so that the system is fully established once the German baby-boomers start to retire around 2015. Those pensioners who were already retired before the introduction of the NDC system continue to receive their pensions according to the status quo of the German PAYG system. Those who retire during the transitional phase receive a part of their pension benefits according to the current German system and the other part according to the NDC system, starting at a ratio of 'old' to 'new' pensions of 90% in 2005. Cohorts that retire after this transition period receive their full pension according to the new NDC system[42].

4.4.3. Simulation Results

Given the same contribution rate development as projected for the reference scenario, which pension levels can be achieved in the NDC scenario? The results are shown below. However, since the annual budget constraint is abandoned in the NDC scenario, it is no longer sufficient to solely consider pension levels. Thus, in a second step, additional attention is directed to the development of the pension insurance's budget.

Pension Levels

Figure 4.2 illustrates the development of the cohort-specific pension level at the respective retirement entry in the NDC scenario compared to the development of annual pension levels in the reference scenario. As it was explained in section 4.2, the cohort-specific pension level for a year t only represents the pension level of the cohort that retires in the same year, at the statutory retirement age of 65. In Figure 4.2 this means that the 2005 pension level depicts that of the 1940 cohort in its first pension year, while the 2015 pension level corresponds to that of the 1950 cohort in its first pension year. In contrast, in the reference scenario, pension levels in one year t apply to all pensioners, not only to those that retire in that year.

It can be seen that cohort-specific pension levels in the NDC scenario develop quite close, with a maximum deviation of about 5%, to the pension levels projected for the reference scenario. This astonishes since pension levels in the current German system are determined to decline due to the sustainability factor in the benefit indexation formula, that limits the annual rise in pension levels in favor of a less rising contribution rate under the budget constraint of the system. In contrast, the cohort-specific pension levels in the NDC system do not depend on the short-term budget situation of the pension system, but solely on past values such as the cohort-specific earnings history, applicable interest rates and annuity parameters.

[42]In principle, this approach follows the transitional rules applied in Sweden. For a description of the Swedish transition process, see e.g. Sundén (2000).

Figure 4.2. – Cohort-Specific Pension Levels in the NDC Scenario versus Pension Levels in the Reference Scenario

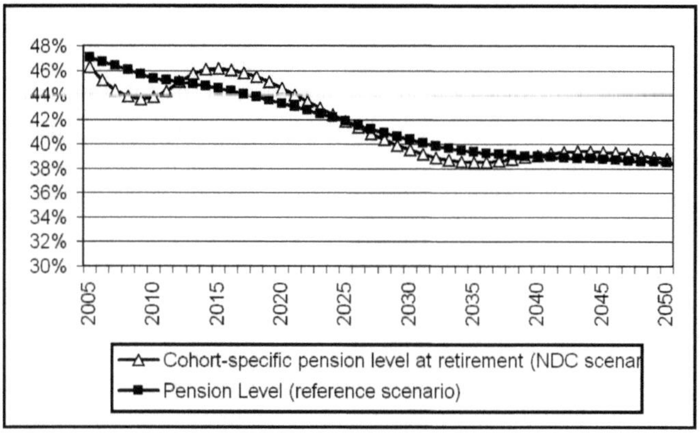

Source: Author's computations.

Cohort-specific pension levels. Even though internal rates of return have been high in the past compared to today's values, pensions for the 1940 cohorts turn out to be lower in the NDC scenario than in the reference scenario. If no transition period was assumed, the pension level of the 1940 cohort would even be lower than that shown in Figure 4.2[43]. This can be explained by relatively low contribution rates around 14% at the start phase of the German PAYG system in the early 1960s, which applies for more than the first fifth of the working period of these cohorts and in addition is weighted more heavily due to effects of compound interest. Cohorts of the 1950s in contrast achieve much higher pension levels under the NDC scenario than under the status quo. They still profit from high internal rates of return, but contributed a significantly higher amount to the pension system due to average contribution rates around 18%. For the 1960 and 1970 cohorts, the decline of the internal rate of return of the system becomes noticeable in generally lower pension levels. The slight rise in pension levels for the 1980 cohorts can be attributed mainly to the assumed increase in the contribution

[43]The effects of the length of the transition period on resulting pension levels are further discussed in the sensitivity analysis in section 4.4.4.

rate to over 23% in 2040.

Benefit indexation. As it is assumed that pensions in the NDC scenario are indexed to nominal wage growth, the cohort specific pension levels remain a constant fraction of wages over their respective retirement period. This is illustrated for selected cohorts in Figure 4.3. Note that this is not the case for pension levels in the reference scenario – the decline of pension levels in the reference scenario shown in Figure 4.2 affects all cohorts equally.

Cohort-specific reform gains and losses. Given the fact that cohort-specific pension levels in the NDC scenario turn out to be lower for some and higher for other cohorts than their respective pension levels at retirement entry in the reference scenario but that they remain constant over the whole retirement period while pension levels in the reference scenario decline further, what are the cohort-specific reform gains and losses? The answer is given in Figure 4.4[44].

As could be expected from the development of pension levels depicted in Figure 4.2, cohorts of the 1940s lose, while cohorts of the 1950s, 1960s and 1980s win. However, in contrast to the results from Figure 4.2, cohorts from 1946 on until 1967 actually win, even though some of their cohort-specific pension levels are lower than their initial pension levels depicted in the reference scenario. This is the case if it is assumed that their respective retirement period equals the cohort-specific remaining life expectancy at the time of retirement. Over the course of the retirement period, the cohort's return from an initially lower, but stable pension level (recall Figure 4.3) is then higher than that of an initially higher, but declining pension level. Of course, this does not apply to the individual that lives for a shorter period than the average remaining life expectancy for the respective cohort.

'Average' pension levels across all cohorts. If in the NDC scenario, at one point in time, pension levels across different cohorts vary so significantly from

[44]The reform gains and losses illustrated in Figure 4.4 were determined by calculating the differences in the rates of return between the reference and the NDC scenario for each cohort. The rate of return was thereby computed as the ratio of total pension benefits to total paid contributions, where the length of the retirement period was set in accordance with the average remaining life expectancy of the respective cohort.

Figure 4.3. – Cohort-Specific Pension Levels in the NDC Scenario for Selected Cohorts

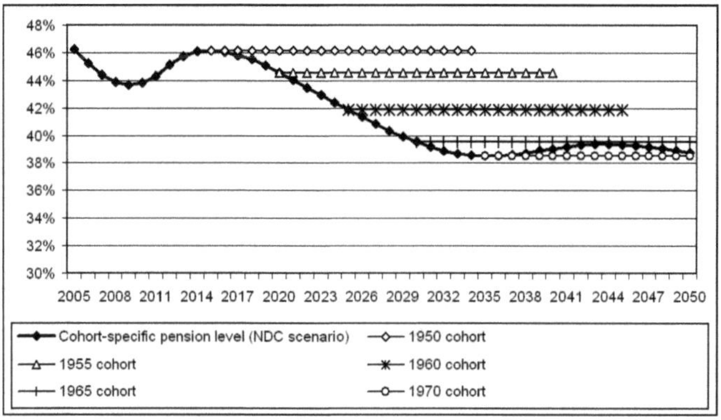

Source: Author's computations.

Figure 4.4. – Reform Gains and Losses of Affected Cohorts

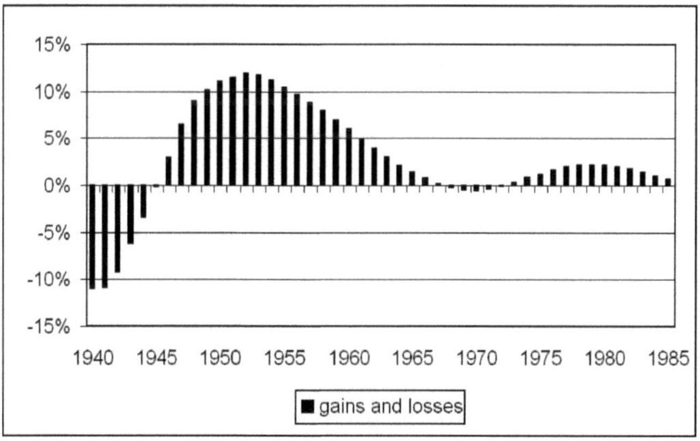

Source: Author's computations.

Figure 4.5. – Total Cohort Pension Levels in the NDC Scenarios versus Pension Levels in the Reference Scenario

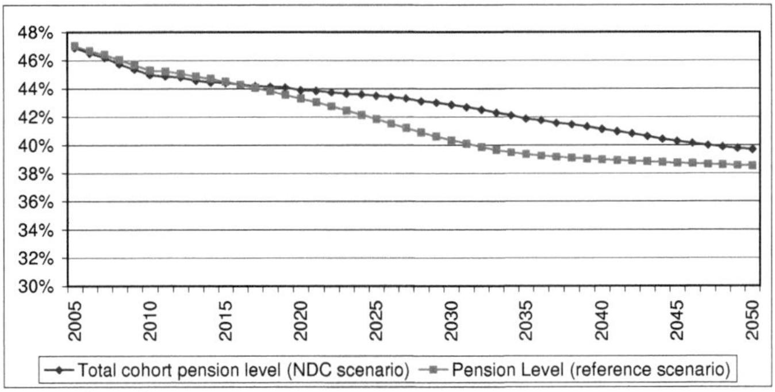

Source: Author's computations.

each other, what can be said about the average situation of all retired cohorts in one specific year? Figure 4.5 shows the development of total cohort pension levels in the NDC system, i.e. the average of all cohort-specific pension levels across cohorts weighted with the respective cohort size[45], in comparison to the pension levels in the reference scenario.

In contrast to the development of the cohort-specific pension levels displayed in Figure 4.2 and Figure 4.3, total cohort pension levels in the NDC scenario turn out to be continuously higher from 2020 on than pension levels in the reference scenario. This means that in the NDC scenario, the annually changing average standard pensioners across all cohorts achieves a higher pension level in each year than the respective standard pensioner in the reference scenario who is the same for all cohorts and years. However, this does not mean that the same necessarily applies for the average pensioner[46] in the two scenarios. For example, differences in pension levels between high-wage and low-wage earners might generally be larger in the NDC scenario than in the reference scenario due to compound interest effects.

Altogether, regarding the development of pension levels, the NDC scenario

[45]Recall the definition of total cohort pension levels given in section 4.2

[46]The average pensioner represents the average across all pensioners, taking account of differences in earnings history, time of retirement entry and age among pensioners.

Figure 4.6. – Budget Development in the NDC Scenario

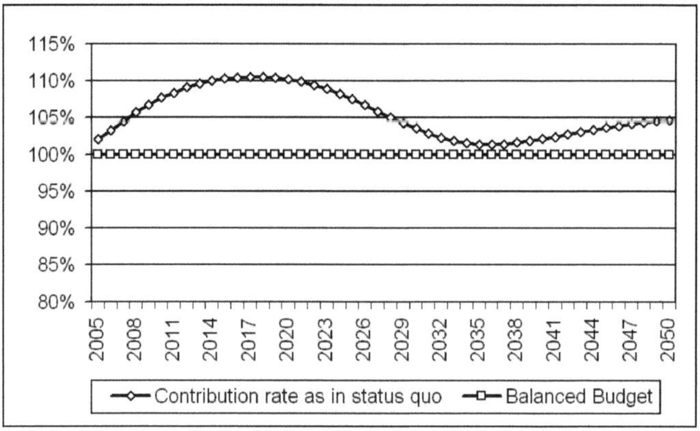

Source: Author's computations.

can be said to be economically feasible. Even though cohort-specific reform losses occur, they are significantly smaller than the gains of the reform. However, this implies a redistribution mainly from the early 1940 cohorts to the baby-boom generation. Given the fact that the baby-boom generation partly induced the demographic challenges the system now has to cope with, this cannot be a political objective.

Budget development

What does the development of pension levels in the NDC scenario displayed in Figure 4.2 to Figure 4.5 imply for the budget of the German pension insurance? In contrast to the reference scenario, an annually balanced budget is no longer ensured in the NDC scenario. Instead, the budget develops as illustrated in Figure 4.4.

Under the given assumptions, revenues turn out to cover pension expenditures throughout the simulation period. At the beginning of the introduction of the NDC system, pension levels for the first cohorts that retire in the NDC scenario, the 1940 cohorts, are lower than pension levels projected for the reference scenario – and they stay at this level over the whole retirement period of these cohorts – so that revenues are larger than pension expenditures. Note also, that the early cohorts of the 1940s in absolute numbers ar almost as large as the baby boom cohorts of the 1960s, which is the reason for this effect being rather large. For 2015, additional revenues of about 30 billion Euros can be calculated. This amount is equivalent to roughly 40% of the state subsidies the pension system receives in that year. With the rise in pension levels for the 1950s cohorts, the surplus in revenues declines as these cohorts start to retire from 2015 on. Once the 1970s cohorts with much lower pension levels retire from 2035 on and thereby reduce the average pension level across all cohorts, the amount of additional revenues increases again.

The question remains, whether the generated revenue surplus also suffices in order to build up the buffer fund that becomes necessary in the NDC scenario in order to cope with short-term budget deficits. According to Heiss (2003), the German pension system could have overcome past recessions with a buffer fund amounting to two months, that is about 17%, of total annual expenditures. In the NDC scenario, this amount would be reached by means of the accumulated surplus revenues by 2010, which would be early enough in order to countervail potential cyclical effects induced by the retirement of the baby-boom generation from 2015 on.

Thus, from a purely budget oriented perspective, the NDC scenario would be feasible for Germany. However, it should be noted, that the budget surpluses only can be accumulated at the expense of specific cohorts whose pension levels in the NDC scenario is lower at the time of retirement than in the reference scenario.

4.4.4. Sensitivity Analysis

The results presented above only apply under the assumptions underlying the NDC scenario. What happens if some of these assumptions are altered? A thorough sensitivity analysis was conducted on this question. This section points out some selected aspects. Focus is put on the development of pension levels, while budget effects are deliberately excluded, since they are rather straight forward: higher (lower) cohort-specific pension levels in the NDC scenario have a negative (positive) impact on the overall size of the budget.

Figure 4.7. – Development of Pension Levels for a Fixed Contribution Rate

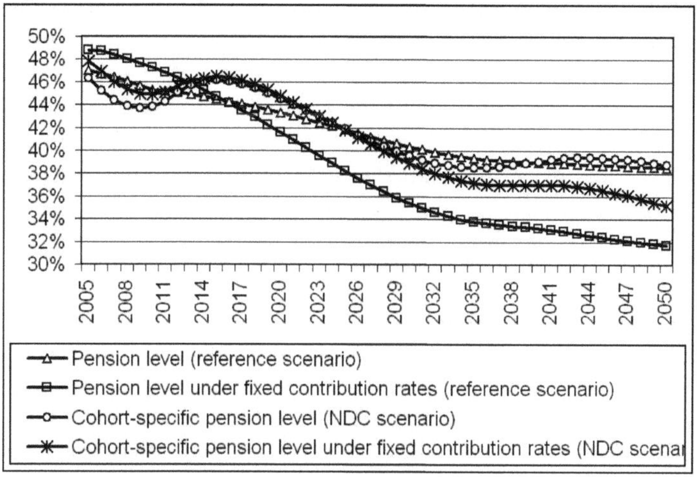

Source: Author's computations.

Altering the contribution rate τ_t. In the literature, it is sometimes claimed that one aim of NDC systems is to stabilize the contribution rate. So far, the simulation analysis only took account of a rising rate, such as in the reference scenario. Figure 4.7 illustrates the effects on pension levels if the contribution rate instead is fixed at 20%. Note, that in this case, pension levels for the reference scenario are no longer calculated via the benefit indexation formula that comprises the sustainability factor but are determined entirely via the annual budget constraint. In contrast, in the NDC scenario, pension levels are determined precisely the same way as before with the only difference being that different contribution amounts are paid onto the individual accounts.

For the reference scenario, a fixed contribution rate of 20% leads to higher pension levels in the short-run as long as the endogenously determined contribution rate would still be lower. As a consequence, in the NDC scenario, cohort-specific pension levels during the transition period also turn out to be higher than before. However, once demographic pressures call for higher contribution rates, pension levels in the reference scenario fall faster than under rising rates. The same effect can be perceived for the NDC scenario from

2030 on. However, while this effect signifies pure intergenerational redistribution in the case of the reference scenario, where the working population pays less contributions thus provoking lower pension levels under the budget constraint of the system, cohorts in the NDC scenario receive lower pension benefits due to the fact that they have acquired lower pension claims as a result of lower contribution rates. In this case, no intergenerational redistribution takes place. Instead, the pension system simply generates less redistribution of income over each individual's life cycle.

Altering the interest rate r_t. In section 4.2 it was stressed that the proper rate of return of an NDC system is the internal rate of return of the system itself. If other interest rates are chosen, the results for the NDC scenario become very different. Figure 4.8 illustrates the development of cohort-specific pension levels in the NDC scenario for alternative interest rates on contributions, i.e. the rate of nominal wage growth and the rate of inflation, that do not take account of changes in demography. It can be seen that, as long as the labor force grows in size, the nominal wage growth rate is smaller than the internal rate of return of the system so that pension levels for cohorts that worked during this time period are smaller than if the internal rate of return was used as the applicable interest rate. However, once the labor force declines, the nominal wage growth rate becomes larger than the internal rate of return and higher pension levels are generated for the respective cohorts. Since projected future nominal wage growth is assumed to be 3% and thus higher than during the nineties, pension levels turn out to be higher for younger cohorts. If interest on the accumulated notional capital is accrued solely according to the inflation rate, resulting pension levels are considerably lower for all cohorts. In this case, no real interest is accrued on the notional capital. Instead, the value of the accumulated capital stock is simply maintained in real values.

Altering the indexing factor δ. So far, pension benefits were assumed to be indexed to nominal wage growth, so that pension levels of specific cohorts remain constant over their respective retirement period (recall Figure 4.3). Figure 4.9 shows how cohort-specific pension levels change, if pensions are solely indexed to the inflation rate or are not indexed at all respectively.

Figure 4.8. – Pension Levels in the NDC Scenario Under Different Interest Rate Scenarios

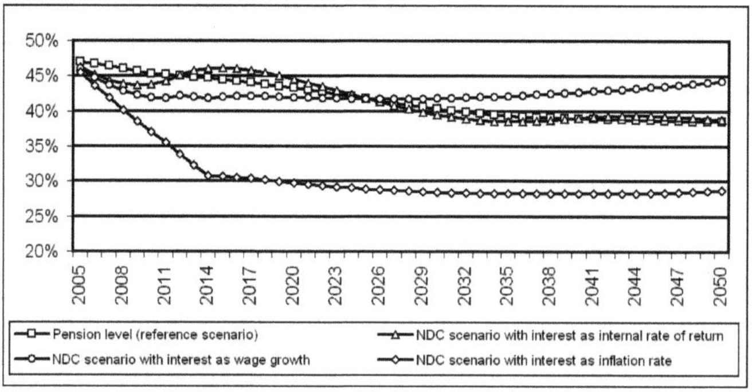

Source: Author's computations.

Figure 4.9. – Trade-off of Cohort-Specific Pension Levels in the NDC Scenario for Selected Cohorts

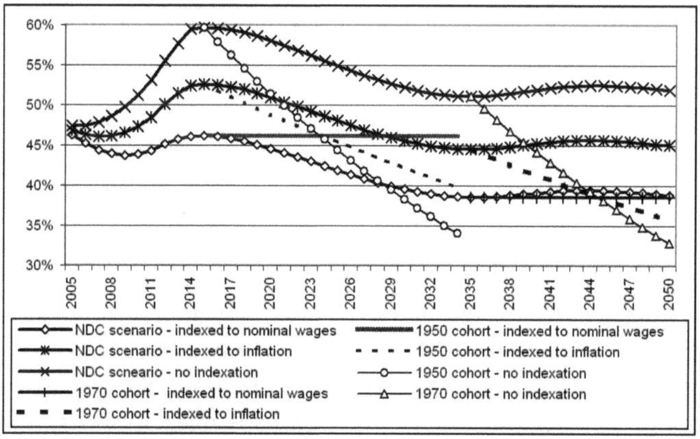

Source: Author's computations.

In both cases, cohort-specific pension levels at the time of retirement are significantly higher since lower future annual increases have to be anticipated at the time of retirement when the pension annuity is calculated. This trade-off in an NDC system, between higher initial cohort-specific pension levels decreasing over the retirement period and lower pension levels decreasing less or remaining constant in fraction of wages is illustrated more explicitly for the 1950 and 1970 cohort respectively (see again Figure 4.9). As long as pensions are indexed to inflation, pension benefits in fact remain equal in real values until the end of the retirement period — the resulting gap to a stable pension level throughout the retirement period thus can be ascribed solely to the difference between nominal wage growth and inflation. If pensions are not indexed at all, they significantly loose in purchasing power.

An important question is whether the decision to index pension benefits to a reference rate or not should be left to the individual pensioner or should be made by the state. It should be noted at this point, that this freedom of choice may not always be affordable in an NDC system if debt financing is to be avoided. This is because the accumulated capital in the system is only notional, while the system itself is still run on a PAYG basis. Thus, if no buffer fund is (not yet) available, existing pension claims have to be financed by sources from outside the system. In the case of Germany, if pension benefits of the 1940 cohorts are not indexed and thus would be a lot higher than in the reference scenario, a large deficit would arise while at the same time it would no longer be possible to build up a buffer fund for future potential crises.

Altering introduction and transition times. For the results in section 4.4 it was assumed that the NDC system was introduced from 2005 on. Whether the NDC system is introduced earlier or later only affects the cohort-specific pension levels of those cohorts that retire during the transitional period. Generally, later introductions lead to lower cohort-specific pension levels for the respective cohorts (see Figure 4.10). This is due to the fact that those cohorts with higher pension levels in the NDC scenario than in the reference scenario now fall into the transition period and receive lower pensions than they otherwise would have.

Figure 4.10. – Transitional Pension Levels in the NDC Scenario for Different Start Years

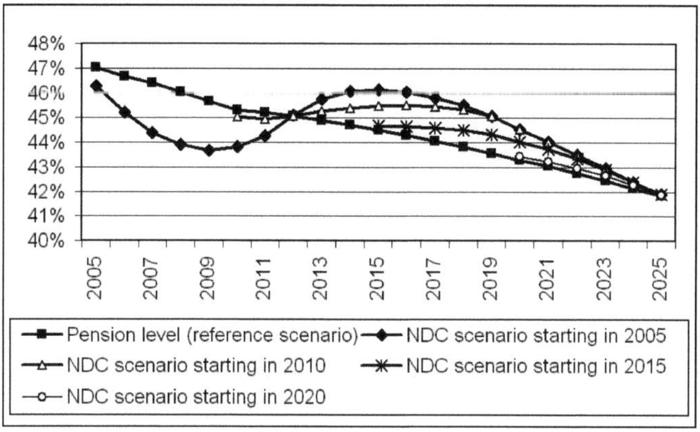

Source: Author's computations.

Similarly, a longer transition period would lead to lower cohort-specific pension levels for those cohorts whose pension is higher in the NDC scenario than in the reference scenario and which then fall into the transition period. On the other hand, for cohorts of the 1940s that receive lower pensions under the NDC scenario, a longer transition period would align their pensions closer along the levels of the reference scenario. In general, it can be found that, for Germany, differences in cohort-specific pension levels across cohorts are leveled off the more the longer the transition period.

Thus, with regard to the size of the reform burden that is carried by the early cohorts of the 1940s in the NDC scenario under the assumptions presented in section 4.4.2, a later introduction or a longer transition period could be suggestive. Respective simulations show the budget would still remain on surplus, even though the prospective to build up a buffer fund diminishes the later the introduction or the longer the transition period. However, this simulation analysis is based on the rather optimistic demographic and labor market forecasts presented in section 2.2. If the labor market develops differently in a way that even more pressure is exerted on the pension system, a delay of the reform or an extension of the transition period may make it impossible to carry out the necessary measures in sufficient time.

4.5. Conclusion

This chapter looked at the question whether the introduction of an NDC system could be a feasible reform alternative for the German PAYG pillar. The simulation analysis conducted in the main part of this chapter showed that a German NDC system would indeed provide (*adequate*) pension levels above, equal or only slightly below those that can be forecasted for the standard pensioner under the present German PAYG pension system that comprises the sustainability factor. However, in terms of *affordability* it was shown that an NDC system may require large buffer funds which are currently not available under the current German pension system and can only be built up under very restrictive assumptions.

Furthermore, the *distribution* of pension income among cohorts would be very different than under the current system, favoring cohorts of the 1950s and 1960s while disadvantaging cohorts of the 1940s that paid lower contribution rates to the system, and cohorts from the 1970s which are affected by the decreasing growth rate of the contribution bill. This clearly is a result that cannot be politically motivated. It illustrates quite clearly the differences between the German time-oriented and the cohort-oriented NDC system where cohort-specific pension levels are largely driven by the past and forecasted demographic and labor market development as well as a country's historic and future economic performance. This issue will play a central role in the next chapter[47].

However, in one point the NDC system still better ensures long-term *sustainability* than the German system: benefits are automatically actuarial fairly adjusted to the retirement age – accounting for future developments in life expectancy. In the German system, in contrast, the adjustment factors are not linked to the future development of life expectancy. This remains

[47]Note that there are also additional *redistributive effects* in an NDC system. In the earnings points based German system, pension levels are proportional to the amount of accumulated earnings points. In the NDC system in contrast, this is no longer the case as pension claims that are collected early during the working life profit from a compound interest effect from which flat income profiles profit more than steep income profiles.

a weakness of the German PAYG pension system, especially in the light of continuous further increases in life expectancy[48].

Regarding the *robustness* of the system, the many ad hoc rulings with regard to benefit adjustments since 2004 as well as the current German debate on an intermission of the Riester staircase for 2008 and 2009 in favor of a higher pension adjustment in these years show that even an automatic balancing mechanism (be it in form of the sustainability factor or be it the automatic balancing mechanism of an NDC system) provides no guarantee against further discretionary interventions.

Finally, in terms of *transparency*, account based systems such as NDC systems naturally provide a larger degree of transparency than defined-benefit based systems where benefit levels change over time[49]. However, the traditional earnings points system along with the recent introduction of so-called 'pension briefs' (*Renteninformation*) that provide insight into peoples accumulated earnings points as well as the earnings points' projected value at retirement may create a similar transparency as that expected from an account-based system[50].

[48]See e.g. Clemens (2006) for an illustration of the past and projected future rises in life expectancy and past and projected future retirement ages.

[49]An interesting discussion of an account-based reform approach of the entire social security system is provided by Orszag, Orszag, Snower, and Stiglitz (1999).

[50]See Börsch-Supan, Ludwig, and Reil-Held (2004) for a description and thorough investigation of these pension briefs.

5. Internal Rates of Return of the German PAYG System: A Comparison of Deterministic and Stochastic Rates

5.1. Introduction

The internal rate of return is one measure for evaluating the proportion of benefits to contributions in a PAYG pension system[1]. It is the rate at which the net present value of benefits received equalizes the net present value of contributions paid. It thus allows to measure the fairness or intergenerational redistribution of the system[2]. In the literature as well as in politics, internal rates of return are therefore frequently used for pension system and policy evaluations.

Intergenerational fairness is a highly disputed issue in the German pension debate[3]. In summer 2004, this issue triggered a public discussion when the chair of the Federal Constitutional Court, Hans-Jürgen Papier, made an official statement that the constitutional conformity of the German public pension system would be threatened should future rates of return become negative for entire cohorts[4]. The statement referred to the previous public debate which had reflected fears that the newly introduced sustainability factor of the 2004 reform would decrease pension levels to such an extent that future cohorts would receive benefits that were smaller than their contributions.

[1]Other so-called money's worth measures are the payback period, the benefit/contribution or benefit/tax ratio and the lifetime transfer. See Leimer (1995) for an overview of these measures.

[2]Other possible measures are the implicit tax rate (see Thum and von Weizsäcker (2000)) or the method of generational accounting (see Boll, Raffelhüschen, and Walliser (1994)).

[3]See e.g. Bäcker and Koch (2003), Börsch-Supan (2003b) and Rürup (2004).

[4]Die Welt (2004).

This raises two questions. First, how high are future rates of return essentially going to be? Several projections based on the 2004 reform are available, however, their results are ambivalent. Clearly positive rates of return are calculated by Ohsmann and Stolz (2004), by the Sozialbeirat (2004) in the context of the 2004 pension insurance report of the government and by the Sachverständigenrat zur Begutachtung der gesamtwirtschaftlichen Entwicklung (2004) in its Annual Report. In contrast, Raffelhüschen (2005), as well as Ottnad and Wahl (2005), calculate (partly) negative rates of return for certain cohorts, based on very different assumptions.

Given these different calculation outcomes, another more fundamental question arises: What is the appropriate calculation method to obtain cohort-specific rates of return? The common approach in the German pension literature is to calculate rates of return for different demographic groups (single men, single women and married couples) and different scenarios (retirement at the statutory retirement age, retirement at earlier ages etc.)[5]. This deterministic approach was used in all of the studies named above. Since it allows only to look at one scenario at a time, the whole range of risks that is covered by the German pension insurance cannot be taken into account adequately. Apart from the longevity risk (covered by old age pensions) and the risk of widowhood (covered by survivor pensions), this is most notably the invalidity risk. Papier (1998) emphasizes that potential benefits from invalidity pensions must be included in the calculation of the rates of return. Moreover, he points out that the constitutional conformity of the system would only be questioned if future rates of return became negative for the *average* pensioner[6]. But what would be an appropriate invalidity scenario for such an *average* pensioner under the deterministic approach? If rates of return are to be used as a measurement of system fairness, all potential risks need to be considered.

This chapter presents an alternative calculation method based on a stochastic rather than the scenario-based, deterministic approach. It computes the rate of return of the expected payment flows (where the expectation includes longevity, survival and invalidity risk as well as the time of retirement) rather than the rate of return of a specific deterministically defined scenario. The

[5]This approach is widely used in the pension literature, see e.g. also Myers and Schobel (1992) for the U.S.
[6]See also Sozialbeirat (2004).

hypothetical and non-representative figure of the standard pensioner here is replaced by the (weighted) average of pensioners in each cohort. This approach is closer to the micro-based approaches based on administrative data and lifetime profiles from longitudinal data[7]. For Germany, it was first introduced by Schnabel (1998).

In the following, internal rates of return will be computed according to both approaches. As in the above named studies, projections are based on the 2004 reform. For the 2007 reform, so far, no data is available that quantifies how the increase in the statutory retirement age will influence retirement behavior nor is the outcome straightforward and clear[8]. For the rate of return computations in this chapter I therefore do not consider the 2007 reform.

This chapter is an updated version of Wilke (2005) that takes account of the new population and labor market projections presented in chapter 2 as well as the new projections on the long-term financial development of the German PAYG system presented in chapter 3. The chapter is structured as follows. Section 5.2 describes how rates of return can be measured according to the two approaches. The results from the deterministic approach are illustrated in section 5.3. Section 5.4 presents the results from the stochastic approach. Section 5.5 concludes.

5.2. How to Measure Rates of Return

This section describes how cohort-specific rates of return of the German PAYG pension system can be measured. Section 5.2.1 explains the underlying internal rate of return concept. For the computations in this chapter, I differentiate two approaches: the deterministic and the stochastic approach. They are presented in sections 5.2.2 and 5.2.3 respectively.

[7]See e.g. Duggan, Gillingham, and Greenless (1996) or Leimer (1999) for the US.

[8]See Bucher-Koenen and Wilke (2008) for a first assessment of the long-term effects of the reform that accounts for the behavioral effects.

5.2.1. The Internal Rate of Return

In general, rates of return describe the size of gains or losses of an investment. In the context of a PAYG pension system, the investment consists of the contributions paid to the system whereas the benefits received during the pension phase represent its pay-off. The rate of return can thus be measured as the proportion of the size of benefits to the size of contributions.

Since contribution payments and pension benefits occur at different points in time, the flow of positive and negative payments has to be discounted to a common date in order to make the different values of the payments comparable. A natural choice for this point in time is the starting point of the payment flow. Here, this is the date of entry into the labor force[9]. The rate of return can then be calculated as the so-called internal rate of return at which the net present value of benefits received equalizes the net present value of contributions paid[10]:

$$\sum_{a=a_{RA}}^{a_{max_c}} P_{c,a} \left(\frac{1}{1+r}\right)^{a-a_0} = \sum_{a=a_0}^{a_{RA}-1} C_{c,a} \left(\frac{1}{1+r}\right)^{a-a_0} \qquad (5.1)$$

with a ... Age index,
a_0 ... Age of entrance into the labor force,
a_{RA} ... Retirement age,
a_{max_c} ... Maximum age/ end of pension period of cohort c,
$P_{c,a}$ ... Pension payments to cohort c at age a,
r ... Internal rate of return,
$C_{c,a}$ ... Contribution payments by cohort c at age a.

[9] For selected questions such as on early retirement incentives, it makes sense to discount the values of the payment flow to a point in time that is close to potential retirement, at which the individual can be assumed to be confronted with the decision on when exactly to retire. Such calculations can e.g. be found in Schnabel (1998). For the rate of return, however, the point in time chosen as t_0 is irrelevant as it does not change the results.

[10] Note that in the calculations in this paper, neither the state subsidy to the pension system nor non-insurance benefits are considered. While they have a different impact on the rate of return for certain individuals which makes the following calculations even more complicated (e.g. mothers, and in the past low wage earners and the highly educated) the aggregate effect is neutral because the state subsidy is meant to exactly cover the non-insurance benefits. Ottnad and Wahl (2005) drop this assumption and calculate rates of return for a scenario where tax-financed government transfers are used to subsidize ordinary insurance benefits, including the additional tax burden on the contribution side. As expected, the resulting rates of return turn out considerably lower and partly even turn negative.

The advantage of this internal rate of return method is that there is no need to determine an appropriate discount rate that otherwise had to be specified in advance. The results are therefore independent of any reference rate.

Gross versus net rates of return. Due to the gradual transition to deferred taxation of old age income which will start in 2010 and will be fully completed by 2050, net values loose their importance within the German public pension system as they will be differing across cohorts. The rates of return projections in this chapter are therefore based on gross values where tax reductions of pension benefits and health and long-term care insurance contributions are not accounted for. Overall, the transition to deferred taxation will have a positive effect on the size of the rates of return. Due to the German tax progression, the transition to deferred taxation will mostly lead to a larger tax relief during the working life than the additional tax burden it creates during the retirement phase as long as retirement income is lower than labor income. From this point of view, the following projections thus will tend to underestimate the true rates of return.

Nominal versus real rates of return. Past as well as current calculations of the rates of return of the German public pension system mostly have been presented in nominal terms[11]. This is typically justified by the fact that most people are more familiar with the concept of nominal rates of return since they know it from the capital market. However, nominal rates of return are strongly biased by inflation. In Germany, inflation reached high rates in the 1970s which deeply affects the real value of contribution payments made during this period. Figure 5.1 shows the development of past (and future) nominal and real average gross wages in Germany. For obvious reasons, real rates are the economically interesting concept. In the following, nominal rates of return are mainly displayed for comparison.

[11]Exceptions are Schnabel (1998, 2001) and the Sozialbeirat (2004) which present both nominal and real rates of return.

Figure 5.1. – Development of Nominal and Real Wage Growth (1950 to 2005)

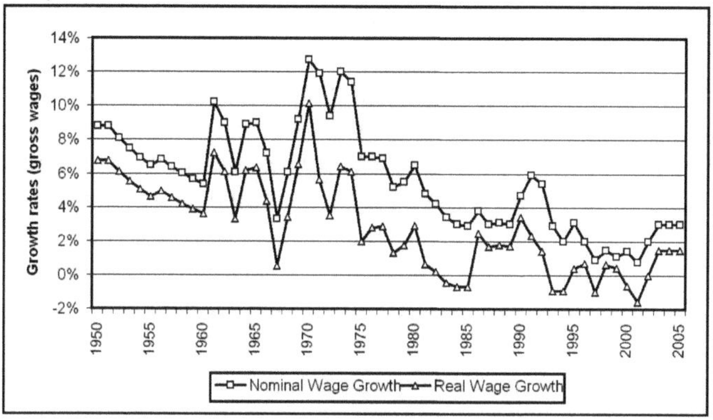

Source: Historical figures are taken from the German Federal Statistical Office (www.destatis.de).

5.2.2. The Deterministic Approach

The deterministic approach takes the view of one selected (fictive) pensioner, who is attributed a certain earnings history, a certain retirement age and the applicable pension benefit over a certain pension period. Different attributes allow looking at different pensioner types. Internal rates of return for the chosen pensioner type are computed for all cohorts. This deterministic approach is predominant in the German pension literature[12] and has also been used for the most recent cohort-specific rate of return calculations by Ohsmann and Stolz (2004), Ottnad and Wahl (2005),Sozialbeirat (2004) and Sachverständigenrat zur Begutachtung der gesamtwirtschaftlichen Entwicklung (2004).

The standard pensioner – male, single. The most frequently used pensioner type is that of the standard pensioner[13]. The size of his pension is

[12]See e.g. Eitenmüller (1996) and Hain, Eitenmüller, and Barth (1997), an earlier paper by Ohsmann and Stolz (1997) or Gliesmann and Horn (1998).

[13]In reality, income usually rises over an individual's working life. This has an effect on the resulting rates of return, since the internal rate of return method weighs earlier contribution payments higher than later ones. I evaluated this effect by introducing an age-specific earnings profile that allows for a rise in wages over the working life but equally results in 45 earnings points. The profile was derived from the medium

derived by multiplying the 45 earnings points he acquired during his working life with the current pension value of the respective year. Since he retires at the statutory retirement age, the adjustment factor is one. Contributions are simply average gross wages times the contribution rate of the same year. The length of the pension period is determined by the remaining life expectancy at age 65. For the female, single standard pensioner, the only difference to the male, single standard pensioner is the higher remaining life expectancy[14]. The internal rate of return r can then be computed from Equation 5.1:

$$\begin{aligned}(5.2)\quad & \sum_{a=RA=65}^{a_{max_c}} \left(\sum_{a=a_0=20}^{64} EP_a \right) \times PV_{c+a} \left(\tfrac{1}{1+r}\right)^{a-a_0} \\ &= \sum_{a=a_0=20}^{64} AGW_{c+a} \times \tau_{c+a} \left(\tfrac{1}{1+r}\right)^{a-a_0}\end{aligned}$$

with

a_{max_c} ...Now: Remaining life expectancy of cohort c at age 65,
EP_a ...Acquired earnings points at age a,
PV_{c+a} ...Current pension value in year $t = c + a$,
AGW_{c+a} ...Average gross wages in year $t = c + a$,
τ_{c+a} ...Contribution rate to the pension system in year $t = c + a$.

The standard pensioner – male, married. If pensioners are married, their spouses obtain survivor benefits if they outlive the pensioner and do not have considerable own pension income. While this is still relevant for many married men, it so far plays a minor role for married women since their husbands mostly have own substantial pension income that is deducted from the survivor pension[15]. Note also that under the deterministic approach there

profile of an estimation of wage trajectories by Fitzenberger, Hujer, McCurdy, and Schnabel (2001) for West Germany. These test calculations showed that for a typical individual this effect is only marginal and thus can be neglected. The result for the stochastic approach is the same.

[14]It could be argued that different earnings points should be considered for different demographic groups (e.g. less earnings points for women than for men). However, since the German pension system ensures relative equivalence, such intra-cohort effects are not subject of this thesis.

[15]A widow pension for the man incurred for less than 25% of all pensioner couples in 2004 and less than 15% of these widow pensions were fully dispensed due to the reduction of existing pension income by the husband (Verband Deutscher Rentenversicherungsträger (VDR) (2004).

are no additional benefits from survivor pensions for the female, married standard pensioner since husbands can never outlive their wives due to their lower remaining life expectancy. Under the deterministic approach, rates of return for single and married women (as standard pensioners) are therefore equal. The subsequent calculations therefore focus on married men. Wives are assumed to be 3 years younger and not to have considerable own pension income. For cohorts before 1962, the adjustment factor for survivor pensions AF^{Surv} is 60%, for younger cohorts it has been lowered to 55% (see also section 3.2). The survivor pension is simply added to the benefit payment flow of the rate of return calculations for the standard pensioner (Equation 5.2):

(5.3)

$$\sum_{a=RA=65}^{a_{max_c}} 45 \times PV_{c+a} \left(\tfrac{1}{1+r}\right)^{a-a_0} + \sum_{a=a_{max_c}+1}^{a_{max_{Spouse}}} AF^{Surv} \times 45 \times PV_{c+a} \left(\tfrac{1}{1+r}\right)^{a-a_0}$$
$$= \sum_{a=a_0=20}^{64} AGW_{c+a} \times \tau_{c+a} \left(\tfrac{1}{1+r}\right)^{a-a_0}$$

with $a_{max_{Spouse}}$ ... Remaining life expectancy of the spouse.

Early retirement. In addition to the standard pensioner, types of early or later retirement entry can be considered if the assumption of retirement at age 65 is dropped. Equation 5.4 gives an example of rate of return calculation for pensioners retiring at age 63. Note that the sum of earnings points is reduced to 43 and annual pension benefits are further reduced by an adjustment factor of 7.2% (0.3 × 24)[16]:

(5.4)

$$\sum_{a=RA=63}^{a_{max_c}} 43 \times 0.928 \times PV_{c+a} \left(\frac{1}{1+r}\right)^{a-a_0} = \sum_{a=a_0=20}^{62} AGW_{c+a} \times \tau_{c+a} \left(\frac{1}{1+r}\right)^{a-a_0}$$

[16]Theoretically, life expectancy then would also have to be adjusted to the age of 63. Due to data restrictions this is typically not done and will not be done here either.

Limits of the deterministic approach. There are several reasons why the deterministic approach is less than satisfactory. First, the use of the remaining life expectancy leads two distorting effects:

1. It is assumed that the pensioner reaches the retirement age with certainty. The probability to decease earlier is not taken into account.

2. It is assumed that the standard pensioner lives exactly according to the cohort's average remaining life expectancy. However, the rate of return for the cohort as a whole is not equal to the rate of return for a person of this cohort with exactly the average life expectancy due to Jensen's inequality[17]: the rate of return is a concave function of its stochastic ingredients such as life length and life-time earnings. The linear approximation implicitly applied in the conventional approach therefore overestimates the true value of the rate of return.

Second, disability benefits are difficult to capture in the deterministic approach since the notion of a 'typical' invalidity scenario is hard to define. On an annual, cross-sectional basis, the share is roughly 80%[18]. The remaining 20% finance rehabilitation and disability expenditures. In the standard calculations, annual contributions are scaled with a correction factor of 80%. However, this contribution correction factor suffers from aggregation bias since the cross-sectional computation of the average budget impact does not represent the true longitudinal payment flow for a specific cohort. Moreover, the bias from Jensen's inequality applies again since different individuals of a certain cohort face different disability risks which do not result in the same rates of return if an average risk is included in the calculations instead.

Finally, the deterministic approach cannot capture the fact that the public pension system insures against all three risks simultaneously. The calculation only captures the pay-off for those risks that apply for the chosen scenario, i.e. a typical person receiving an old age pension, a typical disabled person, or a typical beneficiary of a survivor pension.

[17] According to Jensen's inequality, the expected value $E()$ of a non-linear function $g()$ of a random variable x is not equal to the non-linear function of the expected value of this variable: $E(g(x)) \neq g(E(x))$. For a concave function $g()$, $E(g(x)) < g(E(x))$. See also appendix F.

[18] See Schneider (1997) for a discussion of this ratio.

Figure 5.2. – The Stochastic Approach in a Nutshell

$$PF_a = p_a(alive) \times \begin{pmatrix} p_a(working) \times ContributionPayments_a & ...(j=1) \\ + \; p_a(disabled) \times DisabilityPensionBenefits_a & ...(j=2) \\ + \; p_a(retired) \times OldAgePensionBenefits_a & ...(j=3) \end{pmatrix}$$

$$+ \; p_a(dead) \times p_a(SpouseIsAlive) \times SurviorPensionBenefits_a \quad ...(j=4)$$

PF_a ... Payment flow at age a
p_a ... Probability of a certain scenario to be true at age a

Source: Author's compilation.

5.2.3. The Stochastic Approach

The stochastic approach considers the whole range of scenarios simultaneously instead of looking at one particular case at a time. Every possible scenario is weighted with its probability to occur. This section describes how rates of return are calculated under such a stochastic approach and how this approach differs from the deterministic approach presented above.

Expected cohort-specific payment flows. The deterministic payment flow is turned into a stochastic payment flow by including the probabilities for each possible event j to occur. It comprises the expected values of the net payments for each age a of the life cycle of a cohort c[19]. Four cases are distinguished at any age and may occur with a certain probability: the individual is paying contributions ($j = 1$); the individual receives a disability pension ($j = 2$); the individual receives an old age pension ($j = 3$); the individual's spouse receives a widow pension ($j = 4$). The four cases are illustrated in Figure 5.2.

Note that in the stochastic approach there is no fixed retirement age a_{RA} like in the deterministic approach. Instead, contribution payments as well as

[19]Note that the rate of return calculated on the basis of the *expected* payment flow for a certain cohort is not the same as the expected cohort-specific rate of return. Appendix G explains the differences and the reasons for choosing this approach.

pension benefits are recorded for all years although certain event probabilities may be zero[20].

The calculation of pension benefits under this approach has to account for path dependencies since the size of the applicable pension in a specific year depends on the age at which the individual became disabled or retired. The calculations of the cohort-specific payment flows will therefore be derived step by step as further extensions to the deterministic approach presented above.

Step 1: Introducing probabilities of survival. In the deterministic approach, the individual was assumed to live exactly to his life expectancy. Now it is assumed that the individual survives each year with a certain probability $S_c(a|a = a_0) < 1$. The survival rate $S_c(a|a = 20)$ determines the probability for a member of the cohort c to reach age a given that he reached age 20. Accounting for this probability of survival, the formula for the internal rate of return for a single person who retires at the statutory retirement age can be written as follows:

$$\begin{aligned} &\sum_{a=RA=65}^{a_{max_c}} S_c\left(a\,|a_0 = 20\right) \times P_{c,a}\left(\tfrac{1}{1+r}\right)^{a-a_0} \\ &= \sum_{a=a_0=20}^{64} S_c\left(a\,|a_0 = 20\right) \times C_{c,a}\left(\tfrac{1}{1+r}\right)^{a-a_0} \end{aligned} \tag{5.5}$$

with

a_{max_c}	...Now: Maximum possible age that can be achieved by cohort c,
P	...and
C	...as defined in section 5.2.2.

In the case of married couples, the different respective survival probabilities of the husband and his (younger) wife are used.

[20]The calculations in this thesis ignore the relatively rare events of retiring before age 54 or after age 71. Hence, it is assumed that the probability to receive a pension becomes positive at age 54 (namely in the form of disability pensions) while the probability to pay contributions turns zero after age 70. a_{max} is the maximum age that can be achieved which is assumed to be 100. These boundaries are derived from the underlying empirical data, see Berkel and Börsch-Supan (2004). The assumed time of entry into the labor force a_0 is age 20.

Step 2: Introducing probabilities of disability. Until recently, eligibility regulations for disability pensions were rather weak in Germany and often used as an early retirement option. These eligibility criteria were tightened considerably in the 1992/1999 and 2001 pension reforms (recall chapter 3). As a result of these reform measures, probabilities of retirement due to disability differ not only by age but also across cohorts, depending on whether cohorts are already affected by the reform or not. It is assumed that there is no return to the labor force once a disability pension is received. Accounting for the probability of receiving disability benefits, Equation 5.5 is modified as follows::

(5.6)

$$\sum_{a=65}^{a_{max c}} \left[S_c\left(a|\, a=20\right) \times \left[(1-p_{c,a}\left(Disab\right)) \times P_{c+a} + p_{c,a}\left(Disab\right) \times P_{c+a}^{Disab}\right] \times \left(\frac{1}{1+r}\right)^{a-a_0} \right]$$
$$= \sum_{a=20}^{64} \left[S_c\left(a|\, a=20\right) \times \left[(1-p_{c,a}\left(Disab\right)) \times C_{c+a} - p_{c,a}\left(Disab\right) \times P_{c+a}^{Disab}\right] \times \left(\frac{1}{1+r}\right)^{a-a_0} \right]$$

with

$p_{c,a}\left(Disab\right)$ ... Probability of cohort c to be disabled at age a,
P_{c+a} ... Old age pension of cohort c at age a,
P_{c+a}^{Disab} ... Disability pension of cohort c at age a.

Note that introducing the probability of invalidity affects both the contribution and the pension phase[21]. Also, while P_{c+a} and $C_{c,a}$ are here equivalent to $P_{c,a}$ and $C_{c,a}$ from section 5.2.2, the calculation of $P_{c+a}^{C_{c,a}}$ is more complex. For a given disability retirement age, the size of the disability pension is derived from (1) the sum of earnings points that was collected up to invalidity, (2) additional earnings points that take into account the remaining years until the age of 60 and are granted in the case of disability, (3) an adjustment factor AF_{c+a}^{Disab} which works the same way as the one for early retirement and (4) the current pension value. However, in this stochastic approach, each possible disability retirement age applies with a certain probability $p_{c,a}(DisabEntry)$. All potential possibilities of disability retirement

[21]Recall that for now the pension phase is still assumed to start at age 65. This assumption will be changed in the next step.

entry at and before age a therefore have to be considered in the calculation of $P^{Disab}_{c,a}$:

(5.7)

$$P^{Disab}_{c,a} = p_{c,a}\left(DisabEntry\right) \times \left(\sum_{k=20}^{a-1} EP_{c,k}\right) \times \left(1 + Max\left\{\left(\frac{60-a}{(a-1)-20}\right);0\right\}\right) \times AF^{Disab}_{c+a} \times PV_{c+a}$$
$$+\sum_{i=54}^{a-1}\left[p_{c,i}\left(DisabEntry\right) \times \left(\sum_{k=20}^{i-1} EP_{c,k}\right) \times \left(1 + Max\left\{\left(\frac{60-i}{(i-1)-20}\right);0\right\}\right) \times AF^{Disab}_{c+i} \times PV_{c+a}\right]$$

with $p_{c,a}(DisabEntry)$ ...Probability to become disabled at age a

AF^{Disab}_{c+a} ...Adjustment factor in case of disability at time $t = c + a$

$p_{c,i}(DisabEntry)$ ...Probability to become disabled at any age i before age a

AF^{Disab}_{c+i} ...Adjustment factor in case of disability at any age i before age a

Step 3: Introducing a stochastic retirement age. So far, it was assumed that the individual retires at the statutory retirement age of 65 unless he becomes disabled before that age. However, people may retire before age 65 also because of any of the explicit early retirement options described in chapter 3. The strict confinement of contribution and pension phase pursued above is therefore no longer possible. Equation 5.8 demonstrates how probabilities of invalidity and retirement entry are included in the rate of return calculations:

(5.8)

$$\sum_{a=20}^{a_{max c}} S_c\left(a\,|a_0 = 20\right) \times \left(\frac{1}{1+r}\right)^{a-a_0} \times \left[\begin{array}{l} p_{c,a}\left(OldAge\right) \times P_{c,a} + p_{c,a}\left(Disab\right) \times P^{Disab}_{c,a} \\ -\left(1 - p_{c,a}\left(Disab\right) - p_{c,a}\left(OldAge\right)\right) \times C_{c,a} \end{array}\right] = 0$$

with $p_{c,a}(OldAge)$ ...Probability of cohort c to be retired at age a

Note: $p_{c,72}(Disab) + p_{c,72}(OldAge) = 1$

While the calculation of $P^{Disab}_{c,a}$ and $C_{c,a}$ remains unchanged, $P_{c,a}$ now is determined similarly to $P^{Disab}_{c,a}$:

(5.9) $$P_{c,a} = \sum_{i=60}^{a} \left[p_{c,i}\,(\text{OldAgeEntry}) \times \left(\sum_{k=20}^{i-1} EP_{c,k} \right) \times AF_i \right] \times PV_{c+a}$$

with AF_i [22] ... Adjustment factor in case of old age retirement at age i

The case of married couples. For the reason of simplicity, the above equations solely referred to the demographic group of single men or women. For married men the probability of their spouse's survival after their death has to be taken into account – as it was already shown for the deterministic approach. Adding this probability to the Equation 5.8 gives us equation 5.10:

(5.10)
$$\sum_{a=20}^{a_{maxc}} S_c\,(a\,|a_0 = 20) \times \left[\begin{array}{l} p_{c,a}\,(OldAge) \times P_{c,a} + p_{c,a}\,(Disab) \times P_{c,a}^{Disab} \\ -\,(1 - p_{c,t}\,(Disab) - p_{c,t}\,(OldAge)) \times C_{c,t} \end{array} \right] \times \left(\frac{1}{1+r}\right)^{a-a_0}$$

$$+ \sum_{a=20}^{a_{max_{Spouse}}} \left[(1 - S_c(a\,|a_0 = 20)) \times S_{c_{Spouse}}(a_{Spouse}\,|a_0 = 20) \times P_{c,a}^{Surv} \right] = 0$$

with $S_{c_{Spouse}}$ ... Survival probability of the spouse
$P_{c,a}^{Surv}$ ... Survivor pension the spouse of cohort c receives at age a

$P_{c,a}^{Surv}$ is calculated according to the same concept applied for $P_{c,a}^{Disab}$ and $P_{c,a}$ above. The size of the survivor pension is determined as 60% (or 55% respectively) of the old age pension in the case of death after old age retirement and as 60% (or 55% respectively) of the respective disability pension in the case of death before old age retirement.

5.3. Deterministic Projections on Future Rates of Return

This section presents projections on the future rates of return of the German public pension system based on the deterministic approach as described above. The projections cover cohorts from 1940 to 1980. Thus, data is needed on the past and future development of wages, contribution rates, pension levels and life expectancy. Data and scenario assumptions are explained in section 5.3.1. Section 5.3.2 presents the projection results. In section 5.3.3 it is evaluated to what extent these results depend on the underlying demographic, labor market and growth assumptions.

5.3.1. Data and Scenario Assumptions

2005 is the base year for the projections, the historical data starts in 1950 and the last year of my future projections is 2100[23]. Data on the historical development of annual average gross wages, contribution rates and the current pension value is taken from the statistics provided by the German Pension Insurance[24]. Projections on the future development of contribution rates and pension levels basically depend on the underlying demographic, labor market and growth assumptions as it was explained in chapter 3. I will refer to three different scenarios that cover a wide range of possible future outcomes:

Rürup scenario The Rürup scenario forms the base case scenario for the following rate of return projections. It is based on the Rürup Commission's population and labor market projections as discussed in chapter 2.

Denmark scenario The Denmark scenario is based on the MEA population forecast 3W1.5 and the Denmark labor market scenario (see chapter 2). It results in approximately the same absolute labor supply as the Rürup scenario above. However, decreases in the size of the population are larger and population ageing is stronger as it was explained in chapter 2.

[23]Such a long projection period is necessary in order to allow rate of return computations for cohorts up to the 1990 cohort. Note however, that such long-term forecasts are difficult, especially with respect to the future development of the labor market. In order to better understand how results are driven by these underlying assumptions, a sensitivity analysis at the end of this chapter looks at how results change if a different development of the population, the labor market and growth rates is assumed.

[24]See (Deutsche Rentenversicherung Bund (DRV) 2007e) and www.deutsche-rentenversicherung.de

Status quo scenario The Status Quo scenario is also based on the MEA population forecast 3W1.5 but assumes no further adjustments on the labor market, see again chapter 2.

Additional demographic assumptions. Note that in contrast to chapter 2, projections are now needed until 2100. Some additional assumptions thus have to be made. With regard to *migration*, I assume the same constant annual net inflow as assumed until 2050 (150,000 for the MEA 3W1.5 and 200,000 migrants per year for the Rürup scenario). *Fertility* rates are assumed to remain at a constant level of 1.4 until 2050 and thereafter increase linearly to 1.74 in 2100 for all scenarios[25]. The development of life expectancy follows its previous trend in all three scenarios. As the underlying life expectancy assumptions are crucial for the following rate of return projections, Figure 5.3 shows the past and projected development of the remaining life expectancy for both men and women for the Rürup and the MEA 3W1.5 population projections.

Future development of wages. It is important to note that future real gross wages are assumed to continue to increase at a rate of 1.5%, which means in its economic essence that annual long-run economic growth remains positive[26]. Contribution payments to the pension insurance (in real terms) thus do not remain constant but rise over a cohort's life cycle. This effect is strengthened even more by the projected increases in the contribution rate itself. Due to the compound interest effects in the internal rate of return calculations, the earlier, lower contribution payments are weighted higher which has a favorable effect on the resulting rates of return. If this effect is neglected and constant payments in real values of today are assumed over the entire contribution period, the true rate of return is thus underestimated for those cohorts with a contribution history in the past. Studies that choose a simplified approach based on constant payment flows, such as the one of Raffelhüschen (2005) should therefore be interpreted with care.

[25]For this longer projection horizon a long-term constant fertility rate of 1.4 seems very low and rather unlikely. Therefore, I use the projected fertility rate of 1.74 in 2050 from the medium scenario of the UN population projections for Germany as the target value in 2100 (see (United Nations 2006)).

[26]Even though it is unlikely that future real net growth will turn zero, some studies use this assumption as a worst case scenario, see e.g. Ottnad and Wahl (2005).

Figure 5.3. – Development of the Remaining Life Expectancy at Age 65 (1955 to 2100)

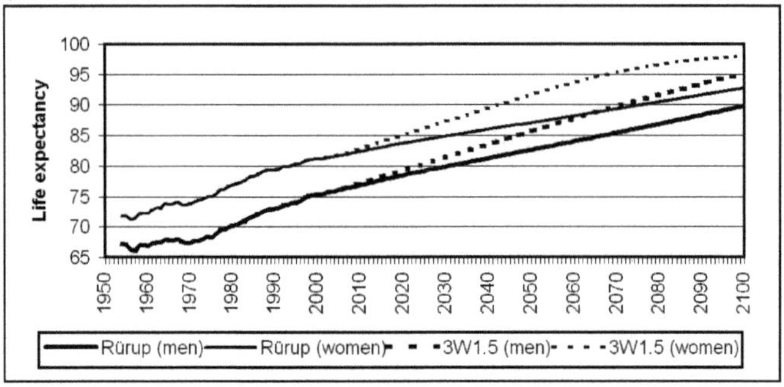

Source: Author's compilation based on historical data taken from the German Federal Statistical Office (www.destatis.de) and the 3W1.5 MEA population projections. Note that the remaining life expectancy at age 65 is added to the latter for illustrative purposes and does not represent life expectancy at birth.

Future development of contribution rates and pension levels. Figure 5.4 shows the projected past and future development of contribution rates and pension levels of the German PAYG system for the three selected scenarios. It can be seen that rates of return of future pensioner cohorts will be affected both by rising contribution rates during their contribution period and declining pension levels during their pension phase. For the Rürup scenario these changes are least pronounced.

5.3.2. Simulation Results

Since I use the same methodology as Ohsmann and Stolz (2004) in my projections based on the deterministic approach, the results for the nominal rates of return are quite similar to theirs. Resulting real rates also roughly correspond to those calculated by Sozialbeirat (2004).

Results for the standard pensioner. Table 5.1 summarizes the results for the standard pensioner and compares them to the results by Ohsmann and Stolz (2004) and Sozialbeirat (2004). Recall that the demographic groups here only differ with regard to their remaining life expectancies at retire-

Figure 5.4. – Development of Contribution Rates and Pension Levels (1950 to 2100)

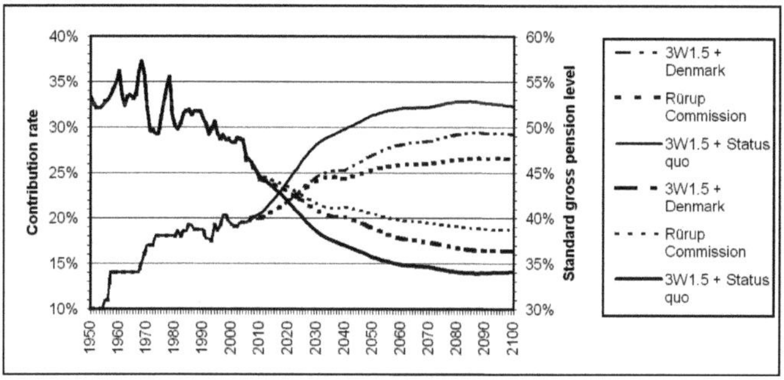

Source: Author's computations. Note that since there is no data on the development of current pension values before 1960, pension levels are displayed only from 1960 on.

ment entry (age 65) and thus the length of their pension phases, while the contribution phases of all three groups are identical. Hence, single women record higher rates of return than single men (roughly 0.6 percentage points) thanks to their higher life expectancy. Likewise, married men record the highest rates of return because of their younger wife whose life expectancy obviously is higher than that of women of the same cohort as the man. Note that the three-years difference is just sufficient in order to compensate for the reduced pension benefits in form of the widow pension. This of course is a co-incidence of our underlying assumption that wives are three years younger than their husbands. With each year the age difference gets smaller, rates of return for married men turn out approximately 2% lower. Husbands with a wife of the same age thus record lower rates by around 6%.

Across cohorts, it can be seen that the rates of return of the younger 1980 cohort turn out lower than those of the 1940 cohort (about 1.1 percentage points in nominal and 0.4 percentage points in real terms). This result is not surprising taking into consideration the development of contribution rates and pension levels depicted in Figure 5.4. Note that the 1940 cohort also is affected by this, since the projected decline in pension levels already fully affects their pension phase.

Table 5.1. – Rates of Return for Selected Cohorts According to the Deterministic Approach

Cohort		*Single, male*			*Single, female*			*Married, male*		
		Ohsmann & Stolz (2004)	*Sozialbeirat (2004)*	*Author's calculations*	*Ohsmann & Stolz (2004)*	*Sozialbeirat (2004)*	*Author's calculations*	*Ohsmann & Stolz (2004)*	*Sozialbeirat (2004)*	*Author's calculations*
1939	Nom.	3,96 %	4,01 %	4,19 %	4,62 %	—	4,79 %	4,71 %	—	4,81 %
	Real	—	1,75 %	1,90 %	—	—	2,50 %	—	—	2,53 %
1940	Nom.	—	—	3,99 %	—	—	4,60 %	—	—	4,66 %
	Real	—	—	1,74 %	—	—	2,35 %	—	—	2,41 %
1944	Nom.	—	3,59 %	3,70 %	—	4,19 %	4,29 %	—	4,09 %	4,34 %
	Real	—	1,56 %	1,62 %	—	2,14 %	2,20 %	—	2,05 %	2,25 %
1975	Nom.	3,00 %	—	2,89 %	3,60 %	—	3,51 %	—	—	3,53 %
	Real	—	—	1,36 %	—	—	1,97 %	—	—	1,99 %
1980	Nom.	—	—	2,87 %	—	—	3,49 %	—	—	3,50 %
	Real	—	—	1,35 %	—	—	1,96 %	—	—	1,97 %

Notes: Deviations between the author's calculations and Ohsmann and Stolz (2004) and Sozialbeirat (2004)are mainly due to differences in the underlying projections. Whereas Ohsmann and Stolz (2004) refer to separate external demographic, labor market and pension system forecasts, my calculations are based on a consistent set of projections. Note that health care contributions by the pension insurance are not included in the calculation. If they were this would lead to an increase of the rates of return by roughly 0.25 percentage points.

However, the decline in the rates of return cannot completely be attributed to the demographic burden and its future negative effects on contribution rates and pension levels. The rates of return for today's retiring cohorts are also higher thanks to the relatively low contribution rates of 14% until 1967[27] that lead to comparably low contribution payments during this period. The sheer development of contribution rates in the past[28] already induces a decline in the rates of return of those cohorts that have entered the labor force at later points in time. In fact, compared to today's older pensioner cohorts, already today's retiring cohorts record lower rates of return since their contribution history also comprises the past 20 years where higher contribution rates around 18% were the case.

Thus, the trend of a decline in the rates of return is not new and can already be observed today – both due to the past institutional and projected future demographic development of the system. However, while for the past the decline in the rates of return can be ascribed solely to the development of the contribution rate, future rates of return will be affected by both the development of contribution rates and that of pension levels. For the 1940 to 1980 cohorts the resulting trend is depicted in Figure 5.5.

Figure 5.5 also displays the difference between nominal and real rates of return. While nominal rates turn out considerably higher for the cohorts of the 1940s due to high and strongly fluctuating inflation particularly in the 1970s, their distance to the real rates reaches a stable 1.5 percentage points for cohorts from 1965 on when the largest part of the contribution phase is solely based on projected wage development. However, note that rates of return clearly remain positive under both terms.

Early retirement. As explained in section 3.3.1 early retirement was possible without reductions before the 1992/1999 reforms. Figure 5.6 shows the results of these reforms for single men of the 1930 to 1950 cohort. For cohorts unaffected by the reforms, rates of return under early retirement at age 63 turned out 0.4 PP higher than under regular retirement at age 65. Likewise, later retirement at age 67 led to lower rates of return in equal mea-

[27]Only in 1973 did the contribution rate reach the 18% mark (recall Figure 5.4). Until the mid 1950s the contribution rate was below 14%.

[28]Note that, in contrast to the projected future rise of the contribution rate that can be attributed to demographic factors, rises in the 1970s and 1980s mainly allowed an increasing generosity of the system.

Figure 5.5. – Rates of Return According to the Deterministic Approach

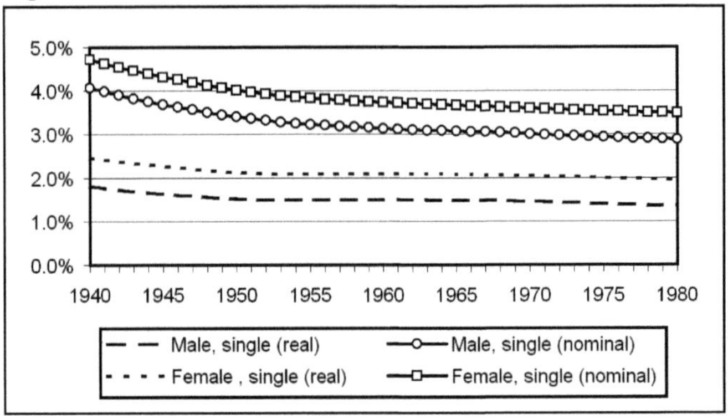

Source: Author's computations.

sure. After the reforms, it can be seen that rates of return for early and regular retirement are almost identical thanks to the adjustment factors[29]. Later retirement now leads to higher rates of return by around 0.1 PP which indicates that adjustment factors for later retirement are slightly too high from the perspective of the pension insurance[30]. This result corresponds to the findings by Sozialbeirat (2004) and shall not be evaluated further here. Note that it is crucial for the analysis to compare pensioners of the same cohort[31].

5.3.3. Sensitivity Analysis

The results presented above were based on the Rürup scenario. In the following, we will look at how these results change if projections are based on the Denmark or Status Quo scenario as defined in section 5.3.1. Furthermore, the effects of different growth rates will be analyzed.

[29]See Ohsmann, Stolz, and Thiede (2003) for a justification of the sizes of the adjustment factors.

[30]This is an interesting aspect which needs to be evaluated also under the latest 2007 reform once appropriate data is available.

[31]Ohsmann and Stolz (2004) e.g. choose to present their scenario results for different cohorts.

Figure 5.6. – Early Retirement Effects on Rates of Return

Note that only rates of return for the single male are displayed.
Source: Author's computations for cohorts 1930 to 1950.

Demographic and labor market effects. The three scenarios introduced in section 5.3.1 can be nicely used to illustrate both, demographic and labor market effects. Regarding demography, the Rürup scenario is based on a lower life expectancy and higher migration than the Denmark and Status Quo scenarios that are based on the MEA 3W1.5 population projections. On the other hand, the absolute development of the labor market are almost identical in the Rürup and the Denmark scenario whereas the Status Quo scenario assumes a much lower labor supply. As a consequence, contribution rates turn out highest (and pension levels lowest) under the Status Quo scenario and lowest (highest) under the Rürup scenario (recall Figure 5.6). Figure 5.7 illustrates the effects on the resulting rates of return for the single, male standard pensioner.

Projected rates of return turn out highest for the Denmark scenario and lowest for the Rürup scenario whereas the Status Quo scenario ends up in the middle. At the first glance, this seems a surprising result as one would expect that the Rürup scenario with the smallest rise in contribution rates (and smallest drop in pension levels) records the highest and the Status Quo scenario the lowest rates of return. However, the negative effect of the lower life expectancy in the Rürup scenario is much stronger than the positive

Figure 5.7. – Demographic and Labor Market Effects on Rates of Return

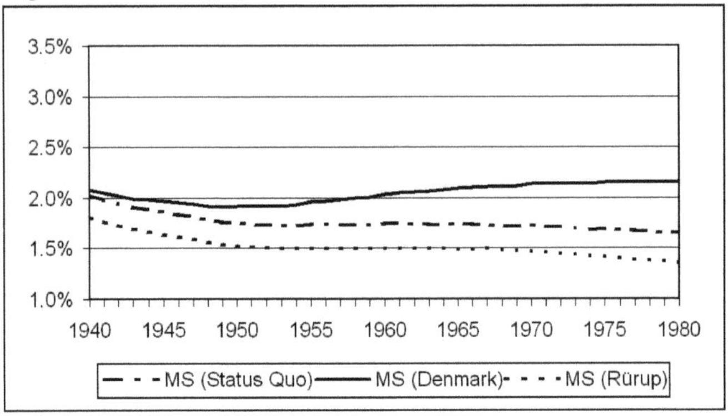

MS = male, single.
Source: Author's computations.

effect of lower contribution rates and higher pension levels – so strong that resulting rates of return end up being lowest for the Rürup scenario.

Effects of different wage growth rates. It was demonstrated in section 3.5.3 that higher wage growth rates lead to lower contribution rates and lower pension levels in the long-run. The resulting net effect on the rates of return is positive. Figure 5.8 illustrates this effect for single men under the Rürup scenario. For the 1940 cohort, which is already close to retirement, a by 0.5 percentage points higher wage growth leads to around a quarter percentage point higher rate of return. For younger cohorts that just entered the labor force, like the 1980 cohort, a by 0.5 percentage points higher growth rate translates directly into 0.5 percentage points higher rates of return. Note also, that rates of return turn negative for cohorts from 1974 on if a zero growth rate (real 1.5% with 1.5% inflation) is assumed.

Thus, how rates of return will develop for future cohorts not only depends on the projected development of contribution rates and pension levels of the German PAYG system but also on the underlying demographic, labor market and growth assumptions.

Figure 5.8. – Wage Growth Effects on Rates of Return

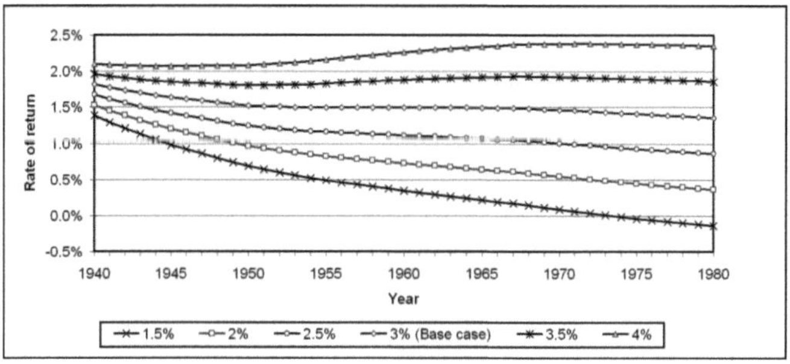

Source: Author's computations.

5.4. Stochastic Projections on Future Rates of Return

This section presents projections on the future rates of return of the German public pension system based on the stochastic approach. Again, projections cover cohorts from 1940 to 1980. For the stochastic approach, additional data on survival and retirement probabilities is needed which is described in section 5.4.1. Taking the deterministic results from the previous section as a starting point, the characteristic features of the stochastic approach are introduced in three consecutive steps in section 5.4.2. Finally, the overall results of the stochastic approach are compared to the deterministic outcomes in section 5.4.3.

5.4.1. Probability Data

The stochastic approach requires additional data on the probabilities of survival, disability and retirement entry which will be described in the following.

Probabilities of survival. Historical survival probabilities are calculated from the age-specific annual mortality rates provided by the German Sta-

Figure 5.9. – Conditional Survival Rates for Men and Women (Cohorts 1940 and 1980)

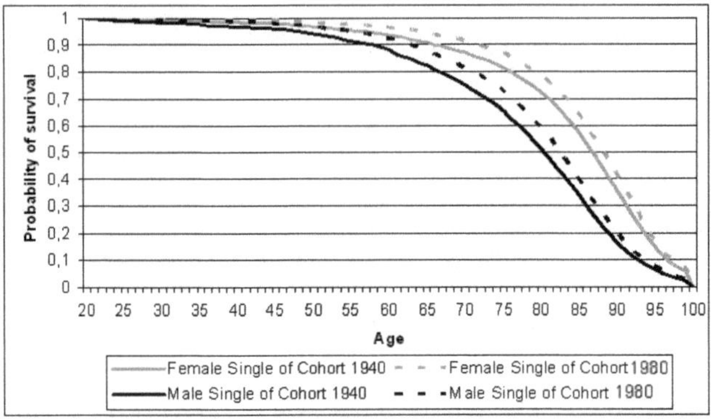

Source: Historical figures are taken from the German Federal Statistical Office (www.destatis.de), while future figures are consistent with the demographic forecast used by the Rürup Commission (Kommission für die Nachhaltigkeit in der Finanzierung der Sozialen Sicherungssysteme (2003a)).

tistical Office[32]. Future probabilities are consistent with the underlying demographic Rürup population projections described in chapter 2. Figure 5.9 illustrates the survival probabilities for men and women of the 1940 and 1980 cohort across age. It can be seen how the curve shifts outward for the 1980 cohorts as life expectancy is projected to increase.

Estimated probabilities of retirement entry. As was explained in chapter 3, the 1992 and 1999 pension reforms shifted the statutory retirement ages for women and disabled workers upwards and introduced adjustments for early retirement[33]. In addition, the 2001 reform toughened eligibility rules for disability pensions. Depending on the extent to which cohorts are affected by these reforms, their probabilities of retirement both for disability as well as for old age retirement will therefore change. For the following computa-

[32]See www.destatis.de. Note that data on mortality rates is available only from 1954 on. For our calculations we assume mortality rates before 1954 to be equivalent to those in 1954.

[33]Note that disabled workers in Germany can get a disability pension at any age (if they fulfill eligibility rules). At the statutory retirement age this pension is turned into a lifelong pension.

tions, I use the results of Berkel and Börsch-Supan (2004) who model these behavioral effects by predicting retirement decisions based on an option-value approach[34]. Since Berkel and Börsch-Supan (2004) do not explicitly differentiate between disability and old age retirement, their results are split into two respective probability matrices. I do this on the basis of the institutional transitional rules on the cohort-specific earliest possible retirement ages with and without adjustments, as it was depicted in Figure 3.1 on page 58.

Probabilities of disability retirement. For the probabilities of disability retirement, I take the values for the 1940 cohort (not affected by the 1992 and 1999 reforms) and for the 1944 cohort (fully affected) from the estimations by Berkel and Börsch-Supan (2004). For the 1941 to 1943 cohorts the respective probability values are derived by linear interpolation of the pre- and post-reform probabilities. The probabilities are displayed in Table H.1. The earliest age for a significantly positive probability of disability retirement in the data is age 54 for both men and women. Probabilities after age 62 are zero since it is assumed that old age retirement turns more favorable then. Until age 62 for men probabilities are positive for all cohorts since their earliest possible old age retirement age is 63, both before (without reductions) and after the reforms (with reductions). However, probabilities decline for younger cohorts due to the toughened disability eligibility rules. For women, probabilities for cohorts not affected by the reforms are only positive until age 59 since old age retirement is possible from age 60 on and probabilities of disability retirement turn zero then. For younger women affected by the reforms, probabilities eventually remain positive until age 62. Thus, for women, probabilities up to age 59 decline for younger cohorts and increase up to age 62.

Probabilities of old age retirement. For the probabilities of old age retirement, I again take the values for the pre- (1936 for men and 1939 for

[34]This option value approach goes back to Stock and Wise (1990) and can be regarded as an approximation of the 'stochastic dynamic programming model' developed by Rust (1989). A discussion of different approaches on modeling retirement behavior can be found in Lumbsdaine, Stock, and Wise (1992). The study by Berkel and Börsch-Supan (2004) is based on the econometric analysis of Börsch-Supan, Kohnz, Mastrobuoni, and Schnabel (2004) that was conducted in the framework of an international social security project on the causes and implications of early retirement, see Gruber and Wise (1999) and Gruber and Wise (2004).

Table 5.2. – Step-wise Analysis of the Stochastic Approach – Conceptual Overview

	Life length	*Disability*	*Retirement Age*
Step 1	a) stochastic contributions[1]	deterministic	deterministic
	b) stochastic benefits[2]		
	c) total effect		
Step 2	stochastic	stochastic	deterministic
Step 3	stochastic	stochastic	stochastic

[1] Accounting separately for the first bias that does not account for possible death before age 65.
[2] Accounting separately for the second bias that results from neglecting Jensen's inequality.
Source: Author's compilation.

women) and post-reform (1944 for men and 1945 for women) cohorts from the estimations by Berkel and Börsch-Supan (2004). Probabilities for cohorts in between these dates are interpolated such that accumulated disability and retirement probabilities after age 72 - when everybody retired - add up to one. The probabilities are displayed in Table H.2. Probabilities are positive from age 63 on when old age retirement becomes possible for those with an earnings history of at least 35 years. For men, probabilities from age 63 on increase for younger cohorts since former pathways of earlier retirement can no longer be used. For women, retirement probabilities up to age 62 decrease for younger cohorts and eventually turn zero. This is due to the increase of the statutory retirement age for women from age 60 to 65. From age 63 on, as for men, probabilities for women increase for younger cohorts.

5.4.2. A Stepwise Introduction of Stochastic Elements

In order to demonstrate the different impacts of the stochastic compared to the deterministic approach, I will analyze the results from the stochastic approach in three consecutive steps – similar to my proceedings in section 5.2.3. Table 5.2 gives an overview of the parameters introduced deterministically and stochastically in the single steps.

Step 1: Introducing probabilities of survival. In a first step, the life expectancy data used in the deterministic approach is replaced by the respective survival probabilities. Figure 5.10 depicts the way in which this affects the size of the payment flow for the contribution and the pension phase respectively[35].

For the contribution phase (Step 1a), contributions are slightly lower as compared to the deterministic approach because there is a probability that contributors die before reaching the normal retirement age. Around age 50, contribution payments are more than 5%, around age 60 already more than 10% lower than the contribution payments recorded under the deterministic approach[36].

For the pension phase (Step 1b), Figure 5.10 depicts a totally different picture. Under the scenario-based approach, survival until the remaining life expectancy age 81.5 is sure and benefits increase according to real wage adjustment. After age 81.5, benefits are zero. In the stochastic approach, however, expected benefits decline steadily because the probabilities of survival decrease faster than the wage adjustment[37].

The next question is which impact these two effects have on the resulting rates of return. Figure 5.11 shows the resulting real internal rates of return for the 1940 cohort for all three demographic groups. The effects on the contribution phase (Step 1a) and on the pension phase (Step 1b) are illustrated separately before the combined effect is shown as Step 1c.

The internal rates of return turn out higher if the probability of death before retirement is taken into account (Step 1a) since expected contribution payments are lower. On the other hand, internal rates of return are lower if remaining life expectancies are replaced by survival probabilities (Step 1b) due to the concave survival probability function and Jensen's inequality as it was explained at the end of section 5.2.2. The overall effect (Step 1c) is a decrease in the rates of return. For women, whose survival probabilities are clearly higher than those of men (recall Figure 5.9) the effects are considerably smaller than for single men.

Married men are the only group recording higher rates of return in the

[35]Note that the only difference between the two payment flows shown in Figure 5.10 lies in the use of the remaining life expectancy and survival probability respectively. In particular, this means that contribution payments are only considered with 80% according to the usual practices common for the deterministic approach. The contribution correction factor will be introduced in step 2.

[36]Figure 5.10 is based on real values for 2004.

[37]For data reasons, the maximum age for the calculations presented in this chapter is assumed to be 100 years.

Figure 5.10. – Introducing Probabilities of Survival – Contribution and Pension Phase of the Single Male of the 1940 Cohort

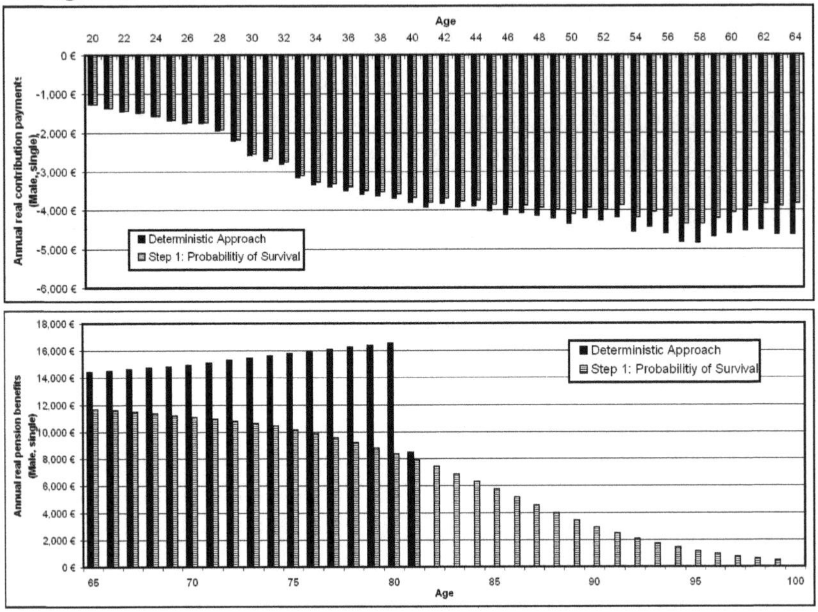

Source: Author's computations.

stochastic approach. This is due to two effects. On the one hand, there is already a positive probability of death and survival of the spouse before retirement (recall section 5.2.3) which is not taken into account under the deterministic approach and which has a positive effect on the rate of return. On the other hand, this probability rises with age which means that according to Jensen's inequality the true rate of return is underestimated in the case the remaining life expectancy and a subsequent survivor pension are assumed as it is done under the deterministic approach. Figure 5.12 illustrates these effects on the overall payment flow.

Step 2: Introducing probabilities of disability. As it was explained in section 5.2.2, the deterministic approach does not include benefits from dis-

Figure 5.11. – Introducing Probabilities of Survival – Rates of Return for the 1940 Cohort

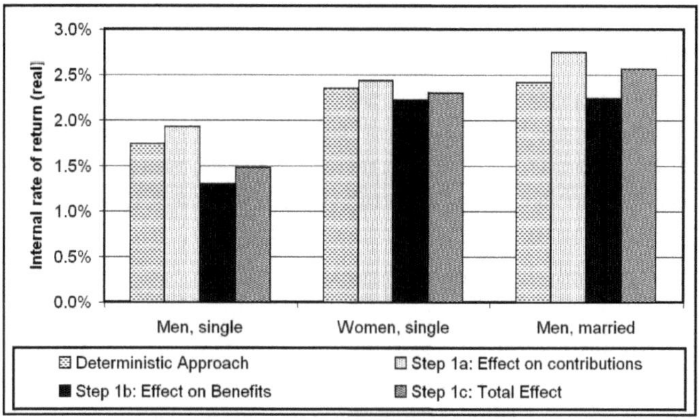

Source: Author's computations.

Figure 5.12. – Introducing Probabilities of Survival – Contribution and Pension Phase of the Married Male of the 1940 Cohort

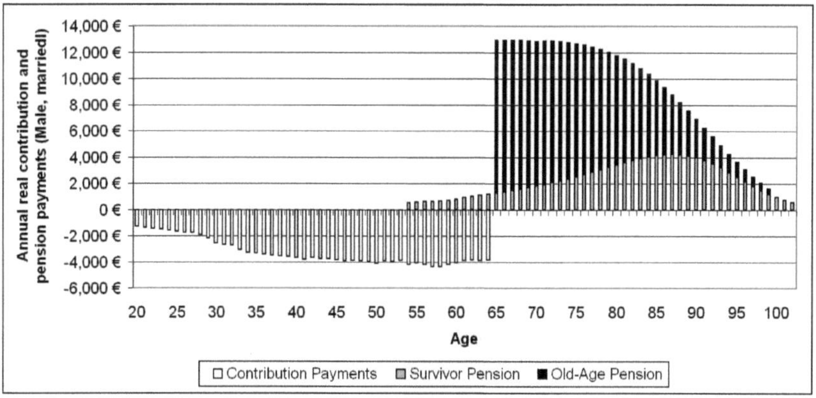

Source: Author's computations.

ability pensions but instead uses a contribution correction factor that reduces the applicable contribution payment size by the percentage that is assumed to finance the invalidity risk.

In Step 2 I now explicitly consider disability risk. The contribution correction factor is abandoned and probabilities of disability are introduced instead. Since the pool of pensioners for a specific cohort remains unchanged, this means that less people retire at the statutory retirement age of 65 but retire earlier due to disability. They thus receive lower pensions, but for a longer time period[38]. The net effect is negative. As Figure 5.13 shows, resulting rates of return for Step 2 are lower than for Step 1.

However, a second effect counteracts this first one. The higher the probability of disability for younger ages near age 54, the higher the weight of these potential pension benefits for the remaining payment flow calculation, since for each subsequent age the potential benefit flow from an earlier claimed disability pension is considered. For this reason, the decline in the resulting rates of return turns out highest for single women. As was explained in section 5.4.1, women of the 1940 cohort have a much lower probability to retire before age 60 than men.

The effect of the change in retirement behavior can also be shown nicely for single men. Figure 5.14 compares the effects for the 1940 and 1980 cohort. The size of potential disability pension flows clearly diminishes from about two thirds for the 1940 to one third of the overall pension flow for the 1980 cohort, as was to be expected from the assumptions made above.

Step 3: Introducing a stochastic retirement age. In contrast to the deterministic approach, the stochastic approach allows taking into account all potentially possible early, normal and late retirement scenarios. Step 3 replaces the statutory, fixed retirement age by a flexible one based on the old age retirement probabilities displayed in Table H.2. The results are shown in Figure 5.15. Note that a positive old age pension flow for ages below the statutory retirement age of 65 is now recorded.

[38] It is likely that those people receiving a disability pension in general have a lower life expectancy than healthy people that work until the statutory retirement age. Since data on this feedback effects is not readily available, this aspect is neglected here.

Figure 5.13. – Introducing Probabilities of Disability – Rates of Return for the 1940 Cohort

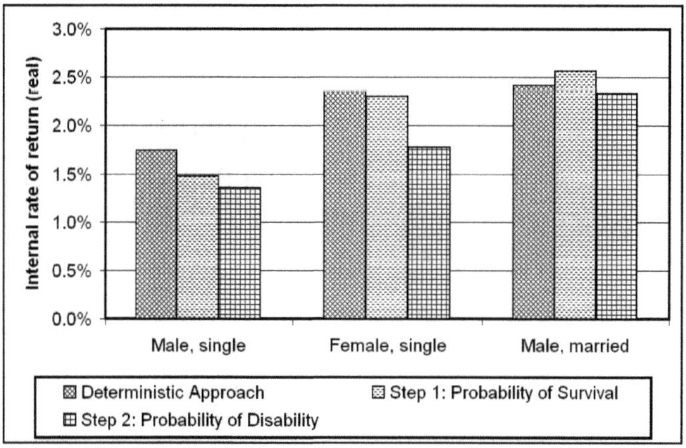

Source: Author's computations.

The effect of the introduction of the stochastic retirement age on the resulting rates of return is shown in Figure 5.16 for the 1940 and 1980 cohort. While the effect is positive for the 1940 cohort across all demographic groups, the results from Step 2 remain almost unchanged for the 1980 cohort. This result nicely demonstrates the effects of the introduction of adjustment factors for early retirement with the 1992 and 1999 German pension reforms and also shows that these adjustment factors are indeed roughly actuarially neutral from the viewpoint of the pension insurance[39]. Remember the reforms are phased in gradually and don't affect the 1940 cohort fully. The slight decrease in the rates of return (compared to Step 2) for single men and women of the 1980 cohort indicates that the concept of adjustment factors probably also goes back to a deterministic approach based on remaining life expectancy figures and that once survival probabilities are applied this actuarial fairness no longer fully holds. As could be seen from Step 1, the

[39]For a discussion on this subject, see Ohsmann, Stolz, and Thiede (2003) who justify the current adjustment factors and Börsch-Supan (2004a)? who argues they should be higher. The Rürup Commission (Kommission für die Nachhaltigkeit in der Finanzierung der Sozialen Sicherungssysteme (2003a)) takes a neutral view.

Figure 5.14. – Introducing Probabilities of Disability – Contribution and Pension Phase of the Single Male for the 1940 and 1980 Cohorts

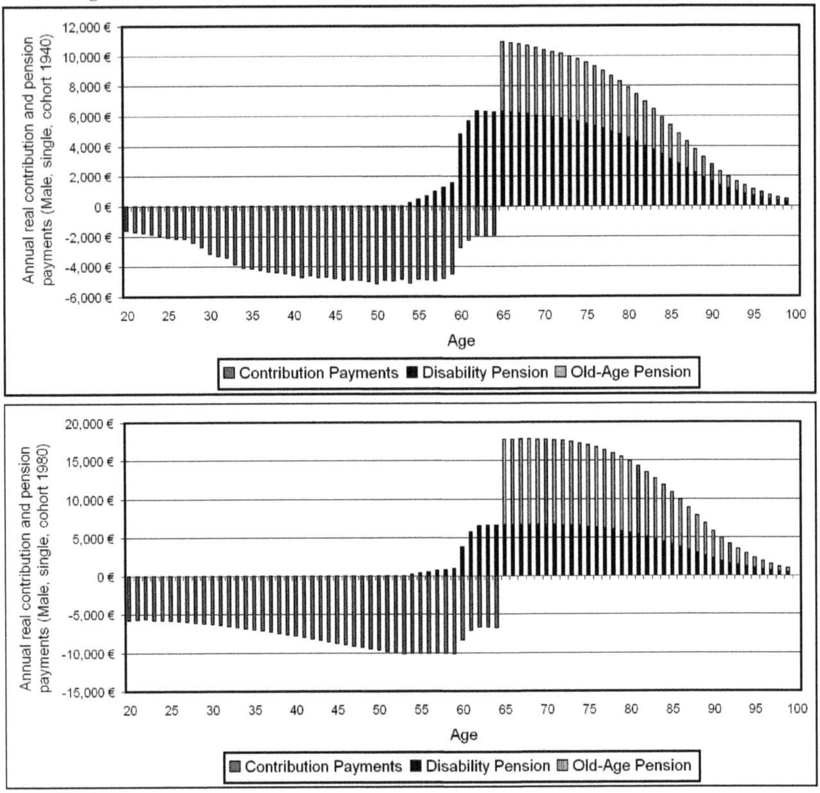

Source: Author's computations.

introduction of survival probabilities leads to a negative effect on the rates of return.

5.4.3. Simulation Results

The previous three steps transformed the deterministic approach into a stochastic one. Under this stochastic approach, married women no longer

Figure 5.15. – Introducing a Stochastic Retirement Age – Contribution and Pension Phase for the Married Male of the 1940 Cohort

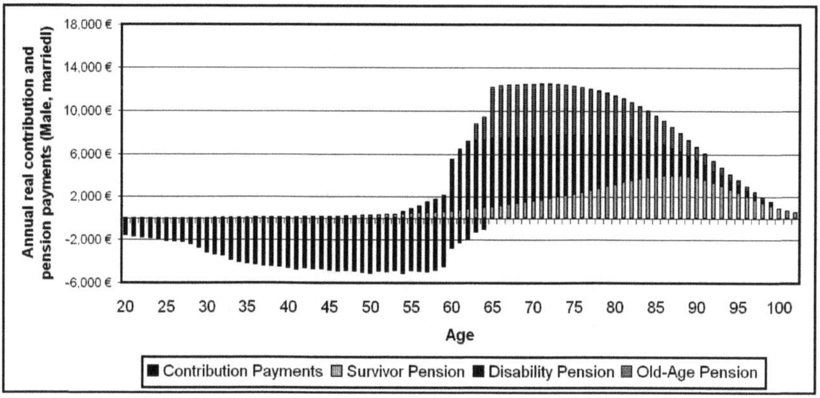

Source: Author's computations.

record the same rates of return as single women since their husbands may still outlive them with a certain probability. In the following, I therefore present results for all four demo-graphic groups. In contrast to the deterministic approach, contributions as well as pension phases now differ among all groups because of different survival and retirement probabilities throughout both phases.

Results for the weighted average pensioner. The results of the stochastic approach are depicted in Figure 5.17. Real rates of return in general turn out lower than under the deterministic approach. For the 1940 cohort, single women and married men nearly record equal rates of about 3.1%. Rates of return of married women are at 3.3% slightly higher while those for single men are again lowest at scarcely 2.2%. For the 1980 cohort, real rates of return are reduced to 2.0% for single women and married men, to 2.1% for married women and to 1,5% for single men.

Across demographic groups, married women now record the highest rates of return because of the probability that their husbands might outlive them. Rates of return for married men and single women are no longer equal but

Figure 5.16. – Introducing a Stochastic Retirement Age – Rates of Return for the 1940 and 1980 Cohorts

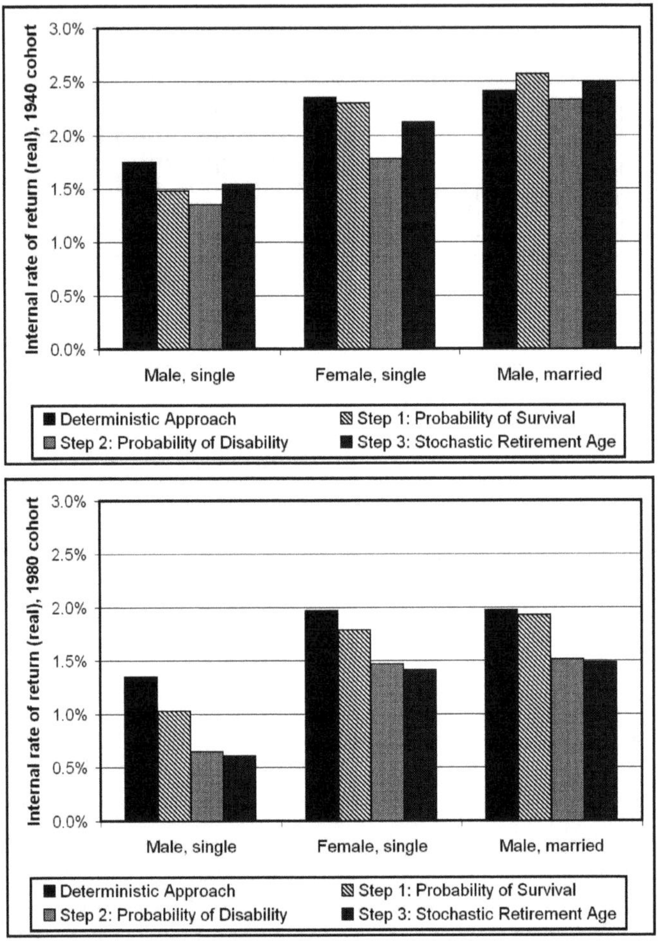

Source: Author's computations.

Figure 5.17. – Rates of Return According to the Stochastic Approach

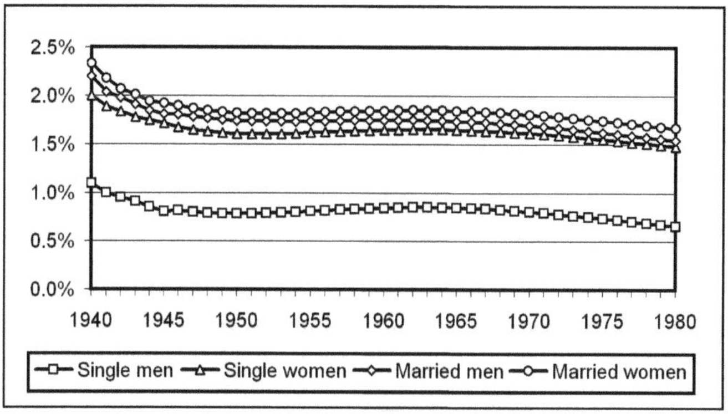

Source: Author's computations.

turn out higher for married men. As under the deterministic approach, distances between the rates of return of the several demographic groups get smaller over time, however, overall, they are larger. While rates of return for single women of the 1940 cohort are approximately 0.9 PP or 29% higher than for single men of this cohort, they are only higher by 0.5 PP or 24% for the 1980 cohort. In contrast to the deterministic approach, this is no longer purely the effect of differences in life expectancy or survival probabilities respectably but also differences in retirement probabilities which show into the opposite direction.

For the comparison of results across cohorts, the same up-and-down-pattern as under the deterministic approach can be observed. In addition, there is an upward kink for men and a downward kink for women during the transitional period of the 1992 and 1998 pension reforms. The upward kink for men can be explained by declining probabilities of disability retirement and later probabilities of old age retirement leading to higher pension payments. During the transitional phase. The downward kink for women can be explained by the rise in disability retirement and declining probabilities of old age retirement despite a later retirement age in case of old age.

Table 5.3. – Rates of Return for the 1940 and 1980 Cohorts According to the Deterministic and the Stochastic Approach

	Cohort 1940				*Cohort 1980*			
	Nominal		*Real*		*Nominal*		*Real*	
	Det.	*Stoch.*	*Det.*	*Stoch.*	*Det.*	*Stoch.*	*Det.*	*Stoch.*
Single, male	3,99%	3,83%	1,74%	1,54%	2,87%	2,12%	1,35%	0,61%
Single, female	4,60%	4,40%	2,35%	2,12%	3,49%	2,95%	1,96%	1,41%
Married, male	4,66%	4,79%	2,41%	2,49%	3,50%	2,91%	1,97%	1,47%

Source: Author's compilation.

A comparison of the results of the two approaches. A summary of the results of the two approaches for both the 1940 and 1980 cohort is given in Table 5.3. Across demographic groups, it can be seen that both for single men and for single women rates of return turn out lower under the stochastic approach. In contrast, rates of return for married men turn out slightly higher for the 1940 and slightly lower for the 1980 cohort than under the deterministic approach. Across cohorts, both approaches deliver very similar results for the 1940 cohort that hardly differ by more than 0.2 percentage points. However, projections for younger cohorts like the 1980 cohort turn out considerably different under the two approaches. The results here differ by 0.5 to about 0.7 percentage points.

This outcome shows that for today's retiring cohorts the differences between the two approaches in the end are surprisingly small, given the differences that could be seen during the step-wise transformation above. However, the fact that the results vary significantly for younger cohorts calls into mind that both approaches are based on very different concepts and assumptions that react very differently to longer life spans and different retirement behavior of future cohorts. Still, rates of return remain positive under both approaches as long as positive real wage growth is assumed.

5.5. Conclusion

The calculations presented in this chapter show that under realistic assumptions of future demographic and labor market development, rates of return of the German public pension system will indeed decline in the future but they will remain positive.

In contrast to the deterministic approach typically applied in the German pension literature, this chapter picks up a stochastic approach that allows to consider the entire range of possible scenarios simultaneously instead of restricting the analysis to one selected scenario at a time. Hence, all risks covered by the German pension insurance can be adequately captured in the rate of return calculations, which is not possible under the deterministic approach. Therefore these rates of return more adequately reflect the situation of the "average" pensioner of a certain cohort. Real rates for the 1980 cohort are projected to be around 0.6%, 1.4% and 1.5% for single men, women and married men respectively in contrast to 1.5%, 2.1% and 2.5% for the 1940 cohort. Future nominal rates of return are of course much higher than the real rates. The results show that they will remain above 2% for all demographic groups. Since the juridical debate refers to nominal rates of return, the future constitutionality of the German public pension system thus seems to be warranted also in the future.

While the stochastic approach presented in this chapter allows for a more precise calculation of the size of future rates of returns, its application requires appropriate data on the respective survival and retirement probabilities. This is not much of a problem concerning the age- and cohort-specific survival probabilities as concerning the probabilities of retirement entry. For the calculations in this chapter, this data was available thanks to the estimation of these probabilities by Berkel and Börsch-Supan (2004) that adequately reflects projected future changes in response to the recent reform measures in this area. If such data is not available as is currently the case for the latest 2007 reform, a stochastic computation that adequately considers all risks is no longer possible. However, as a first step towards a more proper computation of cohort-specific rates of return, the introduction of age- and cohort-specific survival probabilities into an otherwise deterministic approach could at least correct for the two mistakes named above.

With regard to *fairness*, the question of course is how low rates can fall until the system is perceived to be unfair. This question is hard to answer, especially as the notion of intergenerational fairness requires a much broader view which cannot as easily be expressed in numbers.[40] Given the demographic trends it is clear, however, that some *intergenerational redistribution* cannot be prevented. The baby-boom cohorts will end up with much lower public pension income then their parent cohorts. This gap can only be filled with supplementary private old age income.

[40]See Börsch-Supan (2003b) and Rürup (2004) for a thorough discussion of the concept of intergenerational fairness.

6. Summary and Concluding Remarks

This thesis delivered an assessment of the German pension system and its past reforms. It showed that the demographic transition in Germany will more than double old age dependency ratios by 2050, creating enormous pressure. Some of this pressure can be reduced if labor force participation of the young, women and the elderly are increased and unemployment is decreased. However, even if it is assumed that Germany will reach the current Danish participation rates by 2040, thanks to profound and consistent labor market reforms as outlined by the former Schröder government in the Agenda 2010, the pensioner ratio is projected to rise from 55% today, to around 78% in 2040. Without any labor market reforms, this ratio is expected to rise even more steeply to 105% in 2040. In this case, roughly one worker has to finance one pensioner in 2040. This rise in the pensioner ratio is projected to continue after 2040.

In order to cope with these challenges, past reforms have shifted the German pension system from the former monolithic system towards a multi-pillar system, with an increasing emphasis on supplementary private pension income in old age to fill the gap caused by the anticipated future cuts in public pension levels. In addition, the previous generosity of the system established under the 1972 reform, which provided numerous early retirement options, has been cut considerably. This began with the 1992 reform and culminated in the increase of the statutory retirement age from 65 to 67 with the 2007 reform. This thesis looked at whether pension reforms of the past quarter century have been successful in stabilizing the system. My assessment of these reforms has focused on five selected dimensions: (1) Adequacy, (2) affordability and sustainability, (3) fairness and redistribution, (4) robustness and (5) transparency. In the following, I will briefly summarize the main findings.

Adequacy The 2001 Riester reform set an upper limit for the future development of contribution rates of 20% in 2020 and 22%, in 2030, as well as lower limits for the future development of (modified) net pension levels before tax of 46% in 2020, and 43% in 2030. Pension levels above this limit were still considered to be adequate compared to average wages. The projections in chapter 3 have shown that these targets can be met if the demographic and labor market projections of the Rürup Commission are assumed. Higher increases in life expectancy, only moderately increasing labor force participation rates, or lower wage growth, can shift the Riester targets out of sight. The scale of the reductions in pension levels also demonstrates that public pension benefits will no longer be sufficient to safeguard pensioners' standards of living in old age.

Affordability and sustainability The introduction of the sustainability factor into the German benefit indexation formula in 2004, linked the development of benefits to the development of the pensioner ratio, the most crucial internal system parameter. Depending on the size of α, the system now technically can either follow a defined benefit approach ($\alpha = 0$) or a defined-contribution approach ($\alpha = 1$). With the setting of $\alpha = 0.25$, the German public pension system was effectively shifted from the formerly defined-benefit to a defined-contribution oriented system. Given this development as well as its earnings points system and the actuarial adjustment of benefits to the retirement age, the German pension system now largely resembles an notional defined contribution (NDC) system. As argued in chapter 4 an NDC system – such as the Swedish PAYG system – would not have been a suitable reform alternative for Germany as it leads to large distributional effects, mainly due to the development of contribution rates and wages. Moreover, it was shown that an NDC system may require large buffer funds which are not available under the current German pension system. However, in one point the NDC system still better ensures long-term sustainability than the German system: benefits are automatically actuarially fair adjusted to the retirement age – accounting for future developments in life expectancy. In the German system, in contrast, the adjustment factors are not linked to the future development of life expectancy. They were once computed on a given set of assumptions and are now simply retained. This remains a weak point spot of the German PAYG pension system.

Fairness and Redistribution As a consequence of the further increasing contribution rates and simultaneously decreasing pension levels, internal rates of return will decrease for future pensioner cohorts. It was shown in chapter 5, however, that – even under very different demographic, labor market and growth settings – rates of return are unlikely to turn negative. The simulations showed that for single men of the 1980 cohort, real rates of return are still around 0.6% compared to a rate of 1.5% for single men of the 1940 cohort – if all risks are considered in the calculations. The question of course is how low rates can fall until the system is perceived to be unfair. This question is hard to answer, especially as the notion of intergenerational fairness requires a much broader view which cannot as easily be expressed in numbers.[1] Given the demographic trends, it becomes clear that some intergenerational redistribution cannot be prevented. The baby boom cohorts will end up with much lower public pension income then their parent cohorts. This gap can only be filled with supplementary private old age income. In terms of intra-generational redistribution, the German system contains few redistributive elements. With the introduction of the tax-financed minimum pension guarantee in 2001, the last redistributive elements besides additional credits for child raising have been basically abolished.

Robustness Thanks to the shift from the former monolithic to a multi-pillar system, the German pension system as a whole has become a lot more robust as risks have been diversified better. Public pension benefits of course are still subject to political risk even though the introduction of the sustainability factor, a somewhat automatic balancing mechanism, has reduced this risk considerably. However, the many ad hoc rulings with regard to benefit adjustments since 2004 as well as the current debate on an intermission of the Riester staircase for 2008 and 2009 in favor of a higher pension adjustment in these years show that

[1]See Börsch-Supan (2003b) and Rürup (2004) for a thorough discussion of the concept of intergenerational fairness.

even such an automatic balancing mechanism provides no guarantee against further discretionary interventions. Supplementary private old age income in contrast is subject to the rate of return risk on the capital market. However, as it was discussed, pertinent model calculations show that the demographically-induced fall in rates of return will not be as dramatic as often predicted in the popular press[2].

Transparency Finally, it can be argued that account based systems such as NDC systems naturally provide a larger degree of transparency than traditional PAYG systems. However, it was shown that the German earnings points system along with the recent introduction of so-called 'pension briefs' (*Renteninformation*) that provide insight into peoples' accumulated earnings points as well as the earnings points' projected value at retirement actually may create a similar transparency as expected from account-based systems.

Overall, past reforms have put the German pension system back onto a stable path and moved it towards a multi-pillar system. There remain some unresolved issues, however, the main one being the discrete adjustment factors that do not automatically adjust for future rises in life expectancy and therefore cannot be actuarially fair in the long run. In addition, if Germany does not succeed in cushioning some of the demographic pressures via the labor market, the demographic burden eventually could necessitate a further increase in the statutory retirement age.

For the moment, further fundamental reforms seem unlikely. On the contrary, after the courageous reform propositions of the Rürup Commission, politics in Germany right now seem to try to soften down already the first sensible effects of the past reforms. However, the transition towards a more sustainable system with scaled-back public benefits supplemented by growing funded private pillars has only just begun. It will be essential to continue the new direction set by the past reforms if this transition shall be successful.

[2]See e.g. (Börsch-Supan, Ludwig, and Winter (2006) and Ludwig and Krüger (2007) who find that the capital market rate of return, owing to demographic factors, will fall by merely one percentage point if diversification within the EU region is assumed.

A. Variations of the 'Denmark' Scenario

In the 'Denmark' scenario a convergence of the German to the Danish labor force participation rates is assumed until the year 2040. If this convergence happens quicker or slower, the labor supply will develop significantly differently in the mid-term (see Figure A.1).

Figure A.1. – Different Convergence Speeds in the 'Denmark' Scenario.

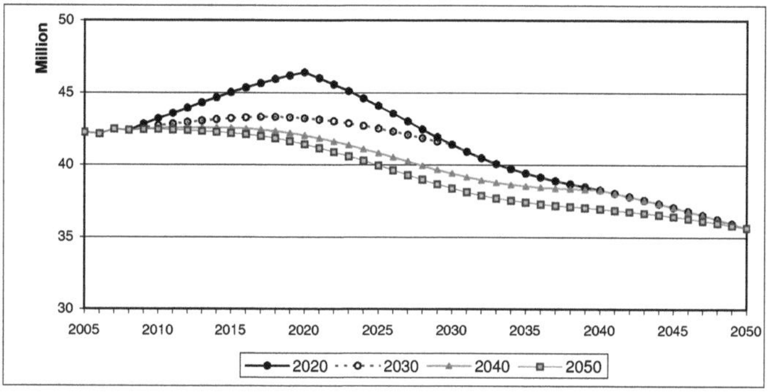

Source: Author's computations.

If the German rates would reach the Danish level already in 2020, the labor force size would rise to nearly 46.5 million, which corresponds to a rise of 4 million. This is caused by a strong increase of participation rates in a short period while the population decrease is still moderate. However, this increase in labor force size is not sustainable. After 2020, the labor force size decreases again, following the same trend as the other scenario variants with a constant labor force participation. In this case only the population and the age structure determine the development of the labor force size. If the convergence takes place until 2030, there is no kink of these dimensions. Instead, the labor force size increases only moderately to 43 million in 2020.

It will then fall slightly below today's levels by 2030 and thereafter follow the underlying demographic trends. If convergence is even slower and is reached only by 2050, the labor force size between 2020 and 2045 is nearly one million lower than if the convergence was reached by 2040.

B. The German Public Pension System from Bismarck until Today

1889/1991

- Introduction of capital funded disability pension
- Old age pension for workers age 70 and older
- Employer and employee share contributions equally

1913

- Retirement at age 65 (white-collar workers only)

1916

- Decrease in retirement age for disability pensions from 70 to 65

1921-23

- Inflationary compensation

1923

- Retirement at age 65 (blue-collar workers)

1929

- Retirement at age 60 for elderly unemployed (white-collar workers only)

1957

- Conversion into pay-as-you-go-system
  - Contribution related pension benefits
  - Safeguarding the standard of living in old age is main objective

  - Dynamic benefits: indexed to gross wages and salaries
- Normal retirement age 65
- Retirement at age 60 for elderly unemployed (blue-collar workers)
- Retirement for women at age 60

1968

- Pure pay-as-you-go-system with minimum reserves for three months

1972

- Public retirement insurance system open for all citizens (self-employed, housewives)
- Ex post payment of contributions becomes possible
- Flexible early retirement age for insured with a long service life (63) and disabled persons (60)
- New minimum pension mechanism

1977

- Pension splitting option for divorced couples

1978

- Minimum reserves are reduced to one month

1986

- Benefits for child education (usually one year of service life)
- Equal treatment for men and women regarding survivor's pensions

1992

- Integration of East Germany
- Indexing of pensions to net instead of gross wages and salaries
- Step-wise increase of retirement ages for unemployed, disabled and women

- Introduction of actuarial adjustments for early retirement
- Significant reduction in years of education counting towards service life
- Benefits for child education are raised to three years of service life

1998

- Value added tax is increased in order to stabilize contributions to the pension insurance
- Introduction of the demographic factor

1999

- Introduction of demographic factor is revoked
- Early retirement options for women and unemployed are restricted
  - Early retirement only for the long-insured and with benefit adjustments
  - Exceptions for disabled persons
- Ecological tax is increased in order to stabilize contributions to the pension insurance

2001

- Transition to a multi-pillar pension system ("Riester reform")
  - Reduction of first pillar pensions through modified gross indexation
  - Strengthening of capital funded second and third pillars by subsidies and tax relief
- Redefinition of "disability"
- Further allowances for child education
  - Higher value in terms of recorded years of service life
  - Additive recording of employment becomes possible
  - Bonus for part-time employment
- Reform of survivors pensions

  - Expansion of eligible income base
  - Reduction of survivor's pension benefits
  - Introduction of a child bonus
  - Optional pension splitting for married couples

2002

- Minimum reserves are reduced to two weeks

2003

- Introduction of the means-tested minimum pension (zero pillar)

2004

- Introduction of the sustainability factor
- Full contributions to the long-term care insurance for pensioners
- Minimum/ Sustainability reserve is increased from 0.7 to a maximum of 1.5 of monthly expenditures

2004/2005

- Old Age Income Act: Introduction of deferred taxation for old age income

2007

- Increase in the statutory retirement age from 65 to 67

C. Pension Level Concepts in the German PAYG System

In Germany, pension levels in the official statistics are typically displayed for the so-called standard pensioner. The standard pensioner is a fictitious person who worked for 45 years, always earned the average wage income and retired at the statutory retirement age of 65. He is thus credited 45 earnings points EP_{Strd}, which multiplied by the current pension value PV_t in a specific year t gives his annual pension income (see Equation 3.1 on page 43). The pension level PL_t describes the value of this pension income relative to the average wage income AGW_t of the covered labor force in the same year t:

$$PL_t = \frac{(EP_{Strd} \times PV_t)}{AGW_t} \tag{C.1}$$

The pension level is to be distinguished from the replacement rate that describes the individual pension income relative to the last or average individual wage income during the working life. Pension levels can be expressed in gross or net terms and may comprise additional aspects. In the following, the different concepts that have been applied in Germany are briefly explained.

Net pension level. This measurement was used during the nineties. The net pension level describes the relation between the pension income net of taxes and net average wage income. Hitherto, only the interest portion of the accrued pension benefit was subject to taxation while wage income was fully taxable. As a consequence, net pension levels were distinctively higher than gross pension levels (around 70% compared to roughly 50%).

Modified net pension level accounting for supplementary Riester pension contributions. The Riester reform modified the definition of the net pension level. From 2001 on not only taxes, but also the recommended contributions to the state-subsidized private Riester pension were subtracted from the average net wage income, so that net pension levels turned out to be higher than according to the conventional definition (projected values for 2040 of 67% instead of around 63%).

Net pension level before tax. Since from 2005 on, pension income will step by step become subject to deferred taxation, a universal pension level that is equally applicable to all pensioners, will no longer exist. Instead, during the transition to deferred taxation for pension income, pension levels will vary across cohorts depending on the respective degree of fully taxable pension income of each cohort. The tax adjusted net pension level accounts for this by specifying an annual pension level that is solely applicable to the standard pensioner of the cohort that retires the same year.

Gross pension level. In view of scheduled tax relieves for the labor force as well as the planned introduction of deferred taxation for pension income, the pension level definition was changed to gross terms in the context of the Rürup Commission's work in 2003. The gross pension level describes the relation between gross pension income and gross average wage income (see Equation C.1). It is considerably lower than the net pension level since differences in taxation and labor fringe costs are not taken into account.

D. Riester Criteria for Certified Individual Pension Plans

Individual retirement accounts qualify for state promotion only if they meet criteria laid down in the new Certification of Retirement Pension Contracts Act ('AltZertG'). It originally contained a long list of rules which made the system complex for customers and potential insurers alike. See Börsch-Supan and Wilke (2003). However, these stringent regulations have been dramatically loosened in the course of the 2004 reform. Qualifying pension plans require certification by the Federal Financial Markets Authority ('Bundesanstalt für Finanzdienstleistungs- und Finanzmarktaufsicht') which will be granted automatically if they fulfill the following preconditions:

1. Pension benefits may be paid out only when the beneficiary reaches the age of 60 at the earliest or upon reaching retirement age, unisex rates have to ensure equal treatment of men and women and the possibility to extend benefits to survivor and invalidity benefits must be provided.

2. At the beginning of the disbursement phase, the accrued pension contributions (inclusive of subsidies) must be guaranteed (that is, the nominal rate of return must be nonnegative).

3. Pension payments must be in the form of a life annuity or a disbursement plan linked to lifelong periodic installments with an initial lump-sum payment (up to 30% of the accumulated capital).

4. Initial commission and administrative charges must be spread equally over a period of at least 5 years.

5. The investor must have the right to suspend contributions during the saving phase, to allow the policy to continue running without making additional contributions, to switch policies, to withdraw capital in order to finance privately owned housing or to terminate the policy.

Products eligible for subsidy support and into which old age pension contributions and the proceeds on such contributions may be invested include pension insurance and capitalization products, bank accounts with accumulated interest, and shares in growth and distributing investment funds. These products are offered by life insurance companies, banks, capital investment companies, financial services institutions, and securities services companies.

E. Investment Vehicles for Occupational Pension Plans in Germany

Under the 2001 Riester reform pension funds were introduced as a further vehicle for occupational pensions. Pension funds until then had not been permitted in Germany, even though they were already widely used in other countries. There are now five different investment vehicles in German occupational pension schemes. Table E.1 provides an overview of their specific features as well as their eligibility for Riester subsidies and/or tax relief. Note that only three of them are eligible for Riester incentives: (1) direct insurance, (2) staff pension insurance and (3) pension funds. As the employer has to provide the employee with the possibility to benefit from the Riester incentives, this means – especially for smaller companies – that some companies had to restructure their pension schemes after the 2001 reform.

Table E.1. – Types of occupational pension systems

	Investment Vehicles				
Features	*Direct pension promise*[1]	*Benefit funds*[2]	*Direct insurance*[3]	*Staff pension insurance*[4]	*Pension funds*[5]
Tax on contributions	Tax free		1. Flat-rate tax 2. Fully taxed but Riester subsidy/ tax deductable expense	1. Flat-rate tax 2. Fully taxed but Riester subsidy/ tax deductable expense 3. Tax free until 4% of BMG[7]	1. Fully taxed but Riester subsidy/ tax deductable expense 2. Tax free until 4% of BMG[7]
Tax on benefits	Fully taxed		1. Tax on returns only 2. Fully taxed	1. Tax on returns only 2. Fully taxed 3. Fully taxed	1. Fully taxed 2. Fully taxed
Investment	Internal		external		
Investment rules	None		Acc. Insurance Supervisory Act		None
Insolvency scheme	Membership in pension insurance fund (PSV)		No		Membership in PSV
State supervision	No		Federal Insurance Authority		

[1] *Direktzusage*
[2] *Unterstützungskasse*
[3] *Direktversicherung*
[4] *Pensionskasse*
[5] *Pensionsfonds*
[6] *Bundesaufsichtsamt für das Versicherungswesen*
[7] *Beitragsbemessungsgrenze* = earnings threshold
Source: Author's compilation.

F. Notes on Life Expectancy, Survival Rates and Rates of Return

It was pointed out in section 5.2.2 that under the scenario-based approach the use of the remaining life expectancy in order to determine the relevant retirement period leads to two severe biases: (1) the possible event of death before retirement is neglected and (2) the remaining life expectancy of the cohort is assumed to adequately reflect the 'typical, average' pensioner of that cohort. In the following, it is explained in more detail why resulting rates of return turn out higher if these two biases persist.

Figure F.1 shows how the contribution and pension phase look like if remaining life expectancies or survival probabilities are applied (recall Figure 5.10). The question is why rates of return turn out differently under these two approaches.

The rates of return are derived from the proportion of the size of benefits to the size of contributions as represented by the two rectangles and areas in Figure F.1. However, due to the compound interest effects, this relationship is not linear. Even if the rectangles and areas in Figure F.1 were of equivalent size, the resulting rates of return in all but one case would still differ.

The following stylized example shows in what respect the rates of return calculations differ for the two approaches. Assume an annual net payment flow of -1 and plus 1 for the contribution and pension phase respectively. Using the remaining life expectancy, the rate of return r is derived by solving Equation F.1:

$$\text{(F.1)} \qquad \sum_{a=a_0}^{RA-1} (-1) \times \left(\frac{1}{1+r}\right)^{a-a_0} + \sum_{a=RA}^{a_{RLE}} (1) \times \left(\frac{1}{1+r}\right)^{a-RA} = 0$$

The age of the remaining life expectancy a_{RLE} is thereby determined as follows:

Figure F.1. – Contribution and Pension Phase Based on Remaining Life Expectancy or Survival Probabilities

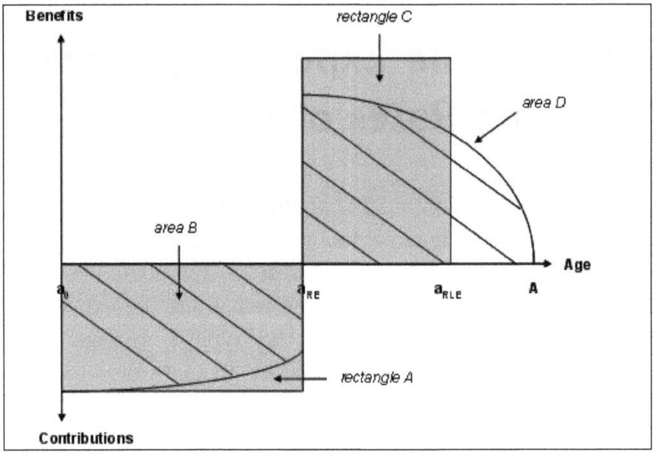

Source: Author's compilation.

$$a_{RLE} = \sum_{a=RA+1}^{a_{max}} S(a\,|RA = 65) + 1 \tag{F.2}$$

where $S(a\,|RA = 65) = S(a - 1\,|RA = 65) \times S(a)$
and $S(a) = 1 - M(a)$

The survival rate $S(a\,|RA = 65)$ determines the probability to reach age a given that the age RA =65 was reached. $S(a)$ represents the conditional survival rate to survive at a certain age while $M(a)$ represents the mortality rate to die from one year to the next.

In contrast, when survival probabilities are used, the rate of return r is to be derived from Equation F.3. Note that the probability p_a is equivalent to the survival rate $S(a\,|a_0 = 20)$ and is now placed in the sum instead of determining the final sum index.

$$\text{(F.3)} \quad \sum_{a=a_0}^{RA-1} (-1) \times p_a \times \left(\frac{1}{1+r}\right)^{a-a_0} + \sum_{a=RA}^{a_{max}} (1) \times p_a \times \left(\frac{1}{1+r}\right)^{a-RA} = 0$$

$$\begin{aligned} &\textit{where} \quad p_a = S\left(a \,|a_0 = 20\right) = S\left(a-1 \,|a_0 = 20\right) \times S\left(a\right) \\ &\textit{and} \quad S\left(a\right) = 1 - M(a) \end{aligned}$$

Apart from the fact that F.1 relies on $S(a\,|RA = 65)$ whereas F.3 relies on $S(a\,|a_0 = 20)$ which alone obviously would lead to higher rates of return for the first approach, the introduction of the survival rates once as the final running index of the sum and once as a part of the sum will in general not lead to identical results.

G. Notes on Expected Payments Flows and Expected Rates of Return

Section 5.2.3 presented a stochastic approach where the rate of return is calculated on the basis of the *expected payment flow* in order to consider all risks that are covered by the German pension insurance simultaneously. Alternatively, one might want to calculate the *expected rate of return* $E(r)$ as it is known from the finance literature. In this case, the rate of return rn is computed for each possible scenario n of a cohort c:

$$\text{(G.1)} \qquad \sum_{a=RA_n}^{a_{max_{c,n}}} P_{c,a,n} \left(\frac{1}{1+r_n}\right)^{a-a_0} - \sum_{a=a_0}^{RA_n-1} C_{c,a,n} \left(\frac{1}{1+r_n}\right)^{a-a_0} = 0$$

with n ... Scenario index with N=maximum number of possible scenarios,

RA_n ... Retirement age in scenario n,

$a_{max_{c,n}}$ ... Maximum age/ end of pension period in scenario n,

Pc, a, n ... Pension payments to cohort c at age a in scenario n,

r_n ... Internal rate of return for scenario n,

$C_{c,a,n}$ ... Contribution payments by cohort c at age a in scenario n.

These scenario-specific rates of return r_n are then weighted according to their probability p_n to occur:

$$\text{(G.2)} \qquad E(r) = \sum_{n=1}^{N} r_n \times p_n$$

with $\quad p_n = \prod_{a=a_0}^{a_{maxc,n}} p_{a,i}$ and $\sum_{i=1}^{I} p_{a,i} = 1$

p_n ...Probability of scenario n to occur

$p_{a,i}$ ...Probability of the event i to occur at age a as assumed in scenario n (e.g. old age retirement at age 65)

i ...Index of possible events (working, receiving a certain pension type, death, survivor pensions) with $I =$ maximum number of possible events at age a

This expected rate of return method, however, has a drawback. For each case where a person dies before retirement the respective scenario-specific rate of return amounts to -100%, since this person receives no benefits at all. This amount enters into the calculation weighted with the respective probability of death at that age and has a large negative impact on the overall expected rate of return. Figure G.1 illustrates this point. It depicts the scenario-specific rates of return for the case of a standard pensioner who – if surviving – retires at age 65. Figure G.1 displays the rate of return by time of death.

Although the scenario-specific rates of return eventually turn positive for ages above 75, they are not sufficiently large in order to make up for the extremely negative rates until age 65. Weighted with their probabilities to occur and accounting for all possible scenarios including disability, early retirement and survivor pensions, the scenario-specific rates of return lead to a highly negative expected rate of return E(r). Calculations show that the latter amounts to about –28% for the 1940 and about –22% for the 1980 cohort.[1]

[1]Note that the expected rate of return for the 1980 cohort is lower since it records considerably lower probabilities of death for younger ages (recall Figure 5.9).

Figure G.1. – Scenario-Specific Rates of Return for Retirement at Age 65

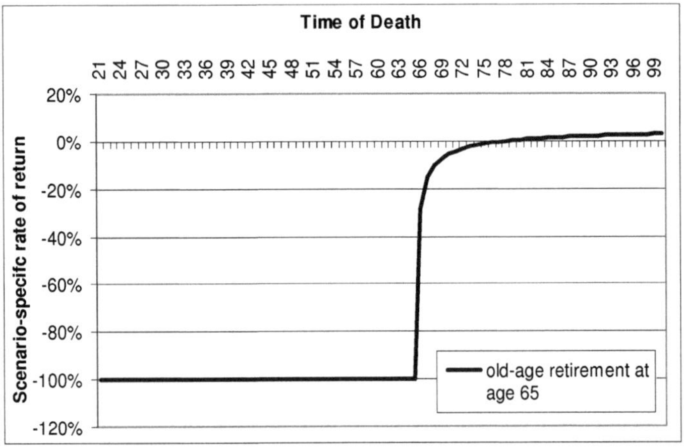

Source: Author's computations. Figures are based on calculations for the 1940 cohort.

H. Estimated Disability and Old Age Retirement Probabilities

Table H.1. – Probabilities of Disability Retirement

Age	*1940*	*1941*	*1942*	*1943*	*1944*
			Cohort (Men)		
54	0.0214	0.0196	0.0178	0.0160	0.0141
55	0.0200	0.1760	0.0153	0.0129	0.0105
56	0.0230	0.0197	0.0164	0.0131	0.0097
57	0.0264	0.0224	0.0183	0.0143	0.0103
58	0.0262	0.0215	0.0169	0.0123	0.0077
59	0.0267	0.0215	0.0163	0.0111	0.0059
60	0.3125	0.2799	0.2446	0.2093	0.1739
61	0.0797	0.0885	0.0974	0.1062	0.1151
62	0.0602	0.0572	0.0543	0.0513	0.0484
			Cohort (Women)		
54	0.0176	0.0163	0.0151	0.0138	0.0125
55	0.0179	0.0163	0.0147	0.0131	0.0115
56	0.0192	0.0175	0.0159	0.0143	0.0126
57	0.0172	0.0155	0.0137	0.0120	0.0102
58	0.0186	0.0158	0.0129	0.0101	0.0073
59	0.0171	0.0150	0.0130	0.0110	0.0089
60	0	0.0381	0.3628	0.2450	0.3272
61	0	0	0.0795	0.0850	0.0915
62	0	0	0	0.0306	0.0304

Source: Probabilities for the 1940 cohort (that was not affected by the reform) and for the 1944 cohort (for which the reform changes will be already fully implemented) are taken from estimations by Berkel and Börsch-Supan (2004) who explicitly model the behavioral effects of this reform. For the 1941 to 1943 cohorts that are directly affected by the phase-in of the new regulations, the respective probability values were derived by linear interpolation of the pre- and post-reform probabilities. In addition, the probabilities account for the fact that women can no longer receive their old age pension at the age of 60 with their earliest possibility now being age 63 if they have an earnings history of at least 35 years. Probabilities after age 62 are zero since it is assumed that old age retirement turns more favorable then.

Table H.2. – Probabilities of Old Age Retirement

Age	*1938*	*1939*	*1940*	*1941*	*1942*	*1943*	*1944*	*1945*	*1946*
					Cohort (Men)				
63	0.1303	0.1320	0.2326	0.1333	0.1335	0.1372	0.1424	0.1481	0.1598
64	0.0437	0.0458	0.0478	0.0479	0.0479	0.0530	0.0580	0.0630	0.0841
65	0.2047	0.2053	0.2054	0.2060	0.2066	0.2196	0.2477	0.2808	0.3094
66	0.0074	0.0077	0.0080	0.0083	0.0086	0.0089	0.0092	0.0095	0.0098
67	0.0044	0.0045	0.0046	0.0047	0.0048	0.0049	0.0051	0.0052	0.0053
68	0.0016	0.0029	0.0041	0.0054	0.0067	0.0079	0.0092	0.0105	0.0118
69	0.0023	0.0031	0.0039	0.0047	0.0055	0.0062	0.0070	0.0078	0.0086
70	0.0024	0.0031	0.0037	0.0044	0.0050	0.0057	0.0063	0.0070	0.0076
71	0.0023	0.0026	0.0029	0.0032	0.0036	0.0039	0.0042	0.0045	0.0048
72	0.0020	0.0022	0.0023	0.0024	0.0025	0.0026	0.0028	0.0029	0.0030
					Cohort (Women)				
60		0.4127	0.3985	0	0	0	0	0	
61		0.0654	0.0698	0.0741	0	0	0	0	
62		0.0312	0.0310	0.0309	0.0308	0	0	0	
63		0.2340	0.0250	0.0266	0.0282	0.0298	0.0314	0.0330	
64		0.0284	0.0305	0.0326	0.0347	0.0369	0.0390	0.0411	
65		0.2911	0.3023	0.3134	0.3246	0.3358	0.3469	0.3581	
66		0.0128	0.0131	0.0135	0.0139	0.0143	0.0146	0.0150	
67		0.0021	0.0020	0.0019	0.0018	0.0017	0.0016	0.0015	
68		0.0058	0.0063	0.0068	0.0073	0.0078	0.0083	0.0088	
69		0.0044	0.0053	0.0061	0.0070	0.0078	0.0087	0.0095	
70		0.0068	0.0073	0.0077	0.0082	0.0086	0.0091	0.0095	
71		0.0040	0.0042	0.0045	0.0048	0.0051	0.0054	0.0057	
72		0.0043	0.0045	0.0047	0.0049	0.0051	0.0053	0.0055	

Source: Probabilities for the 1938 and 1939 cohorts (that were not affected by the reforms) and for the 1945 and 1946 cohort (for which the reform changes will be fully implemented) are again taken from estimations by Berkel and Börsch-Supan (2004). For the 1940 to 1944 cohorts that are directly affected by the phase-in of the new regulations, the respective probability values were again derived by linear interpolation of the pre- and post-reform probabilities.

References

Aaron, H. (1966). The social insurance paradox. *Canadian Journal of Economics and Political Science XXXII (3)*, 371–374.

Abel, A. (2001). Will bequests attentuate the predicted meltdown in stock prices when baby boomers retire? *The Review of Economics and Statistics 83*(4), 589–595.

Allmendiger, J. and C. Ebner (2005). Demographischer Wandel. Chancengleichheit für Frauen auf dem Arbeitsmarkt – was ist zu tun? In *Demographischer Wandel – Herausforderung und Chance für den Arbeitsmarkt.* Wiesbaden: ESF Kongress Hessen 2005.

Barr, N. (2003). Notional defined contribution pensions: Mapping the terrain. Paper presented at the World Bank and Swedish Social Insurance Board Conference on NDC Pensions, Sandhamn, September 28-30, 2003.

Bäcker, G. (1999). Von der Frühverrentung zur Altersteilzeit: Alter Wein in neuen Schläuchen. In G. Naegele and R.-M. Schütz (Eds.), *Soziale Gerontologie und Sozialpolitik für ältere Menschen*, pp. 249–265. Opladen: Westdeutscher Verlag.

Bäcker, G. and A. Koch (2003). Die Jungen als Verlierer? Alterssicherung und Generationengerechtigkeit. *WSI-Mitteilungen* (2), 111–117.

Berkel, B. and A. Börsch-Supan (2004). Pension reform in Germany: The impact on retirement decisions. *Finanzarchiv 60*(3), 393–421.

Boeri, T., A. Börsch-Supan, and G. Tabellini (2001). Would you like to shrink the welfare state? The opinions of European citizens. *Economic Policy 32.*

Boeri, T., A. Börsch-Supan, and G. Tabellini (2002a). How would you like to reform your pension system? The opinions of German and Italian citizens. In R. Brooks and A. Razin (Eds.), *The Politics and Finance of Social Security Reform.* Kluwer.

Boeri, T., A. Börsch-Supan, and G. Tabellini (2002b). Would you like to reform the pension system? The opinions of European citizens. *American Economic Review* (May 2002).

Boll, S., B. Raffelhüschen, and J. Walliser (1994). Social security and intergenerational redistribution: A generational accounting perspective. *Public Choice 81*(1), 79–100.

Bonin, H. (2001). Will it last? An assessment of the 2001 German pension reform. IZA Discussion Paper (343), Bonn.

Bothfeld, S., U. Klammer, and C. Klenner (2005). *WSI-FrauenDatenReport 2005, Handbuch zur wirtschaftlichen und sozialen Situation von Frauen.* Edition Sigma.

Breyer, F. (1989). On the intergenerational pareto-efficiency of Pay-As-You-Go financed pension systems. *Journal of Institutional and Theoretical Economics 145*, 643–658.

Brooks, S. and R. Weaver (2003). Lashed to the mast? The politics of notional defined contribution pension reforms. Paper presented at the World Bank and Swedish Social Insurance Board Conference on NDC Pensions, Sandhamn, September 28-30, 2003.

Börsch-Supan, A. (1998). Zur deutschen Diskussion eines Übergangs vom Umlage- zum Kapitaldeckungsverfahren in der deutschen Rentenversicherung. *Finanzarchiv 55(3)*, 400–428.

Börsch-Supan, A. (2000a). *Data and Research on Retirement in Germany.* Washington, D.C.: National Academy of Sciences.

Börsch-Supan, A. (2000b). Incentive effects of social security on labour force participation: Evidence in Germany and across Europe. *Journal of Public Economics 78*, 25–49.

Börsch-Supan, A. (2002a). A blue print for Germany's pension reform. MEA Discussion Paper 02-02, Mannheim Research Institute for the Economics of Aging, Mannheim University.

Börsch-Supan, A. (2002b). Mehr Zuwanderung? Zur Rolle des Auslands bei der Stabilisierung der gesetzlichen Rentenversicherung in Deutschland. MEA Discussion Paper 22-02, Mannheim Research Institute for the Economics of Aging, Mannheim University.

Börsch-Supan, A. (2003a). Labour market effects of population aging. *Review of Labour Economics and Industrial Relations 17, Special Issue 2003*, 5–44.

Börsch-Supan, A. (2003b). Zum Konzept der Generationengerechtigkeit. *Zeitschrift für Wirtschaftspolitik 52*, 221–226.

Börsch-Supan, A. (2004a, October). Faire Abschläge in der Rentenversicherung. *Sozialer Fortschritt 53*(10), 258–261.

Börsch-Supan, A. (2004b). What are NDC pension systems? What do they bring to reform strategies? MEA Discussion Paper 42-03, Mannheim Research Institute for the Economics of Aging, Mannheim University.

Börsch-Supan, A., S. Kohnz, G. Mastrobuoni, and R. Schnabel (2004). Micro modelling of retirement choices in Germany. In J. Gruber and D. A. Wise (Eds.), *Social Security Programs and Retirement Around the World*, pp. 285–343. Chicago: University of Chicago Press.

Börsch-Supan, A. and M. Lührmann (2000). *Prinzipien der Renten- und Pensionsbesteuerung.* Bad Homburg: Frankfurter Institut - Stiftung Marktwirtschaft und Politik.

Börsch-Supan, A., A. Ludwig, and A. Reil-Held (2004). Hochrechnungsmethoden und Szenarien für gesetzliche und private Renteninformationen. MEA Discussion Paper 49-04, Mannheim Research Institute for the Economics of Aging, Mannheim University.

Börsch-Supan, A., A. Ludwig, and J. Winter (2006). Aging, pension reform, and capital flows: A multi-country simulation model. *Economica 73*, 625–658.

Börsch-Supan, A., M. Miegel, V. Brombacher Steiner, L. Bovenberg, L. Mijdam, R. Disney, D. A. Wise, and K. Schmidt-Hebbel (1999). *Reformerfahrungen im Ausland – Ein systematischer Vergleich aus sechs Ländern.* Köln: DIA.

Börsch-Supan, A., A. Reil-Held, and C. Wilke (2003). Der Nachhaltigkeitsfaktor und andere Formelmodifikationen zur langfristigen Stabilisierung des Beitragssatzes zur GRV. *Sozialer Fortschritt 52, 11-12*, 275–284.

Börsch-Supan, A., A. Reil-Held, and C. Wilke (2004). How an unfunded pension system looks like defined benefits but works like defined contributions: The German pension reform. MEA Discussion Paper 126-07, Mannheim Research Institute for the Economics of Aging, University of Mannheim.

Börsch-Supan, A. and R. Schnabel (1999). Social security and retirement in Germany. In J. Gruber and D. A. Wise (Eds.), *Social Security and Retirement Around the World*, pp. 135–180. Chicago, London: University of Chicago Press.

Börsch-Supan, A. and C. Wilke (2003). The German social security system: How it was and how it will be. *MRRC Discussion Paper UM03-01*. Michigan Retirement Research Center, University of Michigan.

Börsch-Supan, A. and C. Wilke (2007). Szenarien zur mittel- und langfristigen Entwicklung der Anzahl der Erwerbspersonen und der Erwerbstätigen in Deutschland. MEA Discussion Paper 153-2007, Mannheim Research Institute for the Economics of Aging, University of Mannheim.

Brugiavini, A. and V. Galasso (2004). The social security reform process in Italy: Where do we stand? *Journal of Pension Economics and Finance*, July 2004.

Brussig, M. and S. Wojtkowski (2006). Durchschnittliches Renteneintrittsalter steigt weiter. Altersübergangsreport 2006-02, Hans-Böckler-Stiftung, Düsseldorf and Institut Arbeit und Technik, Gelsenkirchen.

Bucher-Koenen, T. and C. Wilke (2008). Die Anhebung der Altersgrenzen: Eine Untersuchung der langfristigen Auswirkungen auf die gesetzliche Rentenversicherung. MEA Discussion Paper, Mannheim Research Institute for the Economics of Aging, University of Mannheim, forthcoming.

Buchheim, C. (1994). *Industrielle Revolutionen.* München: dtv.

Bulmahn, T. (2003). Zur Entwicklung der privaten Altersvorsorge. Vorsorgebereitschaft, Vorsorgeniveau und erwartete Absicherung im Alter. *Kölner Zeitschrift für Soziologie und Sozialpsychologie 55(1)*, 29–54.

Bundesministerium für Arbeit und Sozialordnung (BMA) (2002). *Altersteilzeit.* Berlin: BMA.

Bundesministerium für Gesundheit und Soziale Sicherung (BMGS) (2005). *National Strategy Report on Old-Age Pension Provision.* Berlin: BMGS.

Burniaux, J.-M., T. Dang, D. Fore, M. Förster, M. Mira d'Ercole, and H. Oxley (1998). Income distribution and poverty in selected OECD countries. *OECD Economics Department Working Papers* (189). OECD Publishing.

Carone, G. (2005). Long-term labour force projections for the 25 EU member states: A set of data for assessing the economics impact of ageing. *European Commission Economic Papers 235.*

Casmir, B. (1989). *Staatliche Rentenversicherungssysteme im internationalen Vergleich.* Frankfurt: Lang.

Chlon, A., M. Góra, and M. Rutkowski (1999). Shaping pension reform in Poland: Security through diversity. Social Protection Discussion Paper Series No. 9923, World Bank, Washington, D.C.

Chlon, A.and Góra, M. (2003). The NDC system in Poland - assessment after 5 years. Paper presented at the World Bank and Swedish Social Insurance Board Conference on NDC Pensions, Sandhamn, September 28-30, 2003.

Clemens, J. (2006). Anmerkungen zur geplanten Anhebung des gesetzlichen Rentenalters. *Wirtschaftsdienst* (3), 163–167.

Coppola, M. (2008). Crowding out or crowding in? Evidence from the Riester-Pension. Mimeo, Mannheim Research Institute for the Economics of Aging, University of Mannheim.

Corneo, G., M. Keese, and C. Schröder (2007). Erhöht die Riester-Förderung die Sparneigung von Geringverdienern? *Economics work-*

ing papers 30. Christian-Albrechts-University of Kiel, Department of Economics.

Council of the European Union (2001). *Joint report of the Social protection Committee and the Economic Policy Committee on objectives and working methods in the area of pensions: Applying the open method of coordination.* No. 14098/01, Brussels, November 2001.

Deutsche Bundesbank (2002). Kapitalgedeckte Altersvorsorge und Finanzmärkte. Monatsbericht Juli, Frankfurt am Main.

Deutsche Rentenversicherung Bund (DRV) (2007a). *Erwerbsminderungsrente: Das Netz für alle Fälle.* Number 201, 4/2007. Berlin: Deutsche Rentenversicherung Bund (DRV).

Deutsche Rentenversicherung Bund (DRV) (2007b). *Grundsicherung im Alter oder bei Erwerbsminderung.* Number 102, 4/2007. Berlin: Deutsche Rentenversicherung Bund (DRV).

Deutsche Rentenversicherung Bund (DRV) (2007c). *Rente für Frauen: Mehr Leistung durch sozialen Ausgleich.* Number 500, 4/2007. Berlin: Deutsche Rentenversicherung Bund (DRV).

Deutsche Rentenversicherung Bund (DRV) (2007d). *Renten an Hinterbliebene sichern die Existenz.* Number 202, 7/2007. Berlin: Deutsche Rentenversicherung Bund (DRV).

Deutsche Rentenversicherung Bund (DRV) (2007e). *Rentenversicherung in Zeitreihen.* DRV-Schriften Band 22, Oktober 2007.

Die Welt (2004). Altersrente wird zum Minusgeschäft. June 07th, 2004.

Disney, R. (1999). Notional accounts as a pension reform strategy: An evaluation. Social Protection Discussion Paper Series No. 9928, World Bank, Washington, D.C.

Dressel, C. (2005). Erwerbstätigkeit - Arbeitsmarktintegration von Frauen und Männern. In *1. Datenreport zur Gleichstellung von Frauen und Männern in der Bundesrepublik Deutschland.* Berlin: Bundesministerium für Familie, Senioren, Frauen und Jugend.

Dressel, C., W. Cornelißen, and K. Wolf (2005). Vereinbarkeit von Familie und Beruf. In *1. Datenreport zur Gleichstellung von Frauen und*

Männern in der Bundesrepublik Deutschland. Berlin: Bundesministerium für Familie, Senioren, Frauen und Jugend.

Duggan, J., R. Gillingham, and J. Greenless (1996). Distributional effects of social security: The notch issue revisited. *Public Finance Quarterly* (July), 349–370. Research Paper No. 9303, Office of Economic Policy, U.S. Department of the Treasury.

Eitenmüller, S. (1996). Die Rentabilität der gesetzlichen Rentenversicherung - Kapitalmarktanaloge Renditeberechnungen für die nahe und die ferne Zukunft. *Deutsche Rentenversicherung 12/96*, 784–798.

Essig, L. and A. Reil-Held (2003). Chancen und Risiken der Riester-Rente. MEA Discussion Paper 35-03, Mannheim Research Institute for the Economics of Aging, University of Mannheim.

European Commission (2000). Employment in Europe 2000. Luxemburg.

Fenge, R. (1995). Pareto-efficiency of the Pay-As-You-Go pension system with intergenerational fairness. *Finanzarchiv 52*, 357–363.

Fitzenberger, B., R. Hujer, T. McCurdy, and R. Schnabel (2001). Testing for uniform wage trends in West-Germany: A cohort analysis using quantile regressions for censored data. *Empirical Economics 26*, 41–86.

Franco, D. and N. Sartor (2003). Notional defined contribution in Italy: Unsatisfactory present, uncertain future. Paper presented at the World Bank and Swedish Social Insurance Board Conference on NDC Pensions, Sandhamn, September 28-30, 2003.

Friedman, M. (1968). The role of monetary policy. *American Economic Review 58 (May)*, 1–17.

Fuchs, J. and K. Dörfler (2005a). Projektion des Arbeitsangebots bis 2050 - Demografische Effekte sind nicht mehr zu bremsen. IAB Kurzbericht, Nr. 11/2005.

Fuchs, J. and K. Dörfler (2005b). Projektion des Erwerbspersonenpotenzials bis 2050 - Annahmen und Datengrundlage. IAB Forschungsbericht, Nr. 25/2005.

Fuchs, J. and D. Söhnlein (2007). Einflussfaktoren auf das Erwerbspersonenpotenzial - Demografie und Erwerbsverhalten in Ost- und Westdeutschland. IAB Discussion Paper, No. 12/2007.

Fuchs, R.-M. (2007). Rente mit 67 – Anhebung der Altersgrenzen durch das RV-Altersgrenzenanpassungsgesetz. *RVaktuell 5*, 132–137.

Gerber, H. (1997). *Life Insurance Mathematics.* Zürich: Springer.

German Reform Commission on the Sustainability of the Social Security Systems (2003). Final report. Bundesministerium für Gesundheit und soziale Sicherheit, Berlin.

Gliesmann, H. and E.-J. Horn (1998). Renditen in der deutschen gesetzlichen Alterssicherung. *Wirtschaftsdienst 1998/VIII*, 474–482.

Gronchi, S. and R. Aprile (1998). The 1995 pension reform: Equity, sustainability and indexation. *Labour 12 (1)*, 67–100.

Gruber, J. and D. A. Wise (Eds.) (1999). *Social Security and Retirement Around the World.* University of Chicago Press.

Gruber, J. and D. A. Wise (Eds.) (2004). *Social Security Programs and Retirement Around the World: Micro Estimation.* Chicago: University of Chicago Press.

Gunderson, M. and A. Luchak (2001). Employee preferences for pension plan features. *Journal of Labor Research 22*, 795–808.

Hain, W., S. Eitenmüller, and S. Barth (1997). Von Renditen, Gerechtigkeit und Reformvorschlägen. *Sozialer Fortschritt 9-10/97*, 213–226.

Hauser, R. (1998). Adequacy and poverty among the retired. *Luxembourg Income Study Working Paper Series* (WP 182).

Heiss, F. (2003). Wie groß soll die Schwankungsreserve der gesetzlichen Rentenversicherung sein? MEA Discussion Paper 33-03, Mannheim Research Institute for the Economics of Aging, Mannheim University.

Holzmann, R. and R. Hinz (2005). *Old Age Income Support in the 21st Century – An International Perspective on Pension Systems and Reform.* Washington, D.C.: The World Bank.

Holzmann, R. and R. Palacios (2001). Individual accounts as social insurance: A World Bank perspective. Social Protection Discussion Paper Series No. 0114, World Bank, Washington, D.C.

Hurd, M. D. and S. Rohwedder (2006). *Alternative Measures of Replacement Rates.* Working Paper 2006-132. University of Michigan, Retirement Research Center.

Ippolito, R. (2001). Pension incentives and sorting effects – new developments in pensions, and pension economics. Institute for The Study of Labor Conference on "Pension Reform and Labor Markets" Berlin, May 20, 2001.

Kaldybajewa, K. and E. Kruse (2006). Eine neue, vorgezogene, abschlagsfreie Altersrente für besonders langjährig Versicherte mit 45 'Versicherungsjahren'? *RVaktuell 11*, 434–448.

Kommission für die Nachhaltigkeit in der Finanzierung der Sozialen Sicherungssysteme (2003b). *Abschlußbericht.* Berlin: Bundesministerium für Gesundheit und Soziale Sicherung.

Kommission für die Nachhaltigkeit in der Finanzierung der Sozialen Sicherungssysteme (2003a). *Nachhaltigkeit in der Finanzierung der Sozialen Sicherungssysteme, Bericht der Kommission.* Berlin: Bundesministerium für Gesundheit und Soziale Sicherung.

Leimer, D. (1995). A guide to social security money's worth issues. *Social Security Bulletin 58*(2).

Leimer, D. (1999). Lifetime redistribution under the social security program: A literature synopsis. *Social Security Bulletin 62*(2).

Leinert, J. (2002). Die Riester-Rente: Wer hat sie, wer will sie: Vorausbewertung einer repräsentativen Umfrage zum Vorsorgeverhalten der 30- bis 50-Jährigen. Bertelsmann Stiftung Vorsorgestudien 14, Gütersloh.

Leinert, J. (2003). Es geht auch ohne Zwang: Hohe Teilnahmequoten in der betrieblichen Altersvorsorge durch automatische Entgeltumwandlung. Bertelsmann Stiftung Vorsorgestudien 22, Gütersloh.

Lindbeck, A. and M. Persson (2003). The gains from pension reform. *Journal of Economic Literature XLI*, 74–112.

Ludwig, A. and D. Krüger (2007). On the consequences of demographic change for rates of return to capital, and the distribution of wealth and welfare. *Journal of Monetary Economics 54*(1), 49–87.

Lumbsdaine, R. L., J. H. Stock, and D. A. Wise (1992). Three models of retirement: Computational complexity versus predictive validity. In D. A. Wise (Ed.), *Topics in the Economics of Ageing*, pp. 16–60. Chicago: University of Chicago Press.

Myers, R. and B. Schobel (1992). An updated money's-worth analysis of social security retirement benefits. *Transactions of Society of Actuaries 44*.

Ohsmann, S. and U. Stolz (1997). Beitragszahlungen haben sich gelohnt. *Die Angestelltenversicherung 3/97*, 119–124.

Ohsmann, S. and U. Stolz (2004). Entwicklung der Rendite in der gesetzlichen Rentenversicherung. *Die Angestelltenversicherung 2/04*, 56–62.

Ohsmann, S., U. Stolz, and R. Thiede (2003). Rentenabschläge bei vorgezogenem Rentenbeginn: Welche Abschlagssätze sind "richtig"? *Die Angestelltenversicherung 4/2003*.

O'Neill, B., D. Balk, M. Brickman, and M. Ezra (2001, June). A guide to global population projections. *Demographic Research 4*, 203–288. Max Planck Institute for Demographic Research.

Orszag, M., P. Orszag, D. Snower, and J. Stiglitz (1999). The impact of individual accounts: Piecemeal vs. comprehensive approaches. Presented at the Annual Bank Conference on Development Economics, The World Bank, April 29, 1999.

Ottnad, A. and S. Wahl (2005). *Die Renditen der gesetzlichen Rente: Für Junge ein schlechtes Geschäft.* Frankfurt am Main: Deutsches Institut für Altersvorsorge.

Palmer, E. (2000). The Swedish pension reform model: Framework and issues. Social Protection Discussion Paper Series No. 0012, World Bank, Washington, D.C.

Palmer, E. (2003). Conversion to NDC - issues and models. Paper presented at the World Bank and Swedish Social Insurance Board Conference on NDC Pensions, Sandhamn, September 28-30, 2003.

Pfeiffer, U., R. Braun, A. Grimm, and M. Schmidt (2007). *Altersvorsorge in Deutschland: Verloren im Dschungel der Möglichkeiten.* Deutsches Institut für Altersvorsorge (DIA). Sept. 2006.

Poterba, J. (2001). Demographic structure and asset returns. *The Review of Economics and Statistics 83*(4), 565–584.

Prognos (1987). Gesamtwirtschaftliche Entwicklungen und gesetzliche Rentenversicherung vor dem Hintergrund einer schrumpfenden Bevölkerung. Prognos AG, Basel.

Prognos (2001). Reformoptionen für die gesetzliche Rentenversicherung: Auswirkungen der Rentenreform 2001 und die Verteilung der Umstiegskosten. Prognos AG, Basel.

Raffelhüschen, B. (1993). Funding social security through pareto-optimal conversion policies. *Journal of Economics*, 105–131.

Raffelhüschen, B. (2005). Staatliche Rente oft ohne Rendite. Mitteldeutscher Rundfunk (MDR) Umschau, Juni 2005, http://www.mdr.de/umschau/1980263.html.

Reinberg, A. and M. Hummel (2003). Bildungspolitik: Steuert Deutschland langfristig auf einen Fachkräftemangel hin? IAB Kurzbericht, Nr. 9/2003.

Riphahn, R. T. (1995). Disability retirement among German men in the 1980s. *Münchner Wirtschaftswissenschaftliche Beiträge 95-20.* Ludwig Maximilians Universität München.

Riphahn, R. T. and P. Schmidt (1997). Determinanten des Ruhestandes: Lockt der Ruhestand oder drängt der Arbeitsmarkt? *Jahrbücher für Wirtschaftswissenschaften 48(1)*, 113–147.

Rürup, B. (2004). Generationengerechtigkeit und Rentenversicherung. In *Generationengerechtigkeit - Inhalt, Bedeutung und Konsequenzen für die Alterssicherung*, Schriften Band 51, pp. 39–44. Frankfurt am Main: Verband Deutscher Rentenversicherungsträger (VDR).

Ruprecht, W. (2004). Automatische Entgeltumwandlung in der betrieblichen Altersversorgung – eine Replik. *Wirtschaftsdienst 10*, 651–656.

Rust, J. (1989). A dynamic programming model of retirement behavior. In D. A. Wise (Ed.), *The Economics of Ageing*, pp. 359–398. Chicago: University of Chicago Press for NBER.

Sachverständigenrat zur Begutachtung der gesamtwirtschaftlichen Entwicklung (2004). Erfolge im Ausland - Herausforderungen im Inland, Jahresgutachten. 2004/2005, 237-246.

Samuelson, P. A. (1958). An exact consumption loan model of interest with or without the social contrivance of money. *Journal of Political Economy 66*, 467–482.

Schmidt, P. (1995). *Die Wahl des Rentenalters: Theoretische und empirische Analyse des Rentenzugangsverhältnis in West- und Ostdeutschland.* Frankfurt: Lang.

Schnabel, R. (1998). Rates of return of the German Pay-As-You-Go pension system. *Finanzarchiv 55(3)*, 374–399.

Schnabel, R. (2001). *Die Rentenreform 2001.* Frankfurt am Main: Deutsches Institut für Altersvorsorge.

Schnabel, R. (2003). *Die Rentenlücke. Das Problem wächst.* Köln: Deutsches Institut für Altersvorsorge.

Schnabel, S., K. Kistowski, and J. Vaupel (2005). Immer neue Rekorde und kein Ende in Sicht. In J. M. Hoern and J. Vaupel (Eds.), *Demografische Forschung - Aus Erster Hand*, Volume 2. Rostock: Max-Planck-Institut für demographische Forschung.

Schneider (1997). Versicherungen - Wie hoch ist die Rendite. *Betriebs-Berater* (51/52).

Schnur, P. and G. Zika (2005). Projektion des Arbeitskräftebedarfs bis 2020 - Nur zögerliche Besserung am deutschen Arbeitsmarkt. IAB Kurzbericht, No. 12/2005.

Schwarz, A. M. (2005). Pension system reforms. In A. Condonel and S. Paternostro (Eds.), *Analyzing the Distributional Impact of Reforms.* World Bank Publications.

Settergren, O. (2001a). The automatic balance mechanism of the Swedish pension system. *Wirtschaftspolitische Blätter 4/2001.*

Settergren, O. (2001b). Two thousand five hundred words on the Swedish pension reform. Paper presented at the Workshop on Pension Reform at the German Embassy, Washington, D.C., July 12, 2001.

Settergren, O. (2003). The rate of return of Pay As You Go pension systems. Paper presented at the World Bank and Swedish Social Insurance Board Conference on NDC Pensions, Sandhamn, September 28-30, 2003.

Siddiqui, S. (1997). The pension incentive to retire: empirical evidence for West Germany. *Journal of Population Economics 10(4)*, 463–486.

Sommer, M. (2004). Fiskalische Auswirkungen einer Erweiterung des Förderrahmens von Riester-Renten. MEA Discussion Paper 122-07, Mannheim Research Institute for the Economics of Aging, University of Mannheim.

Sozialbeirat (2004). Gutachten des Sozialbeirats zum Rentenversicherungsbericht 2004. BTD 15/4498.

Statistisches Bundesamt (2006a). *11. koordinierte Bevölkerungsvorausberechnung - Annahmen und Ergebnisse.* Wiesbaden: Statistisches Bundesamt. www.destatis.de.

Statistisches Bundesamt (2006b). *Results of the 11th coordinated population projection.* Wiesbaden: Statistisches Bundesamt, Federal Statistical Office. www.destatis.de.

Stiftung Warentest (2002). Riester-Rentenversicherungen: Die Lücke schließen. FINANZtest, 9/2002.

Stock, J. H. and D. A. Wise (1990, Sep.). Pensions, the option value of work, and retirement. *Econometrica 58*(5), 1151–1180.

Summers, L. (1989). Some simple economics of mandated benefits. *American Economic Review 79*(2, May).

Sundén, A. (2000). How will Sweden's new pension system work? Issue in Brief No. 3-00, Center for Retirement Research, Boston College.

Thum, M. and J. von Weizsäcker (2000). Implizite Einkommensteuer als Messlatte für die aktuellen Rentenreformvorschläge. *Perspektiven der Wirtschaftspolitik 1*, 453–468.

United Nations (2006). *World Population Prospects: The 2006 Revision Population Database.* United Nations Population Division, Department of Economic and Social Affairs. http://esa.un.org/unpp/.

Valdés-Prieto, S. (2000). The financial stability of notional account pensions. *Scandinavian Journal of Economics 102(3)*, 395–417.

Verband Deutscher Rentenversicherungsträger (VDR) (2002). *Die Rentenversicherung in Zeitreihen.* DRV-Schriften 22, Frankfurt am Main.

Verband Deutscher Rentenversicherungsträger (VDR) (2004). *Die Rentenversicherung in Zeitreihen.* Frankfurt am Main.

Verband Deutscher Rentenversicherungsträger (VDR) (2007). *Die Rentenversicherung in Zeitreihen.* Frankfurt am Main.

Von Gaudecker, H.-M. and C. Weber (2004). *Surprises in a Growing Market Niche: An Evaluation of the German Private Annuities Market.* Geneva Papers on Risk an Insurance – Issues and Practice.

Wilke, C. (2004). Ein Simulationsmodell des Rentenversicherungssystems: Konzeption und ausgewählte Anwendungen von MEA-PENSIM. MEA Discussion Paper 48-04, Mannheim Research Institute for the Economics of Aging, University of Mannheim.

Wilke, C. (2005). Rates of return of the German PAYG system – how they can be measured and how they will develop. MEA Discussion Paper 97-05, Mannheim Research Institute for the Economics of Aging, University of Mannheim.

Wissenschaftlicher Beirat beim Bundesministerium für Wirtschaft und Arbeit (2005). *Alterung und Familienpolitik.* Berlin: Bundesministerium für Wirtschaft und Arbeit.

World Bank (1994). *Averting the Old-Age Crisis: Policies to Protect the Old and Promote Growth.* New York: Oxford University Press.

SOZIALÖKONOMISCHE SCHRIFTEN

Herausgegeben von Professor Dr. Dr. h.c. Bert Rürup

Band 1 Marietta Jass: Erfolgskontrolle des Abwasserabgabengesetzes. Ein Konzept zur Erfassung der Gesetzeswirkungen verbunden mit einer empirischen Untersuchung in der Papierindustrie. 1990.

Band 2 Frank Schulz-Nieswandt: Stationäre Altenpflege und "Pflegenotstand" in der Bundesrepublik Deutschland. 1990.

Band 3 Helmut Böhme, Alois Peressin (Hrsg.): Sozialraum Europa. Die soziale Dimension des Europäischen Binnenmarktes. 1990.

Band 4 Stephan Ruß: Telekommunikation als Standortfaktor für Klein- und Mittelbetriebe. Telekommunikative Entwicklungstendenzen und regionale Wirtschaftspolitik am Beispiel Hessen. 1991.

Band 5 Reinhard Grünewald: Tertiärisierungsdefizite im Industrieland Bundesrepublik Deutschland. Nachweis und politische Konsequenzen. 1992.

Band 6 Bert Rürup, Uwe H. Schneider (Hrsg.): Umwelt und Technik in den Europäischen Gemeinschaften. Teil I: Die grenzüberschreitende Entsorgung von Abfällen. Bearbeitet von: Thomas Kemmler, Thomas Steinbacher. 1993.

Band 7 Mihai Nedelea: Erfordernisse und Möglichkeiten einer wachstumsorientierten Steuerpolitik in Rumänien. Dargestellt am Beispiel der Textil- und Bekleidungsindustrie. 1995.

Band 8 Andreas Schade: Ganzjährige Beschäftigung in der Bauwirtschaft – Eine Wirkungsanalyse. Analyse und Ansätze für eine Reform der Winterbauförderung. 1995.

Band 9 Frank Schulz-Nieswandt: Ökonomik der Transformation als wirtschafts- und gesellschaftspolitisches Problem. Eine Einführung aus wirtschaftsanthropologischer Sicht. 1996.

Band 10 Werner Sesselmeier, Roland Klopfleisch, Martin Setzer: Mehr Beschäftigung durch eine Negative Einkommensteuer. Zur beschäftigungspolitischen Effektivität und Effizienz eines integrierten Steuer- und Transfersystems. 1996.

Band 11 Sylvia Liebler: Der Einfluß der Unabhängigkeit von Notenbanken auf die Stabilität des Geldwertes. 1996.

Band 12 Werner Sesselmeier: Einkommenstransfers als Instrumente der Beschäftigungspolitik. Negative Einkommensteuer und Lohnsubventionen im Lichte moderner Arbeitsmarkttheorien und der Neuen Institutionenökonomik. 1997.

Band 13 Stefan Lorenz: Der Zusammenhang von Arbeitsgestaltung und Erwerbsleben unter besonderer Berücksichtigung der Erwerbstätigkeiten von Frauen und Älteren. 1997.

Band 14 Volker Ehrlich: Arbeitslosigkeit und zweiter Arbeitsmarkt. Theoretische Grundlagen, Probleme und Erfahrungen. 1997.

Band 15 Philipp Hartmann: Grenzen der Versicherbarkeit. Private Arbeitslosenversicherung. 1998.

Band 16 Martin Setzer, Roland Klopfleisch, Werner Sesselmeier: Langzeitarbeitslose und Erster Arbeitsmarkt. Eine kombinierte Strategie zur Erhöhung der Wiederbeschäftigungschancen. 1999.

Band 17 Dorothea Wenzel: Finanzierung des Gesundheitswesens und Interpersonelle Umverteilung. Mikrosimulationsuntersuchung der Einkommenswirkung von Reformvorschlägen zur GKV-Finanzierung. 1999.

Band 18 Ingo Schroeter: Analyse und Bewertung der intergenerativen Verteilungswirkungen einer Substitution des Umlage- durch das Kapitalstocksverfahren zur Rentenfinanzierung. 1999.

Band 19 Roland Klopfleisch: Fiskalische Konsequenzen der Europäischen Währungsunion. Die Veränderung des Seigniorage und dessen Bedeutung für die nationalen EWU-11 Haushalte. 2000.

Band 20 Klaus Heubeck, Bert Rürup: Finanzierung der Altersversorgung des öffentlichen Dienstes. Probleme und Optionen. 2000.

Band 21 Manon Pigeau: Der Einfluß der Arbeitszeit auf die Erwerbsbeteiligung von Frauen. Empirische Befunde, mikroökonomische Modellierung und politische Konsequenzen. 2002.

Band 22 Carsten Müller: Existenzgründungshilfen als Instrument der Struktur- und Beschäftigungspolitik. 2002.

Band 23 Stefan Lewe: Wachstumseffiziente Unternehmensbesteuerung. 2003.

Band 24 Robert Coppik: Konzeption eines Transformationsansatzes zur Substitution des kameralen, inputorientierten Budgetkreislaufs der öffentlichen Verwaltung in einen outputorientierten Budgetkreislauf innerhalb des New Public Management.

Band 25 Alexander Meindel: Intergenerative Verteilungswirkung beim Übergang zu einer nachgelagerten Rentenbesteuerung. 2004.

Band 26 Jochen Gunnar Jagob: Das Äquivalenzprinzip in der Alterssicherung. 2004.

Band 27 Tobias Fehr: Recht des außerbörslichen Aktienhandels vor dem Hintergrund des Rechts des börslichen Aktienhandels. Das Kapitalmarktszenario für kapitalmarktaktive Aktiengesellschaften, deren Unternehmensführungen und aktuelle und potentielle Aktionäre und für Wertpapierdienstleister. 2006.

Band 28 Stefan Fetzer: Zur nachhaltigen Finanzierung des gesetzlichen Gesundheitssystems. 2006.

Band 29 Oliver Ehrentraut: Alterung und Altersvorsorge. Das deutsche Drei-Säulen-System der Alterssicherung vor dem Hintergrund des demografischen Wandels. 2006.

Band 30 Martin Debus: Arbeitsmarkteffekte des demografischen Wandels. 2007.

Band 31 Jens Hujer: Regionalökonomische Effekte von Flughäfen. 2008.

Band 32 Zulia Gubaydullina: Nicht-monetäre Inflationsursachen in Russland. Eine empirische Analyse. 2008.

Band 33 Jasmin Häcker: Die Soziale Pflegeversicherung: Eine Generationenbilanz. 2008.

Band 34 Christina Benita Wilke: German Pension Reform. On Road Towards a Sustainable Multi-Pillar System. 2009.